Lab Manual

TO ACCOMPANY

java™
SOFTWARE SOLUTIONS
foundations of program design
fourth edition

LEWIS & LOFTUS

Adrienne Bloss
ROANOKE COLLEGE

N. Jane Ingram
ROANOKE COLLEGE

PEARSON
Addison
Wesley

Boston   San Francisco   New York
London   Toronto   Sydney   Tokyo   Singapore   Madrid
Mexico City   Munich   Paris   Cape Town   Hong Kong   Montreal

ISBN   0-321-27861-5

4 5 6 BB 07 06 05

Java Software Solutions

Lab Exercises

Chapter 1: Introduction
Lab Exercises

Topics	Lab Exercises
Printing strings	Prelab Exercises
	Poem
Documentation	Comments
Identifiers	Program Names
Syntax errors	Recognizing Syntax Errors
	Correcting Syntax Errors

Prelab Exercises

Your task is to write a Java program that will print out the following message (including the row of equal marks):

```
Computer Science, Yes!!!!
=========================
```

An outline of the program is below. Complete it as follows:

a. In the documentation at the top, fill in the name of the file the program would be saved in and a brief description of what the program does.
b. Add the code for the main method to do the printing.

```java
// **************************************************************
// File Name:
//
// Purpose:
// **************************************************************

public class CSYes
{
    // -------------------------------------------------
    //  The following main method prints an exciting
    //  message about computer science
    // -------------------------------------------------




}
```

Poem

Write a Java program that prints the message, "Roses are red". Your program will be a class definition containing a *main* method—see the *Lincoln* example in Listing 1.1 of the text if you need guidance. Remember the following:

☐ The name of the class must match the name of the file (but without the .java extension).
☐ The *main* method must be inside the class definition (between the first { and the last }).
☐ The statement that prints the message must be inside *main*.

Compile and run your program. When it works correctly, modify it so that it prints the entire poem:

```
Roses are red
Violets are blue
Sugar is sweet
And so are you!
```

Comments

File *Count.java* contains a Java program that counts from 1 to 5 in English, French, and Spanish. Save this file to your directory and compile and run it to see what it does. Then modify it as follows:

1. Use // style comments to add a comment header at the top of the file that includes the name of the program, your name, and a brief description of what the program does, neatly formatted. Include a delimiter line (e.g., all stars) at the beginning and end of the header.
2. Add a comment before each println that indicates what language the next line is in. Experiment with leaving a blank line before each of these comment lines (in the program itself, not the output). Is the program easier to read with or without these blank lines?
3. Remove one of the slashes from one of your comment lines and recompile the program, so one of the comments starts with a single /. What error do you get? Put the slash back in.
4. Try putting a comment within a comment, so that a // appears after the initial // on a comment line. Does this cause problems?
5. Consult the documentation guidelines in Appendix F of the text. Have you violated any of them? List two things that you could imagine yourself or someone else doing in commenting this program that these guidelines discourage.

Count.java

```java
public class Count
{

    public static void main (String[] args)
    {

        System.out.println ("one two three four five");
        System.out.println ("un deux trois quatre cinq");
        System.out.println ("uno dos tres cuatro cinco");

    }

}
```

Program Names

File *Simple.java* contains a simple Java program that prints a message. The identifier that represents the name of this program is *Simple*, but we could have chosen a different identifier subject to certain rules and conventions. An identifier may contain any combination of letters, digits, the underscore character, and the dollar sign, but cannot begin with a digit. Furthermore, by convention, identifiers that represent class names (which includes program names) begin with a capital letter. This means that you won't get an error if your program name doesn't start with a capital letter (as long as what it starts with is legal for an identifier), but it's better style if you do. This may seem arbitrary now, but later when you have lots of identifiers in your programs you'll see the benefit. Of course, the program name should always be reasonably descriptive of the program.

Indicate whether each name below is a legal identifier, and if so, whether it is a good choice to name this program. If the answer to either question is no, explain why. Then save Simple.java to your directory and check your answers by modifying it to try each—note that you will have to change the file name each time to match the program name or you will always get an error.

1. simple (Why do you even have to change the name of the file in this case?)
2. SimpleProgram
3. 1Simple
4. _Simple_
5. *Simple*
6. $123_45
7. Simple!

```
// **********************************************
//  Simple.java
//
//  Print a simple message about Java.
//
// **********************************************

public class Simple
{

    public static void main (String[] args)
    {

       System.out.println ("Java rocks!!");

    }
}
```

Recognizing Syntax Errors

When you make syntax errors in your program the compiler gives error messages and does not create the bytecode file. It saves time and frustration to learn what some of these messages are and what they mean. Unfortunately, at this stage in the game many of the messages will not be meaningful *except* to let you know where the first error occurred. Your only choice is to carefully study your program to find the error. In the following you will introduce a few typical errors into a simple program and examine the error messages.

1. Type the following program into a file called Hello.java. (This is the traditional first program a computer scientist writes in a new language.)

    ```
    // *******************************************
    //   Hello.java
    //
    //   Print a Hello, World message.
    // *******************************************

    public class Hello
    {
        // --------------------------------
        // main method -- prints the greeting
        // --------------------------------
        public static void main (String[] args)
        {
            System.out.println ("Hello, World!");
        }
    }
    ```

    Compile and run the program to see what it does. Then make the changes below, answering the questions as you go.

2. **Class name different from file name.** Delete one l (el) from the name of the class (so the first non-comment line is *public class Helo*), save the program, and recompile it. What was the error message?

3. **Misspelling inside string.** Correct the mistake above, then delete one l from the Hello in the message to be printed (inside the quotation marks). Save the program and recompile it. There is no error message—**why not?** Now run the program. What has changed?

4. **No ending quotation mark in a string literal.** Correct the spelling in the string, then delete the ending quotation mark enclosing the string Hello, World!. Save the program and recompile it. What error message(s) do you get?

5. **No beginning quotation mark in a string literal.** Put the ending quotation mark back, then take out the beginning one. Save and recompile. How many errors this time? Lots, even though there is really only one error. **When you get lots of errors always concentrate on finding the first one listed!!** Often fixing that one will fix the rest. After we study variables the error messages that came up this time will make more sense.

6. **No semicolon after a statement.** Fix the last error (put the quotation mark back). Now remove the semicolon at the end of the line that prints the message. Save the program and recompile it. What error message(s) do you get?

Correcting Syntax Errors

File *Problems.java* contains a simple Java program that contains a number of syntax errors. Save the program to your directory, study it and correct as many of the errors as you can find. Then compile the program; if there are still errors, correct them. Some things to remember:

☐ Java is case sensitive, so, for example, the identifiers *public*, *Public*, and *PUBLIC* are all considered different. For reserved words such as *public* and *void* and previously defined identifiers such as *String* and *System*, you have to get the case right. You will learn the conventions about case soon, but for now you can look at a sample program in the text to see what case should be used where.
☐ When the compiler lists lots of errors, fix the first one (or few) and then recompile—often the later errors aren't really errors in the program, they just indicate that the compiler is confused from earlier errors.
☐ Read the error messages carefully, and note what line numbers they refer to. Often the messages are helpful, but even when they aren't, the line numbers usually are.
☐ When the program compiles cleanly, run it.

```
// *********************************************
//    Problems.java
//
//    Provide lots of syntax errors for the user to correct.
//
   *********************************************

public class problems
{

    public Static main (string[] args)
    {

        System.out.println ("!!!!!!!!!!!!!!!!!!!!!!!!!!!!!!!!!!!!!!!!!!!!");
        System.out.println (This program used to have lots of problems,");
        System.Out.println ("but if it prints this, you fixed them all.")
        System.out.println ("           *** Hurray! ***);
        System.out.println ("!!!!!!!!!!!!!!!!!!!!!!!!!!!!!!!!!!!!!!!!!!!!");

    }
}
```

Chapter 2: Data and Expressions
Lab Exercises

Topics	Lab Exercises
Print and println	
String literals	Names and Places
String concatenation	A Table of Student Grades
Escape sequences	Two Meanings of Plus
Variables	Prelab Exercises
Constants	Area and Circumference of a Circle
Assignment	Painting a Room
Integers and Floating point	Ideal Weight
Arithmetic Expressions	Lab Grades
Operator Precedence	Base Conversion
Input using the Scanner class	
HTML	Introduction to HTML
Applets	Drawing Shapes
Graphics	The Java Coordinate System
Colors	Drawing a Face
	Creating a Pie Chart
	Colors in Java

Names and Places

The goal in this exercise is to develop a program that will print out a list of student names together with other information for each. The *tab character* (an escape sequence) is helpful in getting the list to line up nicely. A program with only two names is in the file *Names.java*.

```
//  ************************************************************
//    Names.java
//
//    Prints a list of student names with their hometowns
//    and intended major
//  ************************************************************

public class Names
{
    // -----------------------
    // main prints the list
    // -----------------------
    public static void main (String[] args)
    {
      System.out.println ();
      System.out.println ("\tName\t\tHometown");
      System.out.println ("\t====\t\t========");
      System.out.println ("\tSally\t\tRoanoke");
      System.out.println ("\tAlexander\tWashington");
      System.out.println ();
    }
}
```

1. Save Names.java to your directory. Compile and run it to see how it works.
2. Modify the program so that your name and hometown and the name and hometown of at least two classmates sitting near you in lab also are printed. Save, compile and run the program. Make sure the columns line up.
3. Modify the program to add a third column with the intended major of each person (assume Sally's major is Computer Science and Alexander's major is Math). Be sure to add a label at the top of the third column and be sure everything is lined up (use tab characters!).

A Table of Student Grades

Write a Java program that prints a table with a list of at least 5 students together with their grades earned (lab points, bonus points, and the total) in the format below.

```
///////////////////////\\\\\\\\\\\\\\\\\\\\\
==          Student Points          ==
\\\\\\\\\\\\\\\\\\\\\\\\///////////////////

Name            Lab     Bonus   Total
----            ---     -----   -----
Joe             43      7       50
William         50      8       58
Mary Sue        39      10      49
```

The requirements for the program are as follows:

1. Print the border on the top as illustrated (using the slash and backslash characters).
2. Use tab characters to get your columns aligned and you must use the + operator both for addition and string concatenation.
3. Make up your own student names and points—the ones shown are just for illustration purposes. You need 5 names.

Two Meanings of Plus

In Java, the symbol + can be used to add numbers or to concatenate strings. This exercise illustrates both uses.

When using a string literal (a sequence of characters enclosed in double quotation marks) in Java the complete string must fit on one line. The following is NOT legal (it would result in a compile-time error).

```
System.out.println ("It is NOT okay to go to the next line
                     in a LONG string!!!");
```

The solution is to break the long string up into two shorter strings that are joined using the *concatenation* operator (which is the + symbol). This is discussed in Section 2.1 in the text. So the following would be legal

```
System.out.println ("It is OKAY to break a long string into " +
                    "parts and join them with a + symbol.");
```

So, when working with strings the + symbol means to concatenate the strings (join them). BUT, when working with numbers the + means what it has always meant—add!

1. **Observing the Behavior of +** To see the behavior of + in different settings do the following:
   a. Study the program below, which is in file *PlusTest.java*.

```
// ***************************************************************
//   PlusTest.java
//
//   Demonstrate the different behaviors of the + operator
// ***************************************************************

public class PlusTest
{
    // -------------------------------------------------
    // main prints some expressions using the + operator
    // -------------------------------------------------
    public static void main (String[] args)
    {
       System.out.println ("This is a long string that is the " +
                           "concatenation of two shorter strings.");

       System.out.println ("The first computer was invented about" + 55 +
                           "years ago.");

       System.out.println ("8 plus 5 is " + 8 + 5);

       System.out.println ("8 plus 5 is " + (8 + 5));

       System.out.println (8 + 5 + " equals 8 plus 5.");
    }
}
```

   b. Save PlusTest.java to your directory.
   c. Compile and run the program. For each of the last three output statements (the ones dealing with 8 plus 5) write down what was printed. Now for each explain why the computer printed what it did given that the following rules are used for +. Write out complete explanations.
      □ If both operands are numbers + is treated as ordinary addition. (NOTE: in the expression a + b the a and b are called the operands.)
      □ If at least one operand is a string the other operand is converted to a string and + is the concatenation operator.
      □ If an expression contains more than one operation expressions inside parentheses are evaluated first. If there are no parentheses the expression is evaluated left to right.
   d. The statement about when the computer was invented is too scrunched up. How should that be fixed?

2. **Writing Your Own Program With** + Now write a complete Java program that prints out the following sentence:

```
Ten robins plus 13 canaries is 23 birds.
```

Your program must use only one statement that invokes the *println* method. It must use the + operator both to do arithmetic and string concatenation.

Prelab Exercises

1. What is the difference between a variable and a constant?

2. Explain what each of the lines below does. Be sure to indicate how each is different from the others.
   a. int x;

   b. int x = 3;

   c. x = 3;

3. The following program reads three integers and prints the average. Fill in the blanks so that it will work correctly.

```
//  ************************************************************************
//     Average.java
//
//     Read three integers from the user and print their average
//  ************************************************************************

import java.util.Scanner;
public class Average
{
   public static void main(String[] args)
   {
      int val1, val2, val3;
      double average;
      Scanner scan = new Scanner(System.in) ;

      // get three values from user
      System.out.println("Please enter three integers and " +
                         "I will compute their average");


      _____


      _____


      _____


      //compute the average

      _____


      //print the average

      _____


   }
}
```

4. Given the declarations below, find the result of each expression.

```
int a = 3, b = 10, c = 7;
double w = 12.9, y = 3.2;
```

a. a + b * c

b. a - b - c

c. a / b

d. b / a

e. a - b / c

f. w / y

g. y / w

h. a + w / b

i. a % b / y

j. b % a

k. w % y

5. Carefully study the following program and find and correct all of the syntax errors.

```
// File:      Errors.java
// Purpose:   A program with lots of syntax errors
//            Correct all of the errors (STUDY the program carefully!!)

#import java.util.Scanner;

public class errors
{
    public static void main (String[] args)
    {
        String Name;   / Name of the user
        int number;
        int numSq;
        Scanner scan = new Scanner(System.in);

        System.out.print ("Enter your name, please: ")
        Name = scan.nextInt();

        System.out.print ("What is your favorite number?);
        number = scan.nextInt();

        numSq = number * number;

        System.out.println (Name   ", the square of your number is "
                        numSquared);

    }
}
```

6. Trace the execution of the following program assuming the input stream contains the numbers 10, 3, and 14.3. Use a table that shows the value of each variable at each step. Also show the output (exactly as it would be printed).

```java
// FILE:  Trace.java
// PURPOSE:  An exercise in tracing a program and understanding
//           assignment statements and expressions.

import java.util.Scanner;

public class Trace
{
    public static void main (String[] args)
    {
        int one, two, three;
        double what;
        Scanner scan = new Scanner(System.in);

        System.out.print ("Enter two integers: ");
        one = scan.nextInt();
        two = scan.nextInt();

        System.out.print("Enter a floating point number: ");
        what = scan.nextDouble();

        three = 4 * one + 5 * two;
        two = 2 * one;
        System.out.println ("one " + two + ":" + three);

        one = 46 / 5 * 2 + 19 % 4;
        three = one + two;
        what = (what + 2.5) / 2;
        System.out.println (what + " is what!");
    }
}
```

Area and Circumference of a Circle

Study the program below, which uses both variables and constants:

```java
//**********************************************************
//  Circle.java
//
//  Print the area of a circle with two different radii
//**********************************************************

public class Circle
{
    public static void main(String[] args)
    {
     final double PI = 3.14159;

     int radius = 10;
     double area = PI * radius * radius;

     System.out.println("The area of a circle with radius " + radius +
                        " is " + area);

     radius = 20;
     area = PI * radius * radius;

     System.out.println("The area of a circle with radius " + radius +
                        " is " + area);

    }
}
```

Some things to notice:

☐ The first three lines inside *main* are declarations for PI, radius, and area. Note that the type for each is given in these lines: *final double* for PI, since it is a floating point constant; *int* for radius, since it is an integer variable, and *double* for area, since it will hold the product of the radius and PI, resulting in a floating point value.

☐ These first three lines also hold initializations for PI, radius, and area. These could have been done separately, but it is often convenient to assign an initial value when a variable is declared.

☐ The next line is simply a print statement that shows the area for a circle of a given radius.

☐ The next line is an assignment statement, giving variable radius the value 20. Note that this is not a declaration, so the *int* that was in the previous radius line does not appear here. The same memory location that used to hold the value 10 now holds the value 20—we are not setting up a new memory location.

☐ Similar for the next line—no *double* because area was already declared.

☐ The final print statement prints the newly computed area of the circle with the new radius.

Save this program, which is in file *Circle.java*, into your directory and modify it as follows:

1. The circumference of a circle is two times the product of Pi and the radius. Add statements to this program so that it computes the circumference in addition to the area for both circles. You will need to do the following:
    ☐ Declare a new variable to store the circumference.
    ☐ Store the circumference in that variable each time you compute it.
    ☐ Add two additional print statements to print your results.
    Be sure your results are clearly labeled.

2. When the radius of a circle doubles, what happens to its circumference and area? Do they double as well? You can determine this by dividing the second area by the first area. Unfortunately, as it is now the program overwrites the first area with the second area (same for the circumference). You need to save the first area and circumference you compute instead of overwriting them with the second set of computations. So you'll need two area variables and two

circumference variables, which means they'll have to have different names (e.g., area1 and area2). Remember that each variable will have to be declared. Modify the program as follows:

☐ Change the names of the area and circumference variables so that they are different in the first and second calculations. Be sure that you print out whatever you just computed.

☐ At the end of the program, compute the area change by dividing the second area by the first area. This gives you the factor by which the area grew. Store this value in an appropriately named variable (which you will have to declare).

☐ Add a println statement to print the change in area that you just computed.

☐ Now repeat the last two steps for the circumference.

Look at the results. Is this what you expected?

3. In the program above, you showed what happened to the circumference and area of a circle when the radius went from 10 to 20. Does the same thing happen whenever the radius doubles, or were those answers just for those particular values? To figure this out, you can write a program that reads in values for the radius from the user instead of having it written into the program ("hardcoded"). Modify your program as follows:

☐ At the very top of the file, add the line

```
import java.util.Scanner;
```

This tells the compiler that you will be using methods from the Scanner class. In the main method create a Scanner object called *scan* to read from System.in.

☐ Instead of initializing the radius in the declaration, just declare it without giving it a value. Now add two statements to read in the radius from the user:

☐ A *prompt*, that is, a print statement that tells the user what they are supposed to do (e.g., "Please enter a value for the radius.");

☐ A read statement that actually reads in the value. Since we are assuming that the radius is an integer, this will use the nextInt() method of the Scanner class.

☐ When the radius gets it second value, make it be twice the original value.

☐ Compile and run your program. Does your result from above hold?

Chapter 2: Data and Expressions

Painting a Room

File *Paint.java* contains the partial program below, which when complete will calculate the amount of paint needed to paint the walls of a room of the given length and width. It assumes that the paint covers 350 square feet per gallon.

```java
//******************************************************************
//File: Paint.java
//
//Purpose: Determine how much paint is needed to paint the walls
//of a room given its length, width, and height
//******************************************************************
import java.util.Scanner;

public class Paint
{
    public static void main(String[] args)
    {
        final int COVERAGE = 350;  //paint covers 350 sq ft/gal
        //declare integers length, width, and height;
        //declare double totalSqFt;
        //declare double paintNeeded;
        //declare and initialize Scanner object

        //Prompt for and read in the length of the room

        //Prompt for and read in the width of the room

        //Prompt for and read in the height of the room

        //Compute the total square feet to be painted--think
        //about the dimensions of each wall

        //Compute the amount of paint needed

        //Print the length, width, and height of the room and the
        //number of gallons of paint needed.
    }
}
```

Save this file to your directory and do the following:

1. Fill in the missing statements (the comments tell you where to fill in) so that the program does what it is supposed to. Compile and run the program and correct any errors.
2. Suppose the room has doors and windows that don't need painting. Ask the user to enter the number of doors and number of windows in the room, and adjust the total square feet to be painted accordingly. Assume that each door is 20 square feet and each window is 15 square feet.

Ideal Weight

Write a program to compute the ideal weight for both males and females. According to one study, the ideal weight for a female is 100 pounds plus 5 pounds for each inch in height over 5 feet. For example, the ideal weight for a female who is 5'3" would be 100 + 15 = 115 pounds. For a male the ideal weight is 106 pounds plus 6 pounds for each inch in height over 5 feet. For example, the ideal weight for a male who is 6'2" would be 106 + 14*6 = 190 pounds. Your program should ask the user to enter his/her height in feet and inches (both as integers—so a person 5'3" would enter the 5 and the 3). It should then compute and print both the ideal weight for a female and the ideal weight for a male. The general outline of your main function would be as follows:

- Declare your variables (think about what variables you need—you need to input two pieces of information (what?), then you need some variables for your calculations (see the following steps)
- Get the input (height in feet and inches) from the user
- Compute the total number of inches of height (convert feet and inches to total inches)
- Compute the ideal weight for a female and the ideal weight for a male (here you basically convert the "word" description above to assignment statements)
- Print the answers

Plan your program, then type it in, compile and run it. Be sure it gives correct answers.

Enhance the Program a Bit The weight program would be a bit nicer if it didn't just give one number as the ideal weight for each sex. Generally a person's weight is okay if it is within about 15% of the ideal. Add to your program so that in addition to its current output it prints an okay range for each sex—the range is from the ideal weight minus 15% to the ideal weight plus 15%. You may do this by introducing new variables and assignment statements OR directly within your print statements.

Lab Grades

Suppose your lab instructor has a somewhat complicated method of determining your grade on a lab. Each lab consists of two out-of-class activities—a pre-lab assignment and a post-lab assignment—plus the in-class activities. The in-class work is 60% of the lab grade and the out-of-class work is 40% of the lab grade. Each component of the grade is based on a different number of points (and this varies from lab to lab)—for example, the pre-lab may be graded on a basis of 20 points (so a student may earn 17 out of 20 points) whereas the post-lab is graded on a basis of 30 points and the in-class 25 points. To determine the out-of-class grade the instructor takes the total points earned (pre plus post) divided by the maximum possible number of points, multiplied by 100 to convert to percent; the in-class grade is just the number of points earned divided by the maximum points, again converted to percent.

The program *LabGrade.java* is supposed to compute the lab grade for a student. To do this it gets as input the number of points the student earned on the prelab assignment and the maximum number of points the student could have earned; the number of points earned on the lab itself and the maximum number of points; the number of points earned on the postlab assignment and the maximum number of points. The lab grade is computed as described above: the in-class and out-of-class grades (in percent) are computed separately then a weighted average of these is computed. The program currently assumes the out-of-class work counts 40% and the in-class counts 60%. Do the following:

1. First carefully hand trace the program assuming the input stream contains the values 17, 20, 23, 25, 12, 15. Trace the program exactly as it is written (it is not correct but it will compile and run so the computer would not know it isn't correct). Fill in the answers to the following questions:
    a. Show exactly how the computer would execute the assignment statement that computes the out of class average for this set of input. Show how the expression will be evaluated (the order in which the operations are performed) and what the result will be.
    b. Show how the computer would execute the assignment statement that computes the in-class average. What will the result be?
    c. Show how the computer would execute the assignment statement that computes the lab grade.

2. Now run the program, typing in the input you used in your trace. Compare your answers to the output. Clearly the output is incorrect! Correct the program. This involves writing the expressions to do calculations correctly. The correct answers for the given input should be an out of class average of 82.857 (the student earned 29 points out of a possible 35 which is approximately 82.857%), an in-class average of 92 (23 points out of 25), and a lab grade of 88.34 (40% of 82.857 plus 60% of 92).

3. Modify the program to make the weights for the two components of the grade variable rather than the constants 0.4 and 0.6. To do this, you need to do four things:
    a. Change the declarations so the weights (*IN_WEIGHT* and *OUT_WEIGHT*) are variables rather than constants. Note that you should also change their names from all capital letters (the convention for constants) to lowercase letters with capitals starting new words (the convention for variables). So *IN_WEIGHT* should become *inWeight*. Of course, you'll also have to change it where it's used in the program.
    b. In the input section, add statements that will prompt the user for the weight (in decimal form—for example .4 for 40%) to be assigned to the in-class work, then read the input. Note that your prompt should explain to the user that the weight is expected to be in decimal form.
    c. In the section that calculates the labGrade add an assignment statement that calculates the weight to be assigned to the out of class work (this will be 1 minus the in-class weight).

    Compile and run your program to make sure it is correct.

```
// *******************************************************************
//    LabGrade.java
//    This program computes a student's lab grade from
//    the grades on the three components of lab:  the pre-lab
//    assignment, the lab itself, and the post-lab assignment.
// *******************************************************************

import java.util.Scanner;
```

```java
public class LabGrade
{
    public static void main (String[] args)
    {
      // Declare constants
      final double IN_WEIGHT = 0.6;  // in-class weight is 60%
      final double OUT_WEIGHT = 0.4; // out-of-class weight is 40%

      // Declare variables
      int preLabPts;      //number of points earned on the pre-lab assignment
      int preLabMax;      //maximum number of points possible for pre-lab
      int labPts;         //number of poitns earned on the lab
      int labMax;         //maximum number of points possible for lab
      int postLabPts;     //number of points earned on the post-lab assignment
      int postLabMax;     //maximum number of points possible for the post-lab
      int outClassAvg;    //average on the out of class (pre and post) work
      int inClassAvg;     //average on the in-class work
      double labGrade;    //final lab grade

      Scanner scan = new Scanner(System.in);

      // Get the input
      System.out.println("\nWelcome to the Lab Grade Calculator\n");
      System.out.print("Enter the number of points you earned on the pre-lab: ");
      preLabPts = scan.nextInt();
      System.out.print("What was the maximum number of points you could have earned? ");
      preLabMax = scan.nextInt();
      System.out.print("Enter the number of points you earned on the lab: ");
      labPts = scan.nextInt();
      System.out.print("What was the maximum number of points for the lab? ");
      labMax = scan.nextInt();
      System.out.print("Enter the number of points you earned on the post-lab: ");
      postLabPts = scan.nextInt();
      System.out.print("What was the maximum number of points for the post-lab? ");
      postLabMax = scan.nextInt();
      System.out.println();

      // Calculate the average for the out of class work
      outClassAvg = preLabPts + postLabPts / preLabMax + postLabMax * 100;

      // Calculate the average for the in-class work
      inClassAvg = labPts / labMax * 100;

      // Calculate the weighted average taking 40% of the out-of-class average
      // plus 60% of the in-class
      labGrade = OUT_WEIGHT * outClassAvg + IN_WEIGHT * inClassAvg;

      // Print the results
      System.out.println("Your average on out-of-class work is " + outClassAvg + "%");
      System.out.println("Your average on in-class work is " + inClassAvg + "%");
      System.out.println("Your lab grade is " + labGrade + "%");
      System.out.println();
    }
}
```

Base Conversion

One algorithm for converting a base 10 number to another base b involves repeatedly dividing by b. Each time a division is performed the remainder and quotient are saved. At each step, the dividend is the quotient from the preceding step; the divisor is always b. The algorithm stops when the quotient is 0. The number in the new base is the sequence of remainders in reverse order (the last one computed goes first; the first one goes last).

In this exercise you will use this algorithm to write a program that converts a base 10 number to a 4-digit number in another base (you don't know enough programming yet to be able to convert any size number). The base 10 number and the new base (between 2 and 9) will be input to the program. The start of the program is in the file *BaseConvert.java*. Save this file to your directory, then modify it one step at a time as follows:

1. The program will only work correctly for base 10 numbers that fit in 4 digits in the new base. We know that in base 2 the maximum unsigned integer that will fit in 4 bits is 1111_2 which equals 15 in base 10 (or $2^4 - 1$). In base 8, the maximum number is 7777_8 which equals 4095 in base 10 (or $8^4 - 1$). In general, the maximum base 10 number that fits in 4 base b digits is $b^4 - 1$. Add an assignment statement to the program to compute this value for the base that is input and assign it to the variable *maxNumber*. Add a statement that prints out the result (appropriately labeled). Compile and run the program to make sure it is correct so far.

2. Now add the code to do the conversion. The comments below guide you through the calculations—replace them with the appropriate Java statements.

   ```
   // First compute place0 -- the units place.  Remember this comes
   // from the first division so it is the remainder when the
   // base 10 number is divided by the base (HINT %).
   // Then compute the quotient (integer division / will do it!) -
   // You can either store the result back in base10Num or declare a
   // new variable for the quotient

   // Now compute place1 -- this is the remainder when the quotient
   // from the preceding step is divided by the base.
   // Then compute the new quotient

   // Repeat the idea from above to compute place2 and the next quotient

   // Repeat again to compute place3
   ```

3. So far the program does not print out the answer. Recall that the answer is the sequence of remainders written in reverse order— note that this requires concatenating the four digits that have been computed. Since they are each integers, if we just add them the computer will perform arithmetic instead of concatenation. So, we will use a variable of type String. Note near the top of the program a variable named *baseBNum* has been declared as an object of type String and initialized to an empty string. Add statements to the program to concatenate the digits in the new base to *baseBNum* and then print the answer. Compile and run your program. Test it using the following values: Enter 2 for the base and 13 for the base 10 number—the program should print 1101 as the base 2 value; enter 8 for the base and 1878 for the number—the program should print 3526 for the base 8 value; enter 3for the base and 50 for the number—the program should print 1212.

```java
//  ***************************************************
//    BaseConvert.java
//
//    Converts base 10 numbers to another base
//    (at most 4 digits in the other base).  The
//    base 10 number and the base are input.
//  ***************************************************

import java.util.Scanner;

public class BaseConvert
{
    public static void main (String[] args)
    {
        int base;          // the new base
        int base10Num;     // the number in base 10
        int maxNumber;     // the maximum number that will fit
                           // in 4 digits in the new base

        int place0;        // digit in the 1's (base^0) place
        int place1;        // digit in the base^1 place
        int place2;        // digit in the base^2 place
        int place3;        // digit in the base^3 place

        String baseBNum = new String (""); // the number in the new base
        Scanner scan = new Scanner(System.in);

        // read in the base 10 number and the base
        System.out.println();
        System.out.println ("Base Conversion Program");
        System.out.println();
        System.out.print ("Please enter a base (2 - 9): ");
        base = scan.nextInt();

        // Compute the maximum base 10 number that will fit in 4 digits
        // in the new base and tell the user what range the number they
        // want to convert must be in

        System.out.print ("Please enter a base 10 number to convert: ");
        base10Num = scan.nextInt();


        // Do the conversion (see notes in lab)

        // Print the result (see notes in lab)

    }
}
```

Introduction to HTML

HTML is the HyperText Markup Language. It is used to describe how text, images, and multimedia are displayed by Web browsers. In this lab you will learn a little about HTML so that you can create a web page containing headings, interesting fonts, lists, and links as well as applets.

HTML uses *tags* to describe the layout of a document; the browser then uses these tags to figure out how to display the document. Tags are enclosed in angle brackets. For example, <title> is a tag that indicates that this section contains the title of the document. Many tags, including <title>, have corresponding end tags that indicate where the section ends. The end tags look just like the start tags except that they start with the character /, e.g., </title>. So the following text indicates that the title of the document is `Introduction to HTML`:

```
<title>Introduction to HTML</title>
```

There are a few tags that almost every document will have: <html>, <head>, <title>, and <body>. Here is an example of a simple HTML document:

```
<HTML>
  <HEAD>
    <TITLE>Introduction to HTML</TITLE>
  </HEAD>

  <BODY>
  In this lab you will learn about HTML, which is lots of fun
  to use.  In particular, you will learn how to use fonts,
  paragraphs, lists, links and applets in a web page.  Now you
  can make your own web page for your friends to visit!
  </BODY>
</HTML>
```

To see what this looks like, open the file in the web browser. Change the size of the browser window (click and drag any corner) and see how the text is reformatted as the window changes. Note that the title appears on the window, not as part of the document.

The HEAD of a document (everything between <HEAD> and </HEAD>) contains the introduction to the document. The title goes in the head, but for now we won't use the head for anything else. The BODY of a document (everything between <BODY> and </BODY>) contains everything that will be displayed as part of the document. Both the HEAD and the BODY are enclosed by the HTML tags, which begin and end the document.

This document contains only plain text, but an HTML document can have much more structure: headings, paragraphs, lists, bold and italic text, images, links, tables, and so on. Here is a document containing a heading, two paragraphs, and some fancy fonts:

```
<HTML>
  <HEAD>
    <TITLE>Introduction to HTML</TITLE>
  </HEAD>

  <BODY BGCOLOR="lightgreen">
  <H1 align="center">Introduction to HTML</H1>

  <P>In this lab you will learn about <I>HTML</I>, which
  is lots of fun
  to use.  In particular, you will learn how to use fonts,
  paragraphs, lists, links, and colors in a web page.  Now you
  can make your <B>own</B> web page for your friends to visit!</P>

  <P>Later in this lab you will do some fancier stuff with
  applets and graphics and include an applet on your web page.
  Can't you just feel the job offers start rolling in?</P>
  <U>Yippee!</U>
  </BODY>
</HTML>
```

Run the HTML document to see what this looks like in the browser.

In this document the <H1> tag creates a level 1 heading. This is the biggest heading; it might be used at the beginning of the document or the start of a new chapter. Level 2 through level 6 headings are also available with the <H2> through <H6> tags.

The <P> tag creates a new paragraph. Most browsers leave a blank line between paragraphs. The <B> tag creates bold text, the <I> tag creates italic text, and the <U> tag creates underlined text. Note that each of these tags is closed with the corresponding end tag. The BGCOLOR attribute on the BODY tag sets the background color.

Note that line breaks and blank lines in the HTML document do not matter—the browser will format paragraphs to fit the window. If it weren't for the <P> tag, the blank line between the paragraphs in this document would not show up in the displayed document.

Exercise #1: For a file to be visible on the Web, it must be where the web server knows how to find it. *** Instruct students how to create and/or access the public html directory on the local system. ***

Open a new file called MyPage.html in a directory where it will be accessible from the web. Write a simple web page about things that interest you. Your page should contain at least the following:

☐ A title (using the <TITLE> tag)
☐ Two different levels of headings
☐ Two paragraphs
☐ Some bold, italic, or underlined text

Your name should appear somewhere in the document.

When you are done, view your document from the browser. Just type in the URL, don't use File | Open Page.

More HTML

Lists We often want to add a list to a document. HTML provides two kinds of lists, *ordered* (e.g., 1, 2, 3) and *unordered* (e.g., bulleted). A list is introduced with the <OL> or <UL> tag, depending on whether it is ordered or unordered. Each list item is introduced with a <LI> tag and ended with the </LI> tag. The entire list is then ended with </OL> or </UL>, as appropriate.   For example, the code below creates the list shown; replacing the <OL> and </OL> tags with <UL> and </UL> would produce the same list with bullets instead of numbers.

```
Things I like:
<OL>
<LI>chocolate
<LI>rabbits
<LI>chocolate rabbits
</OL>
```

Things I like:
1. chocolate
2. rabbits
3. chocolate rabbits

Exercise #2: Add a list, either ordered or unordered, of at least three elements to your document.

Links Links connect one document to another. Links are created in HTML with the <A> (anchor) tag. When creating a link you have to specify two things:

☐   The URL of the document to go to when the link is clicked. This is given as the HREF attribute of the A element.

☐   How the link should be displayed (that is, what text or image to click on to go to the linked document). This appears between the <A> and </A> tags.

For example, the code below creates the link shown, which goes to a page about the history of computing:

```
Learn more about <A HREF="http://ei.cs.vt.edu/~history">the history of
computing.</A>
```

Learn more about the history of computing.

Exercise #3: Add at least one link that ties in to the material on your page.

Drawing Shapes

The following is a simple applet that draws a blue rectangle on a yellow background.

```
//  ***********************************************************
//    Shapes.java
//
//    The program will draw two filled rectangles and a
//    filled oval.
//  ***********************************************************

import javax.swing.JApplet;
import java.awt.*;

public class Shapes extends JApplet
{
    public void paint (Graphics page)
    {
      // Declare size constants
      final int MAX_SIZE = 300;
      final int PAGE_WIDTH = 600;
      final int PAGE_HEIGHT = 400;

      // Declare variables
      int x, y;      // x and y coordinates of upper left-corner of each shape
      int width, height; // width and height of each shape

      // Set the background color
      setBackground (Color.yellow);

      // Set the color for the next shape to be drawn
      page.setColor (Color.blue);

      // Assign the corner point and width and height
      x = 200;
      y = 150;
      width = 100;
      height = 70;

      // Draw the rectangle
      page.fillRect(x, y, width, height);
    }
}
```

Study the code, noting the following:

- ☐ The program imports javax.swing.JApplet because this is an applet, and it imports java.awt.* because it uses graphics.
- ☐ There is no *main* method—instead there is a *paint* method. The paint method is automatically invoked when an applet is displayed, just as the main method is automatically invoked when an application is executed.
- ☐ Most of the methods that draw shapes (see the list in Figure 2.12) require parameters that specify the upper left-hand corner of the shape (using the coordinate system described in Section 2.9) and the width and height of the shape. You can see this in the calls to *fillRect*, which draws a rectangle filled with the current foreground color.
- ☐ This applet will be drawn assuming the window for drawing (the Graphics object - named *page* here) is 600 pixels wide and 400 pixels high. These numbers are defined in constants at the beginning of the program. (They currently have no use but you will use them later). The width and height of the applet are actually specified in the HTML file that instructs the Web browser to run the applet (remember applets are executed by Web browsers and Web browsers get their instructions from HTML documents—note that the code executed by the browser is the *bytecode* for the program, the *Shapes.class* file). The code in the HTML document is as follows:

```
<html>
<applet code="Shapes.class" width=600 height=400>
</applet>
</html>
```

Save the files *Shapes.java* and *Shapes.html* to your directory. Now do the following:

1. Compile Shapes.java, but don't run it—this is an applet, so it is run through a browser or a special program called the Applet Viewer.

2. Run the program through your browser. You should see a blue rectangle on a yellow background.

3. Now run the program through the Applet Viewer by typing the command

    ```
    appletviewer Shapes.html
    ```

    You should see a new window open displaying the rectangle.

4. Now open the program in your text editor and change the x and y variables both to 0. Save and recompile the program, then view it in the Applet Viewer (this is generally less trouble when making lots of changes than using the browser). What happened to the rectangle?

5. Now change the width to 200 and the height to 300. Save, recompile and run to see how this affects the rectangle.

6. Change x to 400, y to 40, width to 50 and height to 200. Test the program to see the effect.

7. Modify the program so that it draws four rectangles in all, as follows:
    - One rectangle should be entirely contained in another rectangle.
    - One rectangle should overlap one of the first two but not be entirely inside of it.
    - The fourth rectangle should not overlap any of the others.

8. One last touch to the program ... Change the colors for at least three of the shapes so the background and each of the three shapes are different colors (a list of colors is in Figure 2.10 of the text). Also change two of the *fillRect* methods to *fillOval* so the final program draws two rectangles and two ovals. Be sure that the overlap rules are still met.

The Java Coordinate System

The Java coordinate system is discussed in Section 2.7 & 2.9 of the text. Under this system, the upper left-hand corner of the window is the point (0,0). The X axis goes across the window, and the Y axis goes down the window. So the bigger the X value, the farther a point is to the right. The bigger the Y value, the farther it is down. There are no negative X or Y values in the Java coordinate system. Actually, you can use negative values, but since they're off the screen they won't show up!

1. Save files *Coords.java* and *Coords.html* to your directory. File Coords.java contains an applet that draws a rectangle whose upper lefthand corner is at 0,0. Use the applet viewer to run this applet. Remember that you have to do it through the html file: *appletviewer Coords.html*.

2. Modify the applet so that instead of 0,0 for the upper lefthand corner, you use the coordinates of the middle of the applet window. This applet is set up to be 600 pixels wide and 400 pixels high, so you can figure out where the middle is. Save, compile, and view your applet. Does the rectangle appear to be in the middle of the screen? Modify the coordinates so that it does appear to be in the middle.

3. Now add four more rectangles to the applet, one in each corner. Each rectangle should just touch one corner of the center rectangle and should go exactly to the edges of the window.

4. Make each rectangle be a different color. To do this, use the setColor method of the Graphics class to change the color (this is already done once). **Do not change the background color once it has been set!** Doing so causes the screen to flicker between colors.

```
// *****************************************************************
//   Coords.java
//
//   Draw rectangles to illustrate the Java coordinate system
//
// *****************************************************************

import javax.swing.JApplet;
import java.awt.*;

public class Coords extends JApplet
{
    public void paint (Graphics page)
    {
      // Declare size constants
      final int MAX_SIZE = 300;
      final int PAGE_WIDTH = 600;
      final int PAGE_HEIGHT = 400;

      // Declare variables
      int x, y;      // x and y coordinates of upper left-corner of each shape
      int width, height; // width and height of each shape

      // Set the background color
      setBackground (Color.yellow);

      // Set the color for the next shape to be drawn
      page.setColor (Color.blue);

      // Assign the corner point and width and height
      x = 0;
      y = 0;
```

```
        width = 150;
        height = 100;

        page.fillRect(x, y, width, height);

    }
}
```

Coords.html

```
<html>
<applet code="Coords.class" width=600 height=400>
</applet>
</html>
```

Drawing a Face

Write an applet that draws a smiling face. Give the face eyes with pupils, ears, a nose, and a mouth. Use at least three different colors, and fill in some of the features. Name this file Face.java, and create a corresponding .html file. View your applet using the applet viewer.

Now add your face to a web page you created (you may have created one in an earlier lab exercise). You will do this using the <APPLET> tag that is in the .html file you are using with the applet viewer—you can just copy it out of that file and paste it into your other file. The applet will appear wherever you insert the applet tag.

Creating a Pie Chart

Write an applet that draws a pie chart showing the percentage of household income spent on various expenses. Use the percentages below:

Rent and Utilities	35%
Transportation	15%
Food	15%
Educational	25%
Miscellaneous	10%

Each section of the pie should be in a different color, of course. Label each section of the pie with the category it represents—the labels should appear outside the pie itself.

Embed your applet in an HTML document about managing expenses. It should contain a heading, some text, a relevant list, and at least one link to a relevant page. Your name should also appear somewhere on the page. Embed the applet so that it fits in nicely.

Colors in Java

The basic scheme for representing a picture in a computer is to break the picture down into small elements called *pixels* and then represent the color of each pixel by a numeric code (this idea is discussed in section 1.6 of the text). In most computer languages, including Java, the color is specified by three numbers—one representing the amount of red in the color, another the amount of green, and the third the amount of blue. These numbers are referred to as the *RGB value* of the color. In Java, each of the three primary colors is represented by an 8-bit code. Hence, the possible base 10 values for each have a range of 0-255. Zero means none of that color while 255 means the maximum amount of the color. Pure red is represented by 255 for red, 0 for green, and 0 for blue, while magenta is a mix of red and blue (255 for red, 0 for green, and 255 for blue). In Java you can create your own colors. So far in the graphics programs we have written we have used the pre-defined colors, such as Color.red, from the Color class. However, we may also create our own Color object and use it in a graphics program. One way to create a Color object is to declare a variable of type Color and instantiate it using the constructor that requires three integer parameters—the first representing the amount of red, the second the amount of green, and the third the amount of blue in the color. For example, the following declares the Color object *myColor* and instantiates it to a color with code 255 for red, 0 for green, and 255 for blue.

```
Color myColor = new Color(255, 0, 255);
```

The statement *page.setColor(myColor)* then will set the foreground color for the page to be the color defined by the *myColor* object. The file *Colors.java* contains an applet that defines *myColor* to be a Color object with color code (200, 100, 255) - a shade of purple. Save the program and its associated HTML file *Colors.html* to your directory, compile and run it using the appletviewer. Now make the following modifications:

1. Change the constructor so the color code is (0,0,0) --- absence of color. What color should this be? Run the program to check.
2. Try a few other combinations of color codes to see what you get. The description of the Color class in Appendix M contains documentation that gives the codes for the pre-defined colors.
3. Notice in the Color class in Appendix M there is a constructor that takes a single integer as an argument. The first 8 bits of this integer are ignored while the last 24 bits define the color—8 bits for red, 8 for green, and the last 8 bits for blue. Hence, the bit pattern

    ```
    00000000000000001111111100000000
    ```

    should represent pure green. Its base 10 value is 65280. Change the declaration of the *myColor* object to

    ```
    Color myColor = new Color (65280);
    ```

    Compile and run the program. Do you see green?

4. The Color class has methods that return the individual color codes (for red, green, and blue) for a Color object. For example,

    ```
    redCode = myColor.getRed();
    ```

    returns the code for the red component of the myColor object (redCode should be a variable of type int). The methods that return the green and blue components are *getGreen* and *getBlue*, respectively. Add statements to the program, similar to the above, to get the three color codes for *myColor* (you need to declare some variables). Then add statements such as

    ```
    page.drawString("Red: " + redCode, ____ , ____ );
    ```

    to label the rectangle with the three color codes (fill in the blanks with appropriate coordinates so each string is drawn inside the rectangle—you also need to set the drawing color to something such as black so the strings will show up). Compile and run the program; for the pure green color above, you should get 0 for red and blue and 255 for green. Now change the integer you use to create the color from 65280 to 115 and see what you get (can you predict?), then try it again with 2486921 (harder to predict!).

```
// *************************************************************
//   Colors.java
//
//   Draw rectangles to illustrate colors and their codes in Java
// *************************************************************

import javax.swing.JApplet;
import java.awt.*;

public class Colors extends JApplet
{
    public void paint (Graphics page)
    {
      // Declare size constants
      final int PAGE_WIDTH = 600;
      final int PAGE_HEIGHT = 400;

      // Declare variables
      int x, y;      // x and y coordinates of upper left-corner of each shape
      int width, height; // width and height of each shape

      Color myColor = new Color (200, 100, 255);

      // Set the background color and paint the screen with a white rectangle
      setBackground (Color.white);
      page.setColor(Color.white);
      page.fillRect(0, 0, PAGE_WIDTH, PAGE_HEIGHT);

      // Set the color for the rectangle
      page.setColor (myColor);

      // Assign the corner point and width and height then draw
      x = 200;
      y = 125;
      width = 200;
      height = 150;

      page.fillRect(x, y, width, height);

    }
}
```

Colors.html

```
<html>
<applet code="Colors.class" width=600 height=400>
</applet>
</html>
```

Chapter 3: Using Classes and Objects
Lab Exercises

Topics	Lab Exercises
String Class	Prelab Exercises
	Working with Strings
Random Class	Rolling Dice
Math Class	Computing Distance
Formatting Classes	Formatting Output
Enumerated Types	Playing with Cards
Wrapper Classes	Experimenting with the Integer Class
Panels	Nested Panels

Prelab Exercises
Sections 3.2-3.5

These exercises focus on the String, Random, and Math classes defined in the Java Standard Class Library. The main concepts are in the text in sections 3.2-3.5. The goals of the lab are for you to gain experience with the following concepts:

- Declaring a variable to be a reference to an object—for example, the following declares the variable *quotation* to be a reference to a String object:

  ```
  String quotation;
  ```

- Declaring a variable to be a reference to an object and creating the object (*instantiating* it) using the *new* operator—for example,

  ```
  String quotation = new String("I think, therefore I am.");
  Random generator = new Random();
  ```

- Invoking a method to operate on an object using the *dot operator*—for example,

  ```
  quotation.length()
  ```

  invokes the length method which returns the length of the quotation String or

  ```
  quotation.toLowerCase()
  ```

  quotation except all letters are lower case. These invocations would be used in a program in a place appropriate for an integer (in the first case) or a String (in the second case) such as an assignment statement or a println statement.

- Invoking *static* or *class* methods—these are methods that are invoked using the class name rather than an object name. The methods in the Math class are static methods (basically because we don't need different instances of Math whereas there are lots of different String objects). Examples are

  ```
  Math.sqrt(2)    (which returns the square root of 2)
  ```

  and

  ```
  Math.pow(3, 2)   (which returns 3²)
  ```

- Importing the appropriate packages—usually when you use classes from a library you need to put the *import* declaration at the top of your program. The exception is for classes defined in the java.lang package (this includes String and Math) which is automatically imported into every Java program.

Exercises

1. Fill in the blanks in the program below as follows: (Section 3.2, especially the example in Listing 3.1, should be helpful):
   (a) declare the variable *town* as a reference to a String object and initialize it to "Anytown, USA".
   (b) write an assignment statement that invokes the *length* method of the string class to find the length of the *college* String object and assigns the result to the stringLength variable
   (c) complete the assignment statement so that *change1* contains the same characters as *college* but all in upper case
   (d) complete the assignment statement so that *change2* is the same as *change1* except all capital O's are replaced with the asterisk (*) character.
   (e) complete the assignment statement so that *change3* is the concatenation of *college* and *town* (use the *concat* method of the String class rather than the + operator)

```
//  ***************************************************
//    StringPlay.java
//
//    Play with String objects
//  ***************************************************
public class StringPlay
{
    public static void main (String[] args)
    {
        String college = new String ("PoDunk College");

        _____; // part (a)


        int stringLength;
        String change1, change2, change3;

        _____; // part (b)

        System.out.println (college + " contains " + stringLength + " characters.");

        change1 = _____; // part (c)

        change2 = _____; // part (d)

        change3 = _____; // part (e)

        System.out.println ("The final string is " + change3);
    }
}
```

2. The following program should read in the lengths of two sides of a right triangle and compute the length of the hypotenuse (recall that the length of the hypotenuse is the square root of side 1 squared plus side 2 squared). Complete it by adding statements to read the input from the keyboard and to compute the length of the hypotenuse (you need to use a Math class method for that).

```
// **************************************************************
//    RightTriangle.java
//
//    Compute the length of the hypotenuse of a right triangle
//    given the lengths of the sides
// **************************************************************
import java.util.Scanner;

public class RightTriangle
{
    public static void main (String[] args)
    {
        double side1, side2;  // lengths of the sides of a right triangle
        double hypotenuse;    // length of the hypotenuse

        Scanner scan = new Scanner(System.in);

        // Get the lengths of the sides as input
        System.out.print ("Please enter the lengths of the two sides of " +
                          "a right triangle (separate by a blank space): ");

        _____;

        _____;

        // Compute the length of the hypotenuse

        _____;

        // Print the result
        System.out.println ("Length of the hypotenuse: " + hypotenuse);
    }
}
```

3. In many situations a program needs to generate a random number in a certain range. The Java Random class lets the programmer create objects of type Random and use them to generate a stream of random numbers (one at a time). The following declares the variable *generator* to be an object of type Random and instantiates it with the *new* operator.

```
Random generator = new Random();
```

The *generator* object can be used to generate either integer or floating point random numbers using either the *nextInt* method (either with no parameter or with a single integer parameter) or *nextFloat* (or *nextDouble)* methods, respectively. The integer returned by *nextIn(t* could be any valid integer (positive or negative) whereas the number returned by *nextInt(n)* is a random integer in the range 0 to n-1. The numbers returned by *nextFloat()* or *nextDouble()* are floating point numbers between 0 and 1 (up to but not including the 1). Most often the goal of a program is to generate a random integer in some particular range, say 30 to 99 (inclusive). There are several ways to do this:

- **Using nextInt():** This way we must use the % operator to reduce the range of values—for example,

```
Math.abs(generator.nextInt()) % 70
```

will return numbers between 0 and 69 (because those are the only possible remainders when an integer is divided by 70 - note that the absolute value of the integer is first taken using the *abs* method from the Math class). In general, using % N will give numbers in the range 0 to N - 1. Next the numbers must be shifted to the desired range by adding the appropriate number. So, the expression

```
Math.abs(generator.nextInt()) % 70 + 30
```

will generate numbers between 30 and 99.

- **Using nextInt(70):** The expression

    ```
    generator.nextInt(70)
    ```

    will return numbers between 0 and 69 (inclusive). Next the numbers must be shifted to the desired range by adding the appropriate number. So, the expression

    ```
    generator.nextInt(70) + 30
    ```

    will generate numbers between 30 and 99.

- **Using nextFloat:** In this case, we must multiply the result of nextFloat to expand the range—for example,

    ```
    generator.nextFloat() * 70
    ```

    returns a floating point number between 0 and 70 (up to but not including 70). To get the integer part of the number we use the cast operator:

    ```
    (int) (generator.nextFloat() * 70)
    ```

    The result of this is an integer between 0 and 69, so

    ```
    (int) (generator.nextFloat() * 70) + 30
    ```

    shifts the numbers by 30 resulting in numbers between 30 and 99.

    The method *nextFloat* can be replaced by *nextDouble* to get double precision floating point numbers rather than single precision.

Fill in the blanks in the following program to generate the random numbers as described in the documentation. NOTE that that java.util.Random must be imported to use the Random class.

```
// **************************************************
//   LuckyNumbers.java
//
//   To generate three random "lucky" numbers
// **************************************************

import java.util.Random;

public class LuckyNumbers
{
    public static void main (String[] args)
    {
        Random generator = new Random();
        int lucky1, lucky2, lucky3;

        // Generate lucky1 (a random integer between 50 and 79) using the
        // nextInt method (with no parameter)

        lucky1 = _____ ;

        // Generate lucky2 (a random integer between 90 and 100) using the
        // nextInt method with an integer parameter

        lucky2 = _____ ;
```

Chapter 3: Using Classes and Objects

```java
    // Generate lucky3 (a random integer between 11 and 30) using nextFloat

    lucky3 = _____ ;

    System.out.println ("Your lucky numbers are " + lucky1 + ", " + lucky2
                        + ", and " + lucky3);
    }
}
```

Working with Strings

The following program illustrates the use of some of the methods in the String class. Study the program to see what it is doing.

```
// ****************************************************************
//    StringManips.java
//
//    Test several methods for manipulating String objects
// ****************************************************************

import java.util.Scanner;

public class StringManips
{
    public static void main (String[] args)
    {
      String phrase = new String ("This is a String test.");
      int phraseLength;   // number of characters in the phrase String
      int middleIndex;    // index of the middle character in the String
      String firstHalf;   // first half of the phrase String
      String secondHalf;  // second half of the phrase String
      String switchedPhrase; // a new phrase with original halves switched

      // compute the length and middle index of the phrase
      phraseLength = phrase.length();
      middleIndex = phraseLength / 2;

      // get the substring for each half of the phrase
      firstHalf = phrase.substring(0,middleIndex);
      secondHalf = phrase.substring(middleIndex, phraseLength);

      // concatenate the firstHalf at the end of the secondHalf
      switchedPhrase = secondHalf.concat(firstHalf);

      // print information about the phrase
      System.out.println();
      System.out.println ("Original phrase: " + phrase);
      System.out.println ("Length of the phrase: " + phraseLength +
                  " characters");
      System.out.println ("Index of the middle: " + middleIndex);
      System.out.println ("Character at the middle index: " +
                  phrase.charAt(middleIndex));
      System.out.println ("Switched phrase: " + switchedPhrase);

      System.out.println();
    }
}
```

The file *StringManips.java* contains this program. Save the file to your directory and compile and run it. Study the output and make sure you understand the relationship between the code and what is printed. Now modify the file as follows:

1. Declare a variable of type String named *middle3* (put your declaration with the other declarations near the top of the program) and use an assignment statement and the *substring* method to assign *middle3* the substring consisting of the middle three characters of *phrase* (the character at the middle index together with the character to the left of that and the one to the right – use variables, not the literal indices for this particular string). Add a println statement to print out the result. Save, compile, and run to test what you have done so far.

2. Add an assignment statement to replace all blank characters in *switchedPhrase* with an asterisk (*). The result should be stored back in *switchedPhrase* (so switchedPhrase is actually changed). (Do not add another print—place your statement in the program so that this new value of *switchedPhrase* will be the one printed in the current println statement.) Save, compile, and run your program.

3. Declare two new variables *city* and *state* of type String. Add statements to the program to prompt the user to enter their hometown—the city and the state. Read in the results using the appropriate Scanner class method – you will need to have the user enter city and state on separate lines. Then using String class methods create and print a new string that consists of the state name (all in uppercase letters) followed by the city name (all in lowercase letters) followed again by the state name (uppercase). So, if the user enters Lilesville for the city and North Carolina for the state, the program should create and print the string

    ```
    NORTH CAROLINAlilesvilleNORTH CAROLINA
    ```

Rolling Dice

Write a complete Java program that simulates the rolling of a pair of dice. For each die in the pair, the program should generate a random number between 1 and 6 (inclusive). It should print out the result of the roll for each die and the total roll (the sum of the two dice), all appropriately labeled. You must use the Random class. The RandomNumbers program in listing 3.2 of the text may be helpful.

Computing Distance

The file *Distance.java* contains an incomplete program to compute the distance between two points. Recall that the distance between the two points (x1, y1) and (x2, y2) is computed by taking the square root of the quantity $(x1 - x2)^2 + (y1 - y2)^2$. The program already has code to get the two points as input. You need to add an assignment statement to compute the distance and then a print statement to print it out (appropriately labeled). Test your program using the following data: The distance between the points (3, 17) and (8, 10) is 8.6023... (lots more digits printed); the distance between (–33, 49) and (–9, –15) is 68.352....

```java
// ************************************************************
//    Distance.java
//
//    Computes the distance between two points
// ************************************************************

import java.util.Scanner;

public class Distance
{
    public static void main (String[] args)
    {
      double x1, y1, x2, y2; // coordinates of two points
      double distance;       // distance between the points

      Scanner scan = new Scanner(System.in);

      // Read in the two points
      System.out.print ("Enter the coordinates of the first point " +
              "(put a space between them): ");
      x1 = scan.nextDouble();
      y1 = scan.nextDouble();

      System.out.print ("Enter the coordinates of the second point: ");
      x2 = scan.nextDouble();
      y2 = scan.nextDouble();

      // Compute the distance

      // Print out the answer

    }
}
```

Formatting Output

File *Deli.java* contains a partial program that computes the cost of buying an item at the deli. Save the program to your directory and do the following:

1. Study the program to understand what it does.

2. Add the import statements to import the DecimalFormat and NumberFormat classes.

3. Add the statement to declare *money* to be a NumberFormat object as specified in the comment.

4. Add the statement to declare *fmt* to be a DecimalFormat object as specified in the comment.

5. Add the statements to print a label in the following format (the numbers in the example output are correct for input of $4.25 per pound and 41 ounces). Use the formatting object money to print the unit price and total price and the formatting object fmt to print the weight to 2 decimal places.

    ```
    *****  CS Deli  *****

    Unit Price: $4.25 per pound
    Weight: 2.56 pounds

    TOTAL: $10.89
    ```

```
// ************************************************************
// DeliFormat.java
//
// Computes the price of a deli item given the weight
// (in ounces) and price per pound -- prints a label,
// nicely formatted, for the item.
//
// ************************************************************

import java.util.Scanner;



public class Deli
{
    // ----------------------------------------------------
    //  main reads in the price per pound of a deli item
    //  and number of ounces of a deli item then computes
    //  the total price and prints a "label" for the item
    // ----------------------------------------------------

    public static void main (String[] args)
    {
        final double OUNCES_PER_POUND = 16.0;

        double pricePerPound;   // price per pound
        double weightOunces;    // weight in ounces
        double weight;                  // weight in pounds
        double totalPrice;        // total price for the item

        Scanner scan = new Scanner(System.in);

        // Declare money as a NumberFormat object and use the
        // getCurrencyInstance method to assign it a value


        // Declare fmt as a DecimalFormat object and instantiate
        // it to format numbers with at least one digit to the left of the
        // decimal and the fractional part rounded to two digits.


        // prompt the user and read in each input
        System.out.println ("Welcome to the CS Deli!!\n ");

        System.out.print ("Enter the price per pound of your item: ");
        pricePerPound = scan.nextDouble();

        System.out.print ("Enter the weight (ounces): ");
        weightOunces = scan.nextDouble();

        // Convert ounces to pounds and compute the total price
        weight = weightOunces / OUNCES_PER_POUND;
        totalPrice = pricePerPound * weight;

        // Print the label using the formatting objects
        // fmt for the weight in pounds and money for the prices



    }
}
```

Playing With Cards

Write a class that defines an enumerated type named *Rank* with values ace, two, three, four, five, six, seven, eight, nine, ten, jack, queen, king. The main method should do the following:

1. Declare variables *highCard*, *faceCard*, *card1*, and *card2* of type Rank.

2. Assign highCard to be an ace, faceCard to be a jack, queen or king (your choice), and card1 and card2 to be two different numbered cards (two through ten - your choice).

3. Print a line, using the highCard and faceCard objects, in the following format:

        A blackjack hand: ace and .....

   The faceCard variable should be printed instead of the dots.

4. Declare two variables card1Val and card2Val of type int and assign them the face value of your card1 and card2 objects. Use your card1 and card2 variables and the ordinal method associated with enumerated types. Remember that the face value of two is 2, three is 3, and so on so you need to make a slight adjustment to the ordinal value of the enumerated type.

5. Print two lines, using the card1 and card2 objects and the name method, as follows:

        A two card hand: (print card1 and card2)
        Hand value: (print the sum of the face values of the two cards)

Chapter 3: Using Classes and Objects

Experimenting with the Integer Class

Wrapper classes are described on pages 138-140 of the text. They are Java classes that allow a value of a primitive type to be "wrapped up" into an object, which is sometimes a useful thing to do. They also often provide useful methods for manipulating the associated type. Wrapper classes exist for each of the primitive types: boolean, char, float, double, int, long, short, and byte.

Write a program IntWrapper that uses the constants and methods of the Integer class (page 140 for a short list, pages 819-820 for a complete list) to perform the following tasks. Be sure to clearly label your output and test your code for each task before proceding.

1. Prompt for and read in an integer, then print the binary, octal and hexadecimal representations of that integer.

2. Print the maximum and minimum possible Java integer values. Use the constants in the Integer class that hold these values -- don't type in the numbers themselves. Note that these constants are static (see the description on page 140 and the signature on page 819).

3. Prompt the user to enter two decimal integers, one per line. Use the *next* method of the Scanner class to read each of them in. (The *next* method returns a String so you need to store the values read in String variables, which may seem strange.) Now convert the strings to ints (use the appropriate method of the Integer class to do this), add them together, and print the sum.

Nested Panels

The program NestedPanels.java is from Listing 3.8 of the text. Save the program to your directory and do the following:

1. Compile and run the program. Experiment with resizing the frame and observe the effect on the components.
2. Modify the program by adding a third subpanel that is twice as wide, but the same height, as the other two subpanels. Choose your own label and color for the subpanel (the color should not be red, green, or blue). Add the panel to the primary panel after the other two panels.
3. Compile and run the modified program. Again, experiment with resizing the frame and observe the effect on the components.
4. Now add a statement to the program to set the preferred size of the primary panel to 320 by 260. (What would be the purpose of this?). Compile and run the program to see if anything changed.
5. Now add another panel with background color blue and size 320 by 20. Add a "My Panels" label to this panel and then add this panel to the primary panel before adding the other panels. Compile and run the program. What was the effect of this panel?

```
//**********************************************************************
//  NestedPanels.java        Author: Lewis/Loftus
//
//  Demonstrates a basic component hierarchy.
//**********************************************************************
import java.awt.*;
import javax.swing.*;

public class NestedPanels
{
    //------------------------------------------------------------------
    //  Presents two colored panels nested within a third.
    //------------------------------------------------------------------
    public static void main (String[] args)
    {
        JFrame frame = new JFrame ("Nested Panels");
        frame.setDefaultCloseOperation (JFrame.EXIT_ON_CLOSE);

        // Set up first subpanel
        JPanel subPanel1 = new JPanel();
        subPanel1.setPreferredSize (new Dimension(150, 100));
        subPanel1.setBackground (Color.green);
        JLabel label1 = new JLabel ("One");
        subPanel1.add (label1);

        // Set up second subpanel
        JPanel subPanel2 = new JPanel();
        subPanel2.setPreferredSize (new Dimension(150, 100));
        subPanel2.setBackground (Color.red);
        JLabel label2 = new JLabel ("Two");
        subPanel2.add (label2);

        // Set up primary panel
        JPanel primary = new JPanel();
        primary.setBackground (Color.blue);
        primary.add (subPanel1);
        primary.add (subPanel2);

        frame.getContentPane().add(primary);
        frame.pack();
        frame.setVisible(true);
    }
}
```

Chapter 4: Writing Classes
Lab Exercises

Topics	Lab Exercises
Classes and methods	Prelab Exercises
	A Bank Account Class
	Tracking Grades
	A Band Booster Class
	Representing Names
	Drawing Squares
GUIs: Buttons and Textfields	Voting with Buttons
	Calculating Body Mass Index

Prelab Exercises

1. Constructors are special methods included in class definitions.
   a. What is a constructor used for?
   b. How do constructors differ from other methods in a class?

2. Both methods and variables in a class are declared as either *private* or *public*. Describe the difference between private and public and indicate how a programmer decides which parts of a class should be private and which public.

3. Consider a class that represents a bank account.
   a. Such a class might store information about the account balance, the name of the account holder, and an account number. What instance variables would you declare to hold this information? Give a type and name for each.
   b. There are a number of operations that would make sense for a bank account—withdraw money, deposit money, check the balance, and so on. Write a method header with return type, name, and parameter list, for each such operation described below. Don't write the whole method—just the header. They will all be public methods. The first one is done for you as an example.
      i. Withdraw a given amount from the account. This changes the account balance, but does not return a value.

      ```
      public void withdraw(double amount)
      ```

      ii. Deposit a given amount into the account. This changes the account balance, but does not return a value.
      iii. Get the balance from the account. This does not change anything in the account; it simply returns the balance.
      iv. Return a string containing the account information (name, account number, balance). This does not change anything in the account.
      v. Charge a $10 fee. This changes the account balance but does not return a value.
      vi. Create a new account given an initial balance, the name of the owner, and the account number. Note that this will be a constructor, and that a constructor does not have a return type.

A Bank Account Class

1. File *Account.java* contains a partial definition for a class representing a bank account. Save it to your directory and study it to see what methods it contains. Then complete the Account class as described below. Note that you won't be able to test your methods until you write ManageAccounts in question #2.

   a. Fill in the code for method *toString*, which should return a string containing the name, account number, and balance for the account.
   b. Fill in the code for method *chargeFee*, which should deduct a service fee from the account.
   c. Modify *chargeFee* so that instead of returning void, it returns the new balance. Note that you will have to make changes in two places.
   d. Fill in the code for method *changeName* which takes a string as a parameter and changes the name on the account to be that string.

2. File *ManageAccounts.java* contains a shell program that uses the Account class above. Save it to your directory, and complete it as indicated by the comments.

3. Modify ManageAccounts so that it prints the balance after the calls to chargeFees. Instead of using the getBalance method like you did after the deposit and withdrawal, use the balance that is returned from the chargeFees method. You can either store it in a variable and then print the value of the variable, or embed the method call in a println statement.

```
//***********************************************************
// Account.java
//
// A bank account class with methods to deposit to, withdraw from,
// change the name on, charge a fee to, and print a summary of the account.
//***********************************************************

public class Account
{
  private double balance;
  private String name;
  private long acctNum;

  //-----------------------------------------------
  //Constructor -- initializes balance, owner, and account number
  //-----------------------------------------------
  public Account(double initBal, String owner, long number)
  {
    balance = initBal;
    name = owner;
    acctNum = number;
  }

  //-----------------------------------------------
  // Checks to see if balance is sufficient for withdrawal.
  // If so, decrements balance by amount; if not, prints message.
  //-----------------------------------------------
  public void withdraw(double amount)
  {
    if (balance >= amount)
      balance -= amount;
    else
      System.out.println("Insufficient funds");
  }

  //-----------------------------------------------
  // Adds deposit amount to balance.
```

```java
//-------------------------------------------------
public void deposit(double amount)
{
   balance += amount;
}

//-------------------------------------------------
// Returns balance.
//-------------------------------------------------
public double getBalance()
{
   return balance;
}


//-------------------------------------------------
// Returns a string containing the name, account number, and balance.
//-------------------------------------------------
public String toString()
{

}

//-------------------------------------------------
// Deducts $10 service fee
//-------------------------------------------------
public void chargeFee()
{


}

//-------------------------------------------------
// Changes the name on the account
//-------------------------------------------------
public void changeName(String newName)

{

}

}
```

```
// ****************************************************************
//   ManageAccounts.java
//
//   Use Account class to create and manage Sally and Joe's
//   bank accounts
// ****************************************************************

public class ManageAccounts
{
    public static void main(String[] args)
    {
      Account acct1, acct2;

      //create account1 for Sally with $1000
      acct1 = new Account(1000, "Sally", 1111);

      //create account2 for Joe with $500

      //deposit $100 to Joe's account

      //print Joe's new balance (use getBalance())

      //withdraw $50 from Sally's account

      //print Sally's new balance (use getBalance())

      //charge fees to both accounts

      //change the name on Joe's account to Joseph

      //print summary for both accounts

    }
}
```

Tracking Grades

A teacher wants a program to keep track of grades for students and decides to create a student class for his program as follows:

☐ Each student will be described by three pieces of data: his/her name, his/her score on test #1, and his/her score on test #2.
☐ There will be one constructor, which will have one argument—the name of the student.
☐ There will be three methods: *getName*, which will return the student's name; *inputGrades*, which will prompt for and read in the student's test grades; and *getAverage*, which will compute and return the student's average.

1. File *Student.java* contains an incomplete definition for the Student class. Save it to your directory and complete the class definition as follows:
   a. Declare the instance data (name, score for test1, and score for test2).
   b. Create a Scanner object for reading in the scores.
   c. Add the missing method headers.
   d. Add the missing method bodies.

2. File *Grades.java* contains a shell program that declares two Student objects. Save it to your directory and use the *inputGrades* method to read in each student's test scores, then use the *getAverage* method to find their average. Print the average with the student's name, e.g., "The average for Joe is 87." You can use the *getName* method to print the student's name.

3. Add statements to your Grades program that print the values of your Student variables directly, e.g.:

   ```
   System.out.println("Student 1: " + student1);
   ```

This should compile, but notice what it does when you run it—nothing very useful! When an object is printed, Java looks for a *toString* method for that object. This method must have no parameters and must return a String. If such a method has been defined for this object, it is called and the string it returns is printed. Otherwise the default *toString* method, which is inherited from the Object class, is called; it simply returns a unique hexadecimal identifier for the object such as the ones you saw above.

Add a toString method to your Student class that returns a string containing the student's name and test scores, e.g.:

   ```
   Name: Joe   Test1: 85   Test2: 91
   ```

Note that the toString method does not call System.out.println—it just returns a string.

Recompile your Student class and the Grades program (you shouldn't have to change the Grades program—you don't have to call toString explicitly). Now see what happens when you print a student object—much nicer!

Chapter 4: Writing Classes

```
// ******************************************************************
//     Student.java
//
//     Define a student class that stores name, score on test 1, and
//     score on test 2.  Methods prompt for and read in grades,
//     compute the average, and return a string containing student's info.
// ******************************************************************
import java.util.Scanner;

public class Student
{
    //declare instance data

    //-----------------------------------------------
    //constructor
    //-----------------------------------------------
    public Student(String studentName)
    {
        //add body of constructor
    }

    //-----------------------------------------------
    //inputGrades: prompt for and read in student's grades for test1 and test2.
    //Use name in prompts, e.g., "Enter's Joe's score for test1".
    //-----------------------------------------------
    public void inputGrades()
    {
        //add body of inputGrades
    }

    //-----------------------------------------------
    //getAverage: compute and return the student's test average
    //-----------------------------------------------

    //add header for getAverage
    {
        //add body of getAverage
    }

    //-----------------------------------------------
    //getName: print the student's name
    //-----------------------------------------------

    //add header for printName
    {
        //add body of printName
    }

}
```

```java
// **************************************************************
//    Grades.java
//
//    Use Student class to get test grades for two students
//    and compute averages
//
// **************************************************************
public class Grades
{
    public static void main(String[] args)
    {
      Student student1 = new Student("Mary");
      //create student2, "Mike"

      //input grades for Mary
      //print average for Mary

      System.out.println();

      //input grades for Mike
      //print average for Mike

    }
}
```

Band Booster Class

In this exercise, you will write a class that models a band booster and use your class to update sales of band candy.

1. Write the BandBooster class assuming a band booster object is described by two pieces of instance data: *name* (a String) and *boxesSold* (an integer that represents the number of boxes of band candy the booster has sold in the band fundraiser). The class should have the following methods:

    ☐ A constructor that has one parameter—a String containing the name of the band booster. The constructor should set boxesSold to 0.

    ☐ A method *getName* that returns the name of the band booster (it has no parameters).

    ☐ A method *updateSales* that takes a single integer parameter representing the number of additional boxes of candy sold. The method should add this number to *boxesSold*.

    ☐ A *toString* method that returns a string containing the name of the band booster and the number of boxes of candy sold in a format similar to the following:

    ```
    Joe:   16 boxes
    ```

2. Write a program that uses BandBooster objects to track the sales of 2 band boosters over 3 weeks. Your program should do the following:

    ☐ Read in the names of the two band boosters and construct an object for each.

    ☐ Prompt for and read in the number of boxes sold by each boost for each of the three weeks. Your prompts should include the booster's name as stored in the BandBooster object. For example,

    ```
    Enter the number of boxes sold by Joe this week:
    ```

    For each member, after reading in the weekly sales, invoke the *updateSales* method to update the total sales by that member.

    ☐ After reading the data, print the name and total sales for each member (you will implicitly use the toString method here).

Representing Names

1. Write a class *Name* that stores a person's first, middle, and last names and provides the following methods:
   - public Name(String first, String middle, String last)—constructor. The name should be stored in the case given; don't convert to all upper or lower case.
   - public String getFirst()—returns the first name
   - public String getMiddle()—returns the middle name
   - public String getLast()—returns the last name
   - public String firstMiddleLast()—returns a string containing the person's full name in order, e.g., "Mary Jane Smith".
   - public String lastFirstMiddle()—returns a string containing the person's full name with the last name first followed by a comma, e.g., "Smith, Mary Jane".
   - public boolean equals(Name otherName)—returns true if this name is the same as otherName. Comparisons should not be case sensitive. (Hint: There is a String method *equalsIgnoreCase* that is just like the String method *equals* except it does not consider case in doing its comparison.)
   - public String initials()—returns the person's initials (a 3-character string). The initials should be all in upper case, regardless of what case the name was entered in. (Hint: Instead of using *charAt*, use the *substring* method of String to get a string containing only the first letter—then you can upcase this one-letter string. See Figure 3.1 in the text for a description of the *substring* method.)
   - public int length()—returns the total number of characters in the full name, not including spaces.

2. Now write a program TestNames.java that prompts for and reads in two names from the user (you'll need first, middle, and last for each), creates a Name object for each, and uses the methods of the Name class to do the following:
   a. For each name, print
      - first-middle-last version
      - last-first-middle version
      - initials
      - length
   b. Tell whether or not the names are the same.

Drawing Squares

1. Write a class Square that represents a square to be drawn. Store the following information in instance variables:
   - size (length of any side)
   - x coord of upper left-hand corner
   - y coord of upper left-hand corner
   - color

   Provide the following methods:
   - A parameterless constructor that generates random values for the size, color, x, and y. Make the size between 100 and 200, x between 0 and 600, y between 0 and 400. The squares can be any color—note that you can pass a single int parameter to the Color constructor, but it will only consider the first 24 bits (8 bits for each of R, G, B component).

   - IMPORTANT: Your random number generator must be declared at the class level (not inside the constructor), and must be declared *static*. So its declaration and initialization should appear with the declarations of size, color, x, and y, and should look like this:

   ```
   private static Random generator = new Random();
   ```

   - A *draw* method that draws the square at its x,y coordinate in its color. Note that you need a Graphics object, like the *page* parameter of the paint method, to draw. Your *draw* method should take a Graphics object as a parameter.

2. Now write an applet DrawSquares that uses your Square class to create and draw 5 squares. This code should be very simple; the *paint* method will simply create a Square and then draw it, repeated 5 times. Don't forget to pass the Graphics object to *draw*.

Voting with Buttons

Files *VoteCounter.java* and *VoteCounterPanel.java* contain slightly modified versions of *PushCounter.java* and *PushCounterPanel.java* in listings 4.10 and 4.11 of the text. As in the text the program counts the number of times the button is pushed; however, it assumes ("pretends") each push is a vote for Joe so the button and variables have been renamed appropriately.

1. Compile the program, then run it to see how it works.

2. Modify the program so that there are two candidates to vote for—Joe and Sam. To do this you need to do the following:
   a. Add variables for Sam—a vote counter, a button, and a label.
   b. Add a new inner class named *SamButtonListener* to listen for clicks on the button for Sam. Instantiate an instance of the class when adding the ActionListener to the button for Sam.
   c. Add the button and label for Sam to the panel.

3. Compile and run the program.

```
//***********************************************************
// VoteCounter.java
//
// Demonstrates a graphical user interface and event listeners to
// tally votes for two candidates, Joe and Sam.
//***********************************************************
import javax.swing.JFrame;

public class VoteCounter
{
    //---------------------------------------------
    // Creates the main program frame.
    //---------------------------------------------
    public static void main(String[] args)
    {
        JFrame frame = new JFrame("Vote Counter");
        frame.setDefaultCloseOperation(JFrame.EXIT_ON_CLOSE);

        frame.getContentPane().add(new VoteCounterPanel());

        frame.pack();
        frame.setVisible(true);
    }
}
```

```java
//***********************************************************
// VoteCounterPanel.java
//
// Demonstrates a graphical user interface and event listeners to
// tally votes for two candidates, Joe and Sam.
//***********************************************************

import java.awt.*;
import java.awt.event.*;
import javax.swing.*;

public class VoteCounterPanel extends JPanel
{
    private int votesForJoe;
    private JButton joe;
    private JLabel labelJoe;

    //-----------------------------------------------
    // Constructor: Sets up the GUI.
    //-----------------------------------------------
    public VoteCounterPanel()
    {
        votesForJoe = 0;

        joe = new JButton("Vote for Joe");
        joe.addActionListener(new JoeButtonListener());

        labelJoe = new JLabel("Votes for Joe: " + votesForJoe);

        add(joe);
        add(labelJoe);

        setPreferredSize(new Dimension(300, 40));
        setBackground(Color.cyan);
    }

    //***********************************************************
    // Represents a listener for button push (action) events
    //***********************************************************
    private class JoeButtonListener implements ActionListener
    {
        //-----------------------------------------------
        // Updates the counter and label when Vote for Joe
        // button is pushed
        //-----------------------------------------------
        public void actionPerformed(ActionEvent event)
        {
            votesForJoe++;
            labelJoe.setText("Votes for Joe: " + votesForJoe);
        }
    }
}
```

Calculating Body Mass Index

Body Mass Index (BMI) is measure of weight that takes height into account. Generally, a BMI above 25 is considered high, that is, likely to indicate that an individual is overweight. BMI is calculated as follows for both men and women:

```
(703 * height in inches) / (weight in pounds)2
```

Files *BMI.java* and *BMIPanel.java* contain skeletons for a program that uses a GUI to let the user compute their BMI. This is similar to the Fahrenheit program in listings 4.12 and 4.13 of the text. Fill in the code as indicated by the comments and compile and run this program; you should see the BMI calculator displayed.

```java
//******************************************************************
//  BMI.java
//
//  Sets up a GUI to calculate body mass index.
//******************************************************************

import javax.swing.JFrame;
public class BMI
{
   //-----------------------------------------------------------------
   //  Creates and displays the BMI GUI.
   //-----------------------------------------------------------------
   public static void main (String[] args)
   {

       JFrame frame = new JFrame("BMI");
       frame.setDefaultCloseOperation(JFrame.EXIT_ON_CLOSE);

       BMIPanel panel = new BMIPanel();

       frame.getContentPane().add(panel);
       frame.pack();
       frame.setVisible(true);

   }
}



//******************************************************************
//  BMIPanel.java
//
//  Computes body mass index in a GUI.
//******************************************************************

import java.awt.*;
import java.awt.event.*;
import javax.swing.*;

public class BMIPanel extends JPanel
{
   private int WIDTH = 300;
   private int HEIGHT = 120;
```

```
    private JLabel heightLabel, weightLabel, BMILabel, resultLabel;
    private JTextField height, weight;
    private JButton calculate;

    //-----------------------------------------------------------------
    //  Sets up the GUI.
    //-----------------------------------------------------------------
    public BMIPanel()
    {

        //create labels for the height and weight textfields
        heightLabel = new JLabel ("Your height in inches: ");
        weightLabel = new JLabel ("Your weight in pounds: ");

        //create a "this is your BMI" label
        //create a result label to hold the BMI value

        //create a JTextField to hold the person's height in inches
        //create a JTextField to hold the person's weight in pounds

        //create a button to press to calculate BMI
        //create a BMIListener and make it listen for the button to be pressed


        //add the height label and height textfield to the panel
        //add the weight label and weight textfield to the panel
        //add the button to the panel
        //add the BMI label to the panel
        //add the label that holds the result to the panel

        //set the size of the panel to the WIDTH and HEIGHT constants
        //set the color of the panel to whatever you choose
    }

    //*****************************************************************
    //  Represents an action listener for the calculate button.
    //*****************************************************************
    private class BMIListener implements ActionListener
    {
        //-----------------------------------------------------------------
        //  Compute the BMI when the button is pressed
        //-----------------------------------------------------------------
        public void actionPerformed (ActionEvent event)
        {
            String heightText, weightText;
            int heightVal, weightVal;
            double bmi;

            //get the text from the height and weight textfields

            //Use Integer.parseInt to convert the text to integer values

            //Calculate the bmi = 703 * weight in pounds / (height in inches)^2

            //Put result in result label.  Use Double.toString to convert double to
string.

        }
    }
}
```

Chapter 5: Conditionals and Loops
Lab Exercises

Topics	**Lab Exercises**
Boolean expressions	PreLab Exercises
The **if** statement	Computing a Raise
The **switch** statement	A Charge Account Statement
	Activities at Lake LazyDays
	Rock, Paper, Scissors
	Date Validation
Conditional Operator	Processing Grades
The **while** statement	PreLab Exercises
	Counting and Looping
	Powers of 2
	Factorials
	A Guessing Game
Iterators &	
Reading Text Files	Baseball Statistics
The **do** statement	More Guessing
	Election Day
The **for** statement	Finding Maximum and Minimum Values
	Counting Characters
	Using the Coin Class
Drawing with loops and conditionals	A Rainbow Program
Determining Event Sources	Vote Counter, Revisited
Dialog Boxes	Modifying EvenOdd.java
	A Pay Check Program
Checkboxes & Radio Buttons	Adding Buttons to StyleOptions.java

Prelab Exercises
Sections 5.1-5.3

1. Rewrite each condition below in valid Java syntax (give a boolean expression):
    a. x > y > z
    b. x and y are both less than 0
    c. neither x nor y is less than 0
    d. x is equal to y but not equal to z

2. Suppose *gpa* is a variable containing the grade point average of a student. Suppose the goal of a program is to let a student know if he/she made the Dean's list (the gpa must be 3.5 or above). Write an *if... else...* statement that prints out the appropriate message (either "Congratulations—you made the Dean's List" or "Sorry you didn't make the Dean's List").

3. Complete the following program to determine the raise and new salary for an employee by adding if ... else statements to compute the raise. The input to the program includes the current annual salary for the employee and a number indicating the performance rating (1=excellent, 2=good, and 3=poor). An employee with a rating of 1 will receive a 6% raise, an employee with a rating of 2 will receive a 4% raise, and one with a rating of 3 will receive a 1.5% raise.

```java
//   ****************************************************************
//   Salary.java
//   Computes the raise and new salary for an employee
//   ****************************************************************
import java.util.Scanner;

public class Salary
{
    public static void main (String[] args)
    {
        double currentSalary;   // current annual salary
        double rating;          // performance rating
        double raise;           // dollar amount of the raise

        Scanner scan = new Scanner(System.in);

        // Get the current salary and performance rating
        System.out.print ("Enter the current salary: ");
        currentSalary = scan.nextDouble();
        System.out.print ("Enter the performance rating: ");
        rating = scan.nextDouble();

        // Compute the raise -- Use if ... else ...

        // Print the results
        System.out.println ("Amount of your raise: $" + raise);
        System.out.println ("Your new salary: $" + currentSalary + raise);
    }
}
```

Computing A Raise

File *Salary.java* contains most of a program that takes as input an employee's salary and a rating of the employee's performance and computes the raise for the employee. This is similar to question #3 in the pre-lab, except that the performance rating here is being entered as a String—the three possible ratings are "Excellent", "Good", and "Poor". As in the pre-lab, an employee who is rated excellent will receive a 6% raise, one rated good will receive a 4% raise, and one rated poor will receive a 1.5% raise.

Add the *if... else...* statements to program Salary to make it run as described above. Note that you will have to use the *equals* method of the String class (not the relational operator ==) to compare two strings (see Section 5.3, Comparing Data).

```java
//  ************************************************************
//     Salary.java
//
//     Computes the amount of a raise and the new
//     salary for an employee.  The current salary
//     and a performance rating (a String: "Excellent",
//     "Good" or "Poor") are input.
//  ************************************************************

import java.util.Scanner;
import java.text.NumberFormat;

public class Salary
{
    public static void main (String[] args)
    {
        double currentSalary;   // employee's current  salary
        double raise;           // amount of the raise
        double newSalary;       // new salary for the employee
        String rating;          // performance rating

        Scanner scan = new Scanner(System.in);

        System.out.print ("Enter the current salary: ");
        currentSalary = scan.nextDouble();
        System.out.print ("Enter the performance rating (Excellent, Good, or Poor): ");
        rating = scan.nextLine();

        // Compute the raise using if ...

        newSalary = currentSalary + raise;

        // Print the results
        NumberFormat money = NumberFormat.getCurrencyInstance();
        System.out.println();
        System.out.println("Current Salary:        " + money.format(currentSalary));
        System.out.println("Amount of your raise: " + money.format(raise));
        System.out.println("Your new salary:       " + money.format(newSalary));
        System.out.println();
    }
}
```

A Charge Account Statement

Write a program to prepare the monthly charge account statement for a customer of CS CARD International, a credit card company. The program should take as input the previous balance on the account and the total amount of additional charges during the month. The program should then compute the interest for the month, the total new balance (the previous balance plus additional charges plus interest), and the minimum payment due. Assume the interest is 0 if the previous balance was 0 but if the previous balance was greater than 0 the interest is 2% of the total owed (previous balance plus additional charges). Assume the minimum payment is as follows:

```
        new balance            for a new balance less than $50
          $50.00               for a new balance between $50 and $300 (inclusive)
   20% of the new balance      for a new balance over $300
```

So if the new balance is $38.00 then the person must pay the whole $38.00; if the balance is $128 then the person must pay $50; if the balance is $350 the minimum payment is $70 (20% of 350). The program should print the charge account statement in the format below. Print the actual dollar amounts in each place using currency format from the NumberFormat class—see Listing 3.4 of the text for an example that uses this class.

```
        CS CARD International Statement
        ==================================

        Previous Balance:       $
        Additional Charges:     $
        Interest:               $

        New Balance:            $

        Minimum Payment:        $
```

Activities at Lake LazyDays

As activity directory at Lake LazyDays Resort, it is your job to suggest appropriate activities to guests based on the weather:

```
temp >= 80:          swimming
60 <= temp < 80:     tennis
40 <= temp < 60:     golf
temp < 40:           skiing
```

1. Write a program that prompts the user for a temperature, then prints out the activity appropriate for that temperature. Use a cascading if, and be sure that your conditions are no more complex than necessary.

2. Modify your program so that if the temperature is greater than 95 or less than 20, it prints "Visit our shops!". (Hint: Use a boolean operator in your condition.) For other temperatures print the activity as before.

Rock, Paper, Scissors

Program *Rock.java* contains a skeleton for the game Rock, Paper, Scissors. Open it and save it to your directory. Add statements to the program as indicated by the comments so that the program asks the user to enter a play, generates a random play for the computer, compares them and announces the winner (and why). For example, one run of your program might look like this:

```
$ java Rock
Enter your play: R, P, or S
r
Computer play is S
Rock crushes scissors, you win!
```

Note that the user should be able to enter either upper or lower case r, p, and s. The user's play is stored as a string to make it easy to convert whatever is entered to upper case. Use a switch statement to convert the randomly generated integer for the computer's play to a string.

```java
// ****************************************************************
//    Rock.java
//
//    Play Rock, Paper, Scissors with the user
//
// ****************************************************************
import java.util.Scanner;
import java.util.Random;

public class Rock
{
    public static void main(String[] args)
    {
        String personPlay;     //User's play -- "R", "P", or "S"
        String computerPlay;   //Computer's play -- "R", "P", or "S"
        int computerInt;       //Randomly generated number used to determine
                               //computer's play

        Scanner scan = new Scanner(System.in);
        Random generator = new Random();

        //Get player's play -- note that this is stored as a string
        //Make player's play uppercase for ease of comparison
        //Generate computer's play (0,1,2)
        //Translate computer's randomly generated play to string
        switch (computerInt)
        {

        }

        //Print computer's play
        //See who won.  Use nested ifs instead of &&.
        if (personPlay.equals(computerPlay))
            System.out.println("It's a tie!");
        else if (personPlay.equals("R"))
            if (computerPlay.equals("S"))
                System.out.println("Rock crushes scissors.  You win!!");
            else

                //... Fill in rest of code
    }
}
```

Date Validation

In this exercise you will write a program that checks to see if a date entered by the user is a valid date in the second millenium. A skeleton of the program is in *Dates.java*. Open this program and save it to your directory. As indicated by the comments in the program, fill in the following:

1. An assignment statement that sets monthValid to true if the month entered is between 1 and 12, inclusive.
2. An assignment statement that sets yearValid to true if the year is between 1000 and 1999, inclusive.
3. An assignment statement that sets leapYear to true if the year is a leap year. Here is the leap year rule (there's more to it than you may have thought!):

   If the year is divisible by 4, it's a leap year UNLESS it's divisible by 100, in which case it's not a leap year UNLESS it's divisible by 400, in which case it is a leap year. If the year is not divisible by 4, it's not a leap year.

   Put another way, it's a leap year if a) it's divisible by 400, or b) it's divisible by 4 and it's *not* divisible by 100. So 1600 and 1512 are leap years, but 1700 and 1514 are not.

4. An if statement that determines the number of days in the month entered and stores that value in variable daysInMonth. If the month entered is not valid, daysInMonth should get 0. Note that to figure out the number of days in February you'll need to check if it's a leap year.
5. An assignment statement that sets dayValid to true if the day entered is legal for the given month and year.
6. If the month, day, and year entered are all valid, print "Date is valid" and indicate whether or not it is a leap year. If any of the items entered is not valid, just print "Date is not valid" without any comment on leap year.

```
// ****************************************************************
// Dates.java
//
// Determine whether a 2nd-millenium date entered by the user
// is valid
// ****************************************************************
import java.util.Scanner;

public class Dates
{
    public static void main(String[] args)
    {
        int month, day, year;    //date read in from user
        int daysInMonth;         //number of days in month read in
        boolean monthValid, yearValid, dayValid;  //true if input from user is valid
        boolean leapYear;        //true if user's year is a leap year

        Scanner scan = new Scanner(System.in);

        //Get integer month, day, and year from user

        //Check to see if month is valid

        //Check to see if year is valid

        //Determine whether it's a leap year

        //Determine number of days in month

        //User number of days in month to check to see if day is valid

        //Determine whether date is valid and print appropriate message

    }
}
```

Processing Grades

The file *Grades.java* contains a program that reads in a sequence of student grades and computes the average grade, the number of students who pass (a grade of at least 60) and the number who fail. The program uses a loop (which you learn about in the next section).

1. Compile and run the program to see how it works.
2. Study the code and do the following.
   - ☐ Replace the statement that finds the sum of the grades with one that uses the += operator.
   - ☐ Replace each of three statements that increment a counting variable with statements using the increment operator.

3. Run your program to make sure it works.
4. Now replace the "if" statement that updates the pass and fail counters with the conditional operator.

```java
// ***********************************************************
//   Grades.java
//
//   Read in a sequence of grades and compute the average
//   grade, the number of passing grades (at least 60)
//   and the number of failing grades.
// ***********************************************************
import java.util.Scanner;

public class Grades
{
    //------------------------------------------------------------
    //  Reads in and processes grades until a negative number is entered.
    //------------------------------------------------------------
    public static void main (String[] args)
    {
        double grade;   // a student's grade
        double sumOfGrades; // a running total of the student grades
        int numStudents; // a count of the students
        int numPass;     // a count of the number who pass
        int numFail;     // a count of the number who fail

        Scanner scan = new Scanner(System.in);

        System.out.println ("\nGrade Processing Program\n");

        // Initialize summing and counting variables
        sumOfGrades = 0;
        numStudents = 0;
        numPass = 0;
        numFail = 0;

        // Read in the first grade
        System.out.print ("Enter the first student's grade: ");
        grade = scan.nextDouble();

        while (grade >= 0)
            {
                sumOfGrades = sumOfGrades + grade;
                numStudents = numStudents + 1;

                if (grade < 60)
                    numFail = numFail + 1;
                else
                    numPass = numPass + 1;
```

```java
            // Read the next grade
            System.out.print ("Enter the next grade (a negative to quit): ");
            grade = scan.nextDouble();
         }

      if (numStudents > 0)
         {
            System.out.println ("\nGrade Summary: ");
            System.out.println ("Class Average: " + sumOfGrades/numStudents);
            System.out.println ("Number of Passing Grades: " + numPass);
            System.out.println ("Number of Failing Grades: " + numFail);
         }
      else
         System.out.println ("No grades processed.");
   }
}
```

Prelab Exercises
Section 5.5

In a while loop, execution of a set of statements (the *body* of the loop) continues until the boolean expression controlling the loop (the *condition*) becomes false. As for an if statement, the condition must be enclosed in parentheses. For example, the loop below prints the numbers from 1 to to LIMIT:

```
final int LIMIT = 100;          // setup
int count = 1;

while (count <= LIMIT)          // condition
{                               // body
  System.out.println(count);    //   -- perform task
  count = count + 1;            //   -- update condition
}
```

There are three parts to a loop:

☐   The *setup*, or *initialization*. This comes before the actual loop, and is where variables are initialized in preparation for the first time through the loop.
☐   The *condition*, which is the boolean expression that controls the loop. This expression is evaluated each time through the loop. If it evaluates to true, the body of the loop is executed, and then the condition is evaluated again; if it evaluates to false, the loop terminates.
☐   The *body* of the loop. The body typically needs to do two things:
   ☐   Do some work toward the task that the loop is trying to accomplish. This might involve printing, calculation, input and output, method calls—this code can be arbitrarily complex.
   ☐   Update the condition. Something has to happen inside the loop so that the condition will eventually be false—otherwise the loop will go on forever (an *infinite* loop). This code can also be complex, but often it simply involves incrementing a counter or reading in a new value.
   Sometimes doing the work and updating the condition are related. For example, in the loop above, the print statement is doing work, while the statement that increments count is both doing work (since the loop's task is to print the values of count) and updating the condition (since the loop stops when count hits a certain value).

The loop above is an example of a *count-controlled* loop, that is, a loop that contains a counter (a variable that increases or decreases by a fixed value—usually 1—each time through the loop) and that stops when the counter reaches a certain value. Not all loops with counters are count-controlled; consider the example below, which determines how many even numbers must be added together, starting at 2, to reach or exceed a given limit.

```
final int LIMIT = 16;                          TRACE
int count = 1;                   sum      nextVal      count
int sum = 0;                     ---      -------      -----
int nextVal = 2;

while (sum < LIMIT)
{
  sum = sum + nextVal;
  nextVal = nextVal + 2;
  count = count + 1;
}

System.out.println("Had to add together " + (count-1) + " even numbers " +
               "to reach value " + LIMIT + ".  Sum is " + sum);
```

Note that although this loop counts how many times the body is executed, the condition does not depend on the value of count.

Not all loops have counters. For example, if the task in the loop above were simply to add together even numbers until the sum reached a certain limit and then print the sum (as opposed to printing the number of things added together), there would

           Chapter 5: Conditionals and Loops

be no need for the counter. Similarly, the loop below sums integers input by the user and prints the sum; it contains no counter.

```
int sum = 0;                                              //setup
String keepGoing = "y";
int nextVal;

while (keepGoing.equals("y") || keepGoing.equals("Y"))
{
  System.out.print("Enter the next integer: ");          //do work
  nextVal = scan.nextInt();
  sum = sum + nextVal;

  System.out.println("Type y or Y to keep going");       //update condition
  keepGoing = scan.next();
}

System.out.println("The sum of your integers is " + sum);
```

Exercises

1. In the first loop above, the println statement comes before the value of count is incremented. What would happen if you reversed the order of these statements so that count was incremented before its value was printed? Would the loop still print the same values? Explain.

2. Consider the second loop above.
    a. Trace this loop, that is, in the table next to the code show values for variables nextVal, sum and count at each iteration. Then show what the code prints.
    b. Note that when the loop terminates, the number of even numbers added together before reaching the limit is count-1, not count. How could you modify the code so that when the loop terminates, the number of things added together is simply count?

3. Write a while loop that will print "I love computer science!!" 100 times. Is this loop count-controlled?

4. Add a counter to the third example loop above (the one that reads and sums integers input by the user). After the loop, print the number of integers read as well as the sum. Just note your changes on the example code. Is your loop now count-controlled?

5. The code below is supposed to print the integers from 10 to 1 backwards. What is wrong with it? (Hint: there are two problems!) Correct the code so it does the right thing.

```
count = 10;
while (count >= 0)
{
  System.out.println(count);
  count = count + 1;
}
```

Counting and Looping

The program in *LoveCS.java* prints "I love Computer Science!!" 10 times. Copy it to your directory and compile and run it to see how it works. Then modify it as follows:

```
//   ************************************************************
//   LoveCS.java
//
//   Use a while loop to print many messages declaring your
//   passion for computer science
//   ************************************************************

public class LoveCS
{
    public static void main(String[] args)
    {
      final int LIMIT = 10;

      int count = 1;

      while (count <= LIMIT){
          System.out.println("I love Computer Science!!");
          count++;
      }
    }
}
```

1. Instead of using constant LIMIT, ask the user how many times the message should be printed. You will need to declare a variable to store the user's response and use that variable to control the loop. (Remember that all caps is used only for constants!)

2. Number each line in the output, and add a message at the end of the loop that says how many times the message was printed. So if the user enters 3, your program should print this:

```
1 I love Computer Science!!
2 I love Computer Science!!
3 I love Computer Science!!
Printed this message 3 times.
```

3. If the message is printed N times, compute and print the sum of the numbers from 1 to N. So for the example above, the last line would now read:

```
Printed this message 3 times.  The sum of the numbers from 1 to 3 is 6.
```

    Note that you will need to add a variable to hold the sum.

Powers of 2

File *PowersOf2.java* contains a skeleton of a program to read in an integer from the user and print out that many powers of 2, starting with 20.

1. Using the comments as a guide, complete the program so that it prints out the number of powers of 2 that the user requests. **Do not use Math.pow to compute the powers of 2!** Instead, compute each power from the previous one (how do you get 2^n from 2^{n-1}?). For example, if the user enters 4, your program should print this:

```
Here are the first 4 powers of 2:
1
2
4
8
```

2. Modify the program so that instead of just printing the powers, you print which power each is, e.g.:

```
Here are the first 4 powers of 2:
2^0 = 1
2^1 = 2
2^2 = 4
2^3 = 8
```

```java
// ****************************************************************
//   PowersOf2.java
//
//   Print out as many powers of 2 as the user requests
//
// ****************************************************************
import java.util.Scanner;

public class PowersOf2
{
    public static void main(String[] args)
    {
        int numPowersOf2;          //How many powers of 2 to compute
        int nextPowerOf2 = 1;      //Current power of  2
        int exponent;              //Exponent for current power of 2 -- this
                                   //also serves as a counter for the loop
        Scanner scan = new Scanner(System.in);

        System.out.println("How many powers of 2 would you like printed?");
        numPowersOf2 = scan.nextInt();

        //print a message saying how many powers of 2 will be printed
        //initialize exponent -- the first thing printed is 2 to the what?

        while (  )
        {
            //print out current power of 2

            //find next power of 2 -- how do you get this from the last one?

            //increment exponent

        }
    }
}
```

Factorials

The *factorial* of n (written n!) is the product of the integers between 1 and n. Thus 4! = 1*2*3*4 = 24. By definition, 0! = 1. Factorial is not defined for negative numbers.

1. Write a program that asks the user for a non-negative integer and computes and prints the factorial of that integer. You'll need a while loop to do most of the work—this is a lot like computing a sum, but it's a product instead. And you'll need to think about what should happen if the user enters 0.

2. Now modify your program so that it checks to see if the user entered a negative number. If so, the program should print a message saying that a nonnegative number is required and ask the user the enter another number. The program should keep doing this until the user enters a nonnegative number, after which it should compute the factorial of that number. **Hint:** you will need another while loop **before** the loop that computes the factorial. You should not need to change any of the code that computes the factorial!

A Guessing Game

File *Guess.java* contains a skeleton for a program to play a guessing game with the user. The program should randomly generate an integer between 1 and 10, then ask the user to try to guess the number. If the user guesses incorrectly, the program should ask them to try again until the guess is correct; when the guess is correct, the program should print a congratulatory message.

1. Using the comments as a guide, complete the program so that it plays the game as described above.
2. Modify the program so that if the guess is wrong, the program says whether it is too high or too low. You will need an if statement (inside your loop) to do this.
3. Now add code to count how many guesses it takes the user to get the number, and print this number at the end with the congratulatory message.
4. Finally, count how many of the guesses are too high and how many are too low. Print these values, along with the total number of guesses, when the user finally guesses correctly.

```java
// ****************************************************************
//   Guess.java
//
//   Play a game where the user guesses a number from 1 to 10
//
// ****************************************************************
import java.util.Scanner;
import java.util.Random;

public class Guess
{
    public static void main(String[] args)
    {
       int numToGuess;        //Number the user tries to guess
       int guess;             //The user's guess

       Scanner scan = new Scanner(System.in);
       Random generator = new Random();

       //randomly generate the  number to guess

       //print message asking user to enter a guess

       //read in guess

       while (  )  //keep going as long as the guess is wrong
         {
            //print message saying guess is wrong
            //get another guess from the user
         }

       //print message saying guess is right
    }
}
```

Baseball Statistics

The local Kids' League coach keeps some of the baseball team statistics in a text file organized as follows: each line of the file contains the name of the player followed by a list of symbols indicating what happened on each at bat for the player. The letter h indicates a hit, o an out, w a walk, and s a sacrifice fly. Each item on the line is separated by a comma. There are no blank spaces except in the player name. So, for example the file could look as follows:

Sam Slugger,h,h,o,s,w,w,h,w,o,o,o,h,s
Jill Jenks,o,o,s,h,h,o,o
Will Jones,o,o,w,h,o,o,o,o,w,o,o

The file *BaseballStats.java* contains the skeleton of a program thats reads and processes a file in this format. Study the program and note that three Scanner objects are declared.

- One scanner (*scan*) is used to read in a file name from standard input.
- The file name is then used to create a scanner (*fileScan*) to operate on that file.
- A third scanner (*lineScan*) will be used to parse each line in the file.

Also note that the main method throws an IOException. This is needed in case there is a problem opening the file.

Complete the program as follows:

1. First add a while loop that reads each line in the file and prints out each part (name, then each at bat, without the commas) in a way similar to the URLDissector program in Listing 5.11 of the text. In particular inside the loop you need to
   a. read the next line from the file
   b. create a comma delimited scanner (lineScan) to parse the line
   c. read and print the name of the player, and finally,
   d. have a loop that prints each at bat code.

2. Compile and run the program to be sure it works.

3. Now modify the inner loop that parses a line in the file so that instead of printing each part it counts (separately) the number of hits, outs, walks, and sacrifices. Each of these summary statistics, as well as the batting average, should be printed for each player. Recall that the batting average is the number of hits divided by the total number of hits and outs.

4. Test the program on the file *stats.dat* and *stats2.dat* .

```
// ****************************************************************
//    BaseballStats.java
//
//    Reads baseball data in from a comma delimited file. Each line
//    of the file contains a name followed by a list of symbols
//    indicating the result of each at bat: h for hit, o for out,
//    w for walk, s for sacrifice.  Statistics are computed and
//    printed for each player.
// ****************************************************************

import java.util.Scanner;
import java.io.*;

public class BaseballStats
{
    //----------------------------------------------------
    //  Reads baseball stats from a file and counts
    //  total hits, outs, walks, and sacrifice flies
    //  for each player.
    //----------------------------------------------------
    public static void main (String[] args) throws IOException
```

Chapter 5: Conditionals and Loops

```
   {
      Scanner fileScan, lineScan;
      String fileName;

      Scanner scan = new Scanner(System.in);

      System.out.print ("Enter the name of the input file: ");
      fileName = scan.nextLine();
      fileScan = new Scanner(new File(fileName));

      // Read and process each line of the file



   }
}
```

stats.dat

Willy Wonk,o,o,h,o,o,o,o,h,w,o,o,o,o,s,h,o,h
Shari Jones,h,o,o,s,s,h,o,o,o,h,o,o,o,o
Barry Bands,h,h,w,o,o,o,w,h,o,o,h,h,o,o,w,w,w,h,o,o
Sally Slugger,o,h,h,o,o,h,h,w
Missy Lots,o,o,s,o,o,w,o,o,o
Joe Jones,o,h,o,o,o,o,h,h,o,o,o,o,w,o,o,o,h,o,h,h
Larry Loop,w,s,o,o,o,h,o,o,h,s,o,o,o,h,h
Sarah Swift,o,o,o,o,h,h,w,o,o,o
Bill Bird,h,o,h,o,h,w,o,o,o,h,s,s,h,o,o,o,o,o,o
Don Daring,o,o,h,h,o,o,h,o,h,o,o,o,o,o,o,h
Jill Jet,o,s,s,h,o,o,h,h,o,o,o,h,o,h,w,o,o,h,h,o

stats2.dat

Barry Bands,h,h,w,o,o,o,w,h,o,o,h,h,o,o,w,w,w,h,o,o

More Guessing

File *Guess.java* contains the skeleton for a program that uses a while loop to play a guessing game. (This problem is described in the previous lab exercise.) Revise this program so that it uses a *do ... while* loop rather than a while loop. The general outline using a *do... while* loop is as follows:

```
// set up (initializations of the counting variables)
....

do
{
    // read in a guess
    ...

    // check the guess and print appropriate messages

    ...
}
while ( condition );
```

A key difference between a *while* and a *do ... while* loop to note when making your changes is that the body of the do ... while loop is executed before the condition is ever tested. In the while loop version of the program, it was necessary to read in the user's first guess before the loop so there would be a value for comparison in the condition. In the do... while this "priming" read is no longer needed. The user's guess can be read in at the beginning of the body of the loop.

Election Day

It's almost election day and the election officials need a program to help tally election results. There are two candidates for office—Polly Tichen and Ernest Orator. The program's job is to take as input the number of votes each candidate received in each voting precinct and find the total number of votes for each. The program should print out the final tally for each candidate—both the total number of votes each received and the percent of votes each received. Clearly a loop is needed. Each iteration of the loop is responsible for reading in the votes from a single precinct and updating the tallies. A skeleton of the program is in the file *Election.java*. Open a copy of the program in your text editor and do the following.

1. Add the code to control the loop. You may use either a while loop or a do...while loop. The loop must be controlled by asking the user whether or not there are more precincts to report (that is, more precincts whose votes need to be added in). The user should answer with the character y or n though your program should also allow uppercase repsonses. The variable *response* (type String) has already been declared.
2. Add the code to read in the votes for each candidate and find the total votes. Note that variables have already been declared for you to use. Print out the totals and the percentages after the loop.
3. Test your program to make sure it is correctly tallying the votes and finding the percentages AND that the loop control is correct (it goes when it should and stops when it should).
4. The election officials want more information. They want to know how many precincts each candidate carried (won). Add code to compute and print this. You need three new variables: one to count the number of precincts won by Polly, one to count the number won by Ernest, and one to count the number of ties. Test your program after adding this code.

```
//  ************************************************************
//    Election.java
//
//    This file contains a program that tallies the results of
//    an election.  It reads in the number of votes for each of
//    two candidates in each of several precincts.  It determines
//    the total number of votes received by each candidate, the
//    percent of votes received by each candidate, the number of
//    precincts each candidate carries, and the
//    maximum winning margin in a precinct.
//  ************************************************************

import java.util.Scanner;

public class Election
{
    public static void main (String[] args)
    {
        int votesForPolly;   // number of votes for Polly in each precinct
        int votesForErnest;  // number of votes for Ernest in each precinct
        int totalPolly;      // running total of votes for Polly
        int totalErnest;     // running total of votes for Ernest
        String response;     // answer (y or n) to the "more precincts" question

        Scanner scan = new Scanner(System.in);

        System.out.println ();
        System.out.println ("Election Day Vote Counting Program");
        System.out.println ();

        // Initializations

        // Loop to "process" the votes in each precinct

        // Print out the results
    }
}
```

Finding Maximum and Minimum Values

A common task that must be done in a loop is to find the maximum and minimum of a sequence of values. The file *Temps.java* contains a program that reads in a sequence of hourly temperature readings over a 24-hour period. You will be adding code to this program to find the maximum and minimum temperatures. Do the following:

1. Save the file to your directory, open it and see what's there. Note that a *for* loop is used since we need a count-controlled loop. Your first task is to add code to find the maximum temperature read in. In general to find the maximum of a sequence of values processed in a loop you need to do two things:

    ☐ You need a variable that will keep track of the maximum of the values processed so far. This variable must be initialized before the loop. There are two standard techniques for initialization: one is to initialize the variable to some value *smaller* than any possible value being processed; another is to initialize the variable to the first value processed. In either case, after the first value is processed the maximum variable should contain the first value. For the temperature program declare a variable *maxTemp* to hold the maximum temperature. Initialize it to -1000 (a value less than any legitimate temperature).

    ☐ The maximum variable must be updated each time through the loop. This is done by comparing the maximum to the current value being processed. If the current value is larger, then the current value is the new maximum. So, in the temperature program, add an if statement inside the loop to compare the current temperature read in to maxTemp. If the current temperature is larger set maxTemp to that temperature. NOTE: If the current temperature is NOT larger, DO NOTHING!

2. Add code to print out the maximum after the loop. Test your program to make sure it is correct. Be sure to test it on at least three scenarios: the first number read in is the maximum, the last number read in is the maximum, and the maximum occurs somewhere in the middle of the list. For testing purposes you may want to change the HOURS_PER_DAY variable to something smaller than 24 so you don't have to type in so many numbers!

3. Often we want to keep track of more than just the maximum. For example, if we are finding the maximum of a sequence of test grades we might want to know the name of the student with the maximum grade. Suppose for the temperatures we want to keep track of the time (hour) the maximum temperature occurred. To do this we need to save the current value of the *hour* variable when we update the *maxTemp* variable. This of course requires a new variable to store the time (hour) that the maximum occurs. Declare *timeOfMax* (type int) to keep track of the time (hour) the maximum temperature occurred. Modify your *if* statment so that in addition to updating *maxTemp* you also save the value of *hour* in the *timeOfMax* variable. (WARNING: you are now doing TWO things when the *if* condition is TRUE.)

4. Add code to print out the time the maximum temperature occurred along with the maximum.

5. Finally, add code to find the minimum temperature and the time that temperature occurs. The idea is the same as for the maximum. NOTE: Use a separate *if* when updating the minimum temperature variable (that is, don't add an *else* clause to the *if* that is already there).

```
// ************************************************************
//   Temps.java
//
//   This program reads in a sequence of hourly temperature
//   readings (beginning with midnight) and prints the maximum
//   temperature (along with the hour, on a 24-hour clock, it
//   occurred) and the minimum temperature (along with the hour
//   it occurred).
// ************************************************************

import java.util.Scanner;

public class Temps
{
    //---------------------------------------------------
    //   Reads in a sequence of temperatures and finds the
    //   maximum and minimum read in.
    //---------------------------------------------------
    public static void main (String[] args)
    {
        final int HOURS_PER_DAY = 24;

        int temp;    // a temperature reading

        Scanner scan = new Scanner(System.in);

        // print program heading
        System.out.println ();
        System.out.println ("Temperature Readings for 24 Hour Period");
        System.out.println ();

        for (int hour = 0; hour < HOURS_PER_DAY; hour++)
        {
            System.out.print ("Enter the temperature reading at " + hour +
                         " hours: ");
            temp = scan.nextInt();
        }

        // Print the results
    }
}
```

Counting Characters

The file *Count.java* contains the skeleton of a program to read in a string (a sentence or phrase) and count the number of blank spaces in the string. The program currently has the declarations and initializations and prints the results. All it needs is a loop to go through the string character by character and count (update the *countBlank* variable) the characters that are the blank space. Since we know how many characters there are (the *length* of the string) we use a count controlled loop—*for* loops are especially well-suited for this.

1. Add the *for* loop to the program. Inside the for loop you need to access each individual character—the *charAt* method of the String class lets you do that. The assignment statement

    ```
    ch = phrase.charAt(i);
    ```

    assigns the variable *ch* (type char) the character that is in index i of the String *phrase*. In your for loop you can use an assignment similar to this (replace i with your loop control variable if you use something other than i). NOTE: You could also directly use phrase.charAt(i) in your if (without assigning it to a variable).

2. Test your program on several phrases to make sure it is correct.

3. Now modify the program so that it will count several different characters, not just blank spaces. To keep things relatively simple we'll count the a's, e's, s's, and t's (both upper and lower case) in the string. You need to declare and initialize four additional counting variables (e.g. *countA* and so on). Your current *if* could be modified to cascade but another solution is to use a *switch* statement. Replace the current *if* with a switch that accounts for the 9 cases we want to count (upper and lower case a, e, s, t, and blank spaces). The cases will be based on the value of the *ch* variable. The switch starts as follows—complete it.

    ```
    switch (ch)
    {
        case 'a':
        case 'A':   countA++;
                    break;

        case ....

    }
    ```

    Note that this switch uses the "fall through" feature of switch statements. If *ch* is an 'a' the first case matches and the switch continues execution until it encounters the *break* hence the countA variable would be incremented.

4. Add statements to print out all of the counts.

5. It would be nice to have the program let the user keep entering phrases rather than having to restart it every time. To do this we need another loop surrounding the current code. That is, the current loop will be nested inside the new loop. Add an outer while loop that will continue to execute as long as the user does NOT enter the phrase *quit*. Modify the prompt to tell the user to enter a phrase or *quit* to quit. Note that all of the initializations for the counts should be inside the while loop (that is we want the counts to start over for each new phrase entered by the user). All you need to do is add the while statement (and think about placement of your reads so the loop works correctly). Be sure to go through the program and properly indent after adding code—with nested loops the inner loop should be indented.

```
// ************************************************************
//    Count.java
//
//    This program reads in strings (phrases) and counts the
//    number of blank characters and certain other letters
//    in the phrase.
// ************************************************************

import java.util.Scanner;

public class Count
{
   public static void main (String[] args)
   {
       String phrase;      // a string of characters
       int countBlank;     // the number of blanks (spaces) in the phrase
       int length;         // the length of the phrase
       char ch;            // an individual character in the string

       Scanner scan = new Scanner(System.in);

       // Print a program header
       System.out.println ();
       System.out.println ("Character Counter");
       System.out.println ();

       // Read in a string and find its length
       System.out.print ("Enter a sentence or phrase: ");
       phrase = scan.nextLine();
       length = phrase.length();

       // Initialize counts
       countBlank = 0;

       // a for loop to go through the string character by character
       // and count the blank spaces

       // Print the results
       System.out.println ();
       System.out.println ("Number of blank spaces: " + countBlank);
       System.out.println ();
    }
}
```

Using the Coin Class

The Coin class from Listing 5.4 in the text is in the file *Coin.java*. Copy it to your directory, then write a program to find the length of the longest run of heads in 100 flips of the coin. A skeleton of the program is in the file *Runs.java*. To use the Coin class you need to do the following in the program:

1. Create a coin object.
2. Inside the loop, you should use the *flip* method to flip the coin, the *toString* method (used implicitly) to print the results of the flip, and the *getFace* method to see if the result was HEADS. Keeping track of the current run length (the number of times in a row that the coin was HEADS) and the maximum run length is an exercise in loop techniques!
3. Print the result after the loop.

```java
//  ***************************************************************
//   Coin.java              Author: Lewis and Loftus
//
//   Represents a coin with two sides that can be flipped.
//  ***************************************************************

public class Coin
{
    public final int HEADS = 0;
    public final int TAILS = 1;

    private int face;

    // -----------------------------------------------
    //   Sets up the coin by flipping it initially.
    // -----------------------------------------------
    public Coin ()
    {
       flip();
    }

    // -----------------------------------------------
    //   Flips the coin by randomly choosing a face.
    // -----------------------------------------------
    public void flip()
    {
       face = (int) (Math.random() * 2);
    }

    // -------------------------------------------------------
    //   Returns the current face of the coin as an integer.
    // -------------------------------------------------------
    public int getFace()
    {
       return face;
    }

    // -------------------------------------------------------
    //   Returns the current face of the coin as a string.
    // -------------------------------------------------------
    public String toString()
    {
       String faceName;

       if (face == HEADS)
           faceName = "Heads";
```

```
         else
            faceName = "Tails";

         return faceName;
      }
}



// ******************************************************************
// Runs.java
//
// Finds the length of the longest run of heads in 100 flips of a coin.
// ******************************************************************

import java.util.Scanner;

public class Runs
{
    public static void main (String[] args)
    {
      final int FLIPS = 100; // number of coin flips

      int currentRun = 0; // length of the current run of HEADS
      int maxRun = 0;       // length of the maximum run so far

      Scanner scan = new Scanner(System.in);

      // Create a coin object

      // Flip the coin FLIPS times
      for (int i = 0; i < FLIPS; i++)
         {
            // Flip the coin & print the result

            // Update the run information

         }

      // Print the results

    }
}
```

A Rainbow Program

Write a program that draws a rainbow. (This is one of the Programming Projects at the end of Chapter 5 in the text.) As suggested in the text, your rainbow will be concentric arcs, each a different color. The basic idea of the program is similar to the program that draws a bull's eye in Listing 5.15 and 5.16 of the text. You should study that program and understand it before starting your rainbow. The major difference in this program (other than drawing arcs rather than circles) is making the different arcs different colors. You can do this in several different ways. For example, you could have a variable for the color code, initialize it to some value then either increment or decrement by some amount each pass through the loop (you'll need to experiment with numbers to see the effect on the color). Or you could try using three integer variables—one for the amount of red, one for the amount of green, and the other for the amount of blue—and modify these (by adding or subtracting some amounts) each time through the loop (each of these must be an integer in the range 0 - 255). For this technique you would need to use the constructor for a Color object that takes three integers representing the amount of red, green, and blue as parameters. Other possibilities are to make each arc a different random color, or have set colors (use at least 4 different colors) and cycle through them (using an idea similar to the way the bull's eye program switches between black and white).

Vote Counter, Revisited

Chapter 4 had a lab exercise that created a GUI with two buttons representing two candidates (Joe and Sam) in an election or popularity contest. The program computed the number of times each button was pressed. In that exercise two different listeners were used, one for each button. This exercise is a slight modification. Only one listener will be used and its ActionPerformed method will determine which button was pressed.

The files *VoteCounter.java* and *VoteCounterPanel.java* contain slight revisions to the skeleton programs used in the Chapter 4 exercise. Save them to your directory and do the following:

1. Add variables for Sam - a vote counter, a button, and a label.

2. Add the button and label for Sam to the panel.

3. Modify the ActionPerformed method of the VoteButtonListener class to determine which button was pressed and update the correct counter. (See the LeftRight example or the Quote example for how to determine the source of an event.)

4. Test your program.

5. Now modify the program to add a message indicating who is winning. To do this you need to instantiate a new label, add it to the panel, and add an if statement in ActionPerformed that determines who is winning (also test for ties) and sets the text of the label with the appropriate message.

```
//****************************************************
// VoteCounter.java
//
// Demonstrates a graphical user interface and event
// listeners to tally votes for two candidates, Joe and Sam.
//****************************************************
import javax.swing.JFrame;

public class VoteCounter
{
    //------------------------------------------------
    // Creates the main program frame.
    //------------------------------------------------
    public static void main(String[] args)
    {
        JFrame frame = new JFrame("Vote Counter");
        frame.setDefaultCloseOperation(JFrame.EXIT_ON_CLOSE);

        frame.getContentPane().add(new VoteCounterPanel());

        frame.pack();
        frame.setVisible(true);
    }
}
```

```
//**********************************************************
// VoteCounterPanel.java
//
// Panel for the GUI that tallies votes for two candidates,
// Joe and Sam.
//**********************************************************

import java.awt.*;
import java.awt.event.*;
import javax.swing.*;

public class VoteCounterPanel extends JPanel
{
    private int votesForJoe;
    private JButton joe;
    private JLabel labelJoe;

    //------------------------------------------------
    // Constructor: Sets up the GUI.
    //------------------------------------------------
    public VoteCounterPanel()
    {
        votesForJoe = 0;

        joe = new JButton("Vote for Joe");
        joe.addActionListener(new VoteButtonListener());

        labelJoe = new JLabel("Votes for Joe: " + votesForJoe);

        add(joe);
        add(labelJoe);

        setPreferredSize(new Dimension(300, 40));
        setBackground(Color.cyan);
    }

    //**************************************************
    // Represents a listener for button push (action) events
    //**************************************************
    private class VoteButtonListener implements ActionListener
    {
        //----------------------------------------------
        // Updates the appropriate vote counter when a
        // button is pushed for one of the candidates.
        //----------------------------------------------
        public void actionPerformed(ActionEvent event)
        {
            votesForJoe++;
            labelJoe.setText("Votes for Joe: " + votesForJoe);
        }
    }
}
```

Modifying *EvenOdd.java*

File *EvenOdd.java* contains the dialog box example in Listing 5.21 the text.

1. Compile and run the program to see how it works.
2. Write a similar class named *SquareRoots* (you may modify EvenOdd) that computes and displays the square root of the integer entered.

```java
//************************************************************************
//  EvenOdd.java         Author: Lewis/Loftus
//
//  Demonstrates the use of the JOptionPane class.
//************************************************************************

import javax.swing.JOptionPane;

class EvenOdd
{
    //--------------------------------------------------------------------
    //  Determines if the value input by the user is even or odd.
    //  Uses multiple dialog boxes for user interaction.
    //--------------------------------------------------------------------
    public static void main (String[] args)
    {
        String numStr, result;
        int num, again;

        do
        {
            numStr = JOptionPane.showInputDialog ("Enter an integer: ");

            num = Integer.parseInt (numStr);

            result = "That number is " + ((num%2 == 0) ? "even" : "odd");

            JOptionPane.showMessageDialog (null, result);

            again = JOptionPane.showConfirmDialog (null, "Do Another?");
        }
        while (again == JOptionPane.YES_OPTION);
    }
}
```

A Pay Check Program

Write a class *PayCheck* that uses dialog boxes to compute the total gross pay of an hourly wage worker. The program should use input dialog boxes to get the number of hours worked and the hourly pay rate from the user. The program should use a message dialog to display the total gross pay. The pay calculation should assume the worker earns time and a half for overtime (for hours over 40).

Adding Buttons to *StyleOptions.java*

The files *StyleOptions.java* and *StyleOptionsPanel.java* are from Listings 5.22 and 5.23 of the text (with a couple of slight changes—an instance variable *fontSize* is used rather than the literal 36 for font size and the variable *style* is an instance variable rather than local to the itemStateChanged method). The program demonstrates checkboxes and ItemListeners. In this exercise you will add a set of three radio buttons to let the user choose among three font sizes. The method of adding the radio buttons will be very similar to that in the QuoteOptionsPanel class (Listing 5.25 of the text). Before modifying the program compile and run the current version to see how it works and study the QuoteOptionsPanel example.

Do the following to add the radio buttons to the panel:

1. Declare three objects *small*, *medium*, and *large* of type JRadioButton.

2. Instantiate the button objects labeling them "Small Font," "Medium Font," "Large Font." Initialize the large font button to true. Set the background color of the buttons to cyan.

3. Instantiate a button group object and add the buttons to it.

4. Radio buttons produce action events so you need an ActionListener to listen for radio button clicks. We can use the ItemListener we already have and let it check to see if the source of the event was a radio button. The code you need to add to *actionPerformed* will be similar to that in the QuoteListener in Listing 5.25. In this case you need to set the *fontSize* variable (use 12 for small, 24 for medium, and 36 for large) in the if statement, then call the *setFont* method to set the font for the *saying* object. (Note: the code that checks to see which check boxes have been selected should stay the same.)

5. In *StyleOptionsPanel()* add each button to the ItemListener object. Also add each button to the panel.

6. Compile and run the program. Note that as the font size changes the checkboxes and buttons re-arrange themselves in the panel. You will learn how to control layout later in the course.

```
//*****************************************************************
//   StyleOptions.java          Author: Lewis/Loftus
//
//   Demonstrates the use of check boxes.
//*****************************************************************

import javax.swing.JFrame;

public class StyleOptions
{
    //-------------------------------------------------------------
    //   Creates and presents the program frame.
    //-------------------------------------------------------------
    public static void main (String[] args)
    {
        JFrame frame = new JFrame ("Style Options");
        frame.setDefaultCloseOperation (JFrame.EXIT_ON_CLOSE);

        StyleOptionsPanel panel = new StyleOptionsPanel();
        frame.getContentPane().add (panel);

        styleFrame.pack();
        styleFrame.setVisible(true);
    }
}
```

```java
//********************************************************************
//  StyleOptionsPanel.java        Author: Lewis/Loftus
//
//  Demonstrates the use of check boxes.
//********************************************************************

import javax.swing.*;
import java.awt.*;
import java.awt.event.*;

public class StyleOptionsPanel extends JPanel
{
    private int fontSize = 36;
    private int style = Font.PLAIN;
    private JLabel saying;
    private JCheckBox bold, italic;

    //----------------------------------------------------------------
    //  Sets up a panel with a label and some check boxes that
    //  control the style of the label's font.
    //----------------------------------------------------------------
    public StyleOptionsPanel()
    {
      saying = new JLabel ("Say it with style!");
      saying.setFont (new Font ("Helvetica", style, fontSize));

      bold = new JCheckBox ("Bold");
      bold.setBackground (Color.cyan);
      italic = new JCheckBox ("Italic");
      italic.setBackground (Color.cyan);

      StyleListener listener = new StyleListener();
      bold.addItemListener (listener);
      italic.addItemListener (listener);

      add (saying);
      add (bold);
      add (italic);

      setBackground (Color.cyan);
      setPreferredSize (new Dimension(300, 100));
    }

    //********************************************************************
    //  Represents the listener for both check boxes.
    //********************************************************************
    private class StyleListener implements ItemListener
    {
      //----------------------------------------------------------------
      //  Updates the style of the label font style.
      //----------------------------------------------------------------
      public void itemStateChanged (ItemEvent event)
      {
        style = Font.PLAIN;

        if (bold.isSelected())
            style = Font.BOLD;

        if (italic.isSelected())
            style += Font.ITALIC;
```

```
            saying.setFont (new Font ("Helvetica", style, fontSize));
        }
    }
}
```

Chapter 6: Object-Oriented Design Lab Exercises

Topics	Lab Exercises
Parameter Passing	Changing People
Interfaces	Using the Comparable Interface
Method Decomposition	A Modified MiniQuiz Class
Overloading	A Flexible Account Class A Biased Coin
Static Variables and Methods	Opening and Closing Accounts Counting Transactions Transfering Funds
Overall class design	Random Walks
GUI Layouts	Telephone Keypad

Changing People

The file *ChangingPeople.java* contains a program that illustrates parameter passing. The program uses *Person* objects defined in the file *Person.java*. Do the following:

1. Trace the execution of the program using diagrams similar to those in Figure 6.5 of the text (which is a trace of the program in Listings 6.15 – 6.17). Also show what is printed by the program.
2. Compile and run the program to see if your trace was correct.
3. Modify the *changePeople* method so that it does what the documentation says it does, that is, the two Person objects passed in as actual parameters are actually changed.

```java
// *********************************************************************
//   ChangingPeople.java
//
//   Demonstrates parameter passing -- contains a method that should
//   change to Person objects.
// *********************************************************************
public class ChangingPeople
{
    // --------------------------------------------------------------
    //  Sets up two person objects, one integer, and one String
    //  object.  These are sent to a method that should make
    //  some changes.
    // --------------------------------------------------------------
    public static void main (String[] args)
    {
        Person person1 = new Person ("Sally", 13);
        Person person2 = new Person ("Sam", 15);

        int age = 21;
        String name = "Jill";

        System.out.println ("\nParameter Passing... Original values...");
        System.out.println ("person1: " + person1);
        System.out.println ("person2: " + person2);
        System.out.println ("age: " + age + "\tname: " + name + "\n");

        changePeople (person1, person2, age, name);

        System.out.println ("\nValues after calling changePeople...");
        System.out.println ("person1: " + person1);
        System.out.println ("person2: " + person2);
        System.out.println ("age: " + age + "\tname: " + name + "\n");
    }

    // ------------------------------------------------------------------
    //  Change the first actual parameter to "Jack - Age 101" and change
    //  the second actual parameter to be a person with the age and
    //  name given in the third and fourth parameters.
    // ------------------------------------------------------------------
    public static void changePeople (Person p1, Person p2, int age, String name)
    {
        System.out.println ("\nInside changePeople... Original parameters...");
        System.out.println ("person1: " + p1);
        System.out.println ("person2: " + p2);
        System.out.println ("age: " + age + "\tname: " + name + "\n");
```

```java
        // Make changes
        Person p3 = new Person (name, age);
        p2 = p3;
        name = "Jack";
        age = 101;
        p1.changeName (name);
        p1.changeAge (age);

        // Print changes
        System.out.println ("\nInside changePeople... Changed values...");
        System.out.println ("person1: " + p1);
        System.out.println ("person2: " + p2);
        System.out.println ("age: " + age + "\tname: " + name + "\n");
    }
}


// ***************************************************************
//   Person.java
//
//   A simple class representing a person.
// ***************************************************************
public class Person
{
    private String name;
    private int age;

    // ------------------------------------------------------------
    //   Sets up a Person object with the given name and age.
    // ------------------------------------------------------------
    public Person (String name, int age)
    {
      this.name = name;
      this.age = age;
    }

    // ------------------------------------------------------------
    //   Changes the name of the Person to the parameter newName.
    // ------------------------------------------------------------
    public void changeName (String newName)
    {
      name = newName;
    }

    // ------------------------------------------------------------
    //   Changes the age of the Person to the parameter newAge.
    // ------------------------------------------------------------
    public void changeAge (int newAge)
    {
      age = newAge;
    }

    // ------------------------------------------------------------
    //   Returns the person's name and age as a string.
    // ------------------------------------------------------------
    public String toString()
    {
      return name + " - Age " + age;
    }
}
```

Using the *Comparable* Interface

1. Write a class Compare3 that provides a static method *largest*. Method *largest* should take three *Comparable* parameters and return the largest of the three (so its return type will also be *Comparable*). Recall that method *compareTo* is part of the *Comparable* interface, so *largest* can use the *compareTo* method of its parameters to compare them.

2. Write a class Comparisons whose main method tests your *largest* method above.
    - First prompt the user for and read in three strings, use your *largest* method to find the largest of the three strings, and print it out. (It's easiest to put the call to *largest* directly in the call to println.) Note that since *largest* is a static method, you will call it through its class name, e.g., *Compare3.largest(val1, val2, val3)*.
    - Add code to also prompt the user for three integers and try to use your *largest* method to find the largest of the three integers. Does this work? If it does, it's thanks to *autoboxing*, which is Java 1.5's automatic conversion of ints to Integers. You may have to use the -source 1.5 compiler option for this to work.

A Modified MiniQuiz Class

Files *Question.java*, *Complexity.java*, and *MiniQuiz.java* contain the classes in Listings 6.8-6.10of the text. These classes demonstrate the use of the Complexity interface; class Question implements the interface, and class MiniQuiz creates two Question objects and uses them to give the user a short quiz.

Save these three files to your directory and study the code in MiniQuiz.java. Notice that after the Question objects are created, almost exactly the same code appears twice, once to ask and grade the first question, and again to ask and grade the second question. Another approach is to write a method *askQuestion* that takes a Question object and does all the work of asking the user the question, getting the user's response, and determining whether the response is correct. You could then simply call this method twice, once for *q1* and once for *q2*. Modify the MiniQuiz class so that it has such an *askQuestion* method, and replace the code in *main* that asks and grades the questions with two calls to *askQuestion*. Some things to keep in mind:

☐ The definition of *askQuestion* should be inside the MiniQuiz class but after the *main* method.
☐ Since *main* is a static method, *askQuestion* must be static too. (A static method cannot call an instance method of the same class.) Also, *askQuestion* is for use only by this class, so it should be declared private. So the header for *askQuestion* should look like this:

```
private static void askQuestion(Question question)
```

- String *possible*, which is currently declared in *main*, will need to be defined in *askQuestion* instead.
- The Scanner object *scan* needs to be a static variable and moved outside of main (so it is available to askQuestion).
- You do not need to make any changes to Question.java or Complexity.java.

```java
//******************************************************************
//  Question.java         Author: Lewis/Loftus
//
//  Represents a question (and its answer).
//******************************************************************

public class Question implements Complexity
{
   private String question, answer;
   private int complexityLevel;

   //---------------------------------------------------------------
   //  Sets up the question with a default complexity.
   //---------------------------------------------------------------
   public Question (String query, String result)
   {
      question = query;
      answer = result;
      complexityLevel = 1;
   }

   //---------------------------------------------------------------
   //  Sets the complexity level for this question.
   //---------------------------------------------------------------
   public void setComplexity (int level)
   {
      complexityLevel = level;
   }

   //---------------------------------------------------------------
   //  Returns the complexity level for this question.
   //---------------------------------------------------------------
   public int getComplexity()
```

```java
   {
      return complexityLevel;
   }

   //-----------------------------------------------------------------
   //  Returns the question.
   //-----------------------------------------------------------------
   public String getQuestion()
   {
      return question;
   }

   //-----------------------------------------------------------------
   //  Returns the answer to this question.
   //-----------------------------------------------------------------
   public String getAnswer()
   {
      return answer;
   }

   //-----------------------------------------------------------------
   //  Returns true if the candidate answer matches the answer.
   //-----------------------------------------------------------------
   public boolean answerCorrect (String candidateAnswer)
   {
      return answer.equals(candidateAnswer);
   }

   //-----------------------------------------------------------------
   //  Returns this question (and its answer) as a string.
   //-----------------------------------------------------------------
   public String toString()
   {
      return question + "\n" + answer;
   }
}


//********************************************************************
//  Complexity.java         Author: Lewis/Loftus
//
//  Represents the interface for an object that can be assigned an
//  explicit complexity.
//********************************************************************

public interface Complexity
{
   public void setComplexity (int complexity);
   public int getComplexity();
}
```

```
//************************************************************
//  MiniQuiz.java          Author: Lewis/Loftus
//
//  Demonstrates the use of a class that implements an interface.
//************************************************************

import java.util.Scanner;

public class MiniQuiz
{
    //-----------------------------------------------------------
    //  Presents a short quiz.
    //-----------------------------------------------------------
    public static void main (String[] args)
    {
        Question q1, q2;
        String possible;

        Scanner scan = new Scanner(System.in);

        q1 = new Question ("What is the capital of Jamaica?",
                           "Kingston");
        q1.setComplexity (4);

        q2 = new Question ("Which is worse, ignorance or apathy?",
                           "I don't know and I don't care");
        q2.setComplexity (10);

        System.out.print (q1.getQuestion());
        System.out.println (" (Level: " + q1.getComplexity() + ")");
        possible = scan.nextLine();
        if (q1.answerCorrect(possible))
            System.out.println ("Correct");
        else
            System.out.println ("No, the answer is " + q1.getAnswer());

        System.out.println();
        System.out.print (q2.getQuestion());
        System.out.println (" (Level: " + q2.getComplexity() + ")");
        possible = scan.nextLine();
        if (q2.answerCorrect(possible))
            System.out.println ("Correct");
        else
            System.out.println ("No, the answer is " + q2.getAnswer());
    }
}
```

A Flexible Account Class

File *Account.java* contains a definition for a simple bank account class with methods to withdraw, deposit, get the balance and account number, and return a String representation. Note that the constructor for this class creates a random account number. Save this class to your directory and study it to see how it works. Then modify it as follows:

1. Overload the constructor as follows:

    *   public Account (double initBal, String owner, long number) – initializes the balance, owner, and account number as specified
    *   public Account (double initBal, String owner) – initializes the balance and owner as specified; randomly generates the account number.
    *   public Account (String owner) – initializes the owner as specified; sets the initial balance to 0 and randomly generates the account number.

2. Overload the *withdraw* method with one that also takes a fee and deducts that fee from the account.

File *TestAccount.java* contains a simple program that exercises these methods. Save it to your directory, study it to see what it does, and use it to test your modified Account class.

```
//********************************************************
// Account.java
//
// A bank account class with methods to deposit to, withdraw from,
// change the name on, and get a String representation
// of the account.
//********************************************************

public class Account
{
  private double balance;
  private String name;
  private long acctNum;

  //-----------------------------------------------
  //Constructor -- initializes balance, owner, and account number
  //-----------------------------------------------
  public Account(double initBal, String owner, long number)
  {
    balance = initBal;
    name = owner;
    acctNum = number;
  }

  //-----------------------------------------------
  // Checks to see if balance is sufficient for withdrawal.
  // If so, decrements balance by amount; if not, prints message.
  //-----------------------------------------------
  public void withdraw(double amount)
  {
    if (balance >= amount)
      balance -= amount;
    else
      System.out.println("Insufficient funds");
  }

  //-----------------------------------------------
  // Adds deposit amount to balance.
  //-----------------------------------------------
```

```java
public void deposit(double amount)
{
   balance += amount;
}


//-----------------------------------------------
// Returns balance.
//-----------------------------------------------
public double getBalance()
{
   return balance;
}



//-----------------------------------------------
// Returns a string containing the name, account number, and balance.
//-----------------------------------------------
public String toString()
{
    return "Name:" + name +
          "\nAccount Number: " + acctNum +
          "\nBalance: " + balance;
}
}




//********************************************************
// TestAccount.java
//
// A simple driver to test the overloaded methods of
// the Account class.
//********************************************************

import java.util.Scanner;

public class TestAccount
{
    public static void main(String[] args)
    {
        String name;
        double balance;
        long acctNum;
        Account acct;

        Scanner scan = new Scanner(System.in);

        System.out.println("Enter account holder's first name");
        name = scan.next();
        acct = new Account(name);
        System.out.println("Account for " + name + ":");
        System.out.println(acct);

        System.out.println("\nEnter initial balance");
        balance = scan.nextDouble();
        acct = new Account(balance,name);
        System.out.println("Account for " + name + ":");
        System.out.println(acct);
```

```
        System.out.println("\nEnter account number");
        acctNum = scan.nextLong();
        acct = new Account(balance,name,acctNum);
        System.out.println("Account for " + name + ":");
        System.out.println(acct);

        System.out.print("\nDepositing 100 into account, balance is now ");
        acct.deposit(100);
        System.out.println(acct.getBalance());
        System.out.print("\nWithdrawing $25, balance is now ");
        acct.withdraw(25);
        System.out.println(acct.getBalance());
        System.out.print("\nWithdrawing $25 with $2 fee, balance is now ");
        acct.withdraw(25,2);
        System.out.println(acct.getBalance());

        System.out.println("\nBye!");
    }
}
```

Modifying the Coin Class

1. Create a new class named *BiasedCoin* that models a biased coin (heads and tails are not equally likely outcomes of a flip). To do this modify the coin class from the Listing 5.4 of text (in the file *Coin.java*) as follows:
   - ☐ Add a private data member *bias* of type double. This data member will be a number between 0 and 1 (inclusive) that represents the probability the coin will be HEADS when flipped. So, if bias is 0.5, the coin is an ordinary fair coin. If bias is 0.6, the coin has probability 0.6 of coming up heads (on average, it comes up heads 60% of the time).
   - ☐ Modify the default constructor by assigning the value 0.5 to bias *before* the call to flip. This will make the default coin a fair one.
   - ☐ Modify *flip* so that it generates a random number then assigns *face* a value of HEADS if the number is less than the bias; otherwise it assigns a value of TAILS.
   - ☐ Add a second constructor with a single double parameter—that parameter will be the bias. If the parameter is valid (a number between 0 and 1 inclusive) the constructor should assign the *bias* data member the value of the parameter; otherwise it should assign *bias* a value of 0.5. Call flip (as the other constructor does) to initialize the value of face.

2. Compile your class to make sure you have no syntax errors.

3. Write a program that uses three BiasedCoin objects. Instantiate one as a fair coin using the constructor with no parameter. Read in the biases for the other two coins and instantiate those coins using the constructor with the bias as a parameter. Your program should then have a loop that flips each coin 100 times and counts the number of times each is heads. After the loop print the number of heads for each coin. Run the program several times testing out different biases.

Opening and Closing Accounts

File *Account.java* (see previous exercise) contains a definition for a simple bank account class with methods to withdraw, deposit, get the balance and account number, and return a String representation. Note that the constructor for this class creates a random account number. Save this class to your directory and study it to see how it works. Then write the following additional code:

1. Suppose the bank wants to keep track of how many accounts exist.

    a. Declare a private static integer variable numAccounts to hold this value. Like all instance and static variables, it will be initialized (to 0, since it's an int) automatically.
    b. Add code to the constructor to increment this variable every time an account is created.
    c. Add a static method *getNumAccounts* that returns the total number of accounts. Think about why this method should be static – its information is not related to any particular account.
    d. File *TestAccounts1.java* contains a simple program that creates the specified number of bank accounts then uses the getNumAccounts method to find how many accounts were created. Save it to your directory, then use it to test your modified Account class.

2. Add a method void close() to your Account class. This method should close the current account by appending "CLOSED" to the account name and setting the balance to 0. (The account number should remain unchanged.) Also decrement the total number of accounts.

3. Add a static method *Account consolidate(Account acct1, Account acct2)* to your Account class that creates a new account whose balance is the sum of the balances in acct1 and acct2 and closes acct1 and acct2. The new account should be returned. Two important rules of consolidation:

    *   Only accounts with the same name can be consolidated. The new account gets the name on the old accounts but a new account number.
    *   Two accounts with the same number cannot be consolidated. Otherwise this would be an easy way to double your money!

    Check these conditions before creating the new account. If either condition fails, do not create the new account or close the old ones; print a useful message and return null.

4. Write a test program that prompts for and reads in three names and creates an account with an initial balance of $100 for each. Print the three accounts, then close the first account and try to consolidate the second and third into a new account. Now print the accounts again, including the consolidated one if it was created.

```
//************************************************************
// TestAccounts1
// A simple program to test the numAccts method of the
// Account class.
//************************************************************
import java.util.Scanner;

public class TestAccounts1
{
    public static void main(String[] args)
    {
        Account testAcct;

        Scanner scan = new Scanner(System.in);
```

```
        System.out.println("How many accounts would you like to create?");
        int num = scan.nextInt();

        for (int i=1; i<=num; i++)
            {
                testAcct = new Account(100, "Name" + i);
                System.out.println("\nCreated account " + testAcct);
                System.out.println("Now there are " + Account.numAccounts() +
                                " accounts");
            }
    }
}
```

Chapter 6: Object-Oriented Design

Counting Transactions

File *Account.java* (see **A Flexible Account Class** exercise) contains a definition for a simple bank account class with methods to withdraw, deposit, get the balance and account number, and return a String representation. Note that the constructor for this class creates a random account number. Save this class to your directory and study it to see how it works. Now modify it to keep track of the total number of deposits and withdrawals (separately) for each day, and the total amount deposited and withdrawn. Write code to do this as follows:

1. Add four private static variables to the Account class, one to keep track of each value above (number and total amount of deposits, number and total of withdrawals). Note that since these variables are static, all of the Account objects share them. This is in contrast to the instance variables that hold the balance, name, and account number; each Account has its own copy of these. Recall that numeric static and instance variables are initialized to 0 by default.

2. Add public methods to return the values of each of the variables you just added, e.g., *public static int getNumDeposits()*.

3. Modify the *withdraw* and *deposit* methods to update the appropriate static variables at each withdrawal and deposit

4. File *ProcessTransactions.java* contains a program that creates and initializes two Account objects and enters a loop that allows the user to enter transactions for either account until asking to quit. Modify this program as follows:
    - After the loop, print the total number of deposits and withdrawals and the total amount of each. You will need to use the Account methods that you wrote above. Test your program.
    - Imagine that this loop contains the transactions for a single day. Embed it in a loop that allows the transactions to be recorded and counted for many days. At the beginning of each day print the summary for each account, then have the user enter the transactions for the day. When all of the transactions have been entered, print the total numbers and amounts (as above), then reset these values to 0 and repeat for the next day. Note that you will need to add methods to reset the variables holding the numbers and amounts of withdrawals and deposits to the Account class. Think: should these be static or instance methods?

```
//*********************************************************
// ProcessTransactions.java
//
// A class to process deposits and withdrawals for two bank
// accounts for a single day.
//*********************************************************
import java.util.Scanner;

public class ProcessTransactions
{
    public static void main(String[] args){

        Account acct1, acct2;            //two test accounts
        String keepGoing = "y";          //more transactions?
        String action;                   //deposit or withdraw
        double amount;                   //how much to deposit or withdraw
        long acctNumber;                 //which account to access

        Scanner scan = new Scanner(System.in);

        //Create two accounts
        acct1 = new Account(1000, "Sue", 123);
        acct2 = new Account(1000, "Joe", 456);

        System.out.println("The following accounts are available:\n");
        acct1.printSummary();

        System.out.println();
        acct2.printSummary();
```

```
        while (keepGoing.equals("y") || keepGoing.equals("y"))
            {
            //get account number, what to do, and amount
            System.out.print("\nEnter the number of the account you would like
to access: ");
            acctNumber = scan.nextLong();
            System.out.print("Would you like to make a deposit (D) or withdrawal
(W)? ");

            action = scan.next();
            System.out.print("Enter the amount: ");
            amount = scan.nextDouble();

            if (amount > 0)
                if (acctNumber == acct1.getAcctNumber())
                    if (action.equals("w") || action.equals("W"))
                        acct1.withdraw(amount);
                    else if (action.equals("d") || action.equals("D"))
                        acct1.deposit(amount);
                    else
                        System.out.println("Sorry, invalid action.");
                else if (acctNumber == acct2.getAcctNumber())
                    if (action.equals("w") || action.equals("W"))
                        acct1.withdraw(amount);
                    else if (action.equals("d") || action.equals("D"))
                        acct1.deposit(amount);
                    else
                        System.out.println("Sorry, invalid action.");
                else
                    System.out.println("Sorry, invalid account number.");
            else
                    System.out.println("Sorry, amount must be > 0.");


            System.out.print("\nMore transactions? (y/n)");
            keepGoing = scan.next();
            }


        //Print number of deposits
        //Print number of withdrawals
        //Print total amount of deposits
        //Print total amount of withdrawals


    }
}
```

Transfering Funds

File *Account.java* (see **A Flexible Account Class** exercise) contains a definition for a simple bank account class with methods to withdraw, deposit, get the balance and account number, and print a summary. Save it to your directory and study it to see how it works. Then write the following additional code:

1. Add a method *public void transfer(Account acct, double amount)* to the Account class that allows the user to transfer funds from one bank account to another. If *acct1* and *acct2* are Account objects, then the call *acct1.transfer(acct2,957.80)* should transfer $957.80 from acct1 to acct2. Be sure to clearly document which way the transfer goes!

2. Write a class TransferTest with a main method that creates two bank account objects and enters a loop that does the following:
   - Asks if the user would like to transfer from account1 to account2, transfer from account2 to account1, or quit.
   - If a transfer is chosen, asks the amount of the transfer, carries out the operation, and prints the new balance for each account.
   - Repeats until the user asks to quit, then prints a summary for each account.

3. Add a static method to the Account class that lets the user transfer money between two accounts without going through either account. You can (and should) call the method transfer just like the other one – you are overloading this method. Your new method should take two Account objects and an amount and transfer the amount from the first account to the second account. The signature will look like this:

   public static void transfer(Account acct1, Account acct2, double amount)

   Modify your TransferTest class to use the static transfer instead of the instance version.

Random Walks

In this lab you will develop a class that models a random walk and write two client programs that use the class. A random walk is basically a sequence of steps in some enclosed space where the direction of each step is random. The walk terminates either when a maximum number of steps has been taken or a step goes outside of the boundary of the space. Random walks are used to model physical phenomena such as the motion of molecules and economic phenomena such as stock prices.

We will assume that the random walk takes place on a square grid with the point (0,0) at the center. The boundary of the square will be a single integer that represents the maximum x and y coordinate for the current position on the square (so for a boundary value of 10, both the x and y coordinates can vary from -10 to 10, inclusive). Each step will be one unit up, one unit down, one unit to the left, or one unit to the right. (No diagonal movement.)

The *RandomWalk* class will have the following instance data (all type int):

- the x coordinate of the current position
- the y coordinate of the current position
- the maximum number of steps in the walk
- the number of steps taken so far in the walk
- the boundary of the square (a positive integer -- the x and y coordinates of the position can vary between plus and minus this value)

Create a new file *RandomWalk.java*. You'll define the RandomWalk class incrementally testing each part as you go.

1. First declare the instance data (as described above) and add the following two constructors and toString method.
   o *RandomWalk (int max, int edge)* - Initializes the RandomWalk object. The maximum number of steps and the boundary are given by the parameters. The x and y coordinates and the number of steps taken should be set to 0.
   o *RandomWalk (int max, int edge, int startX, int startY)* -- Initializes the maximum number of steps, the boundary, and the starting position to those given by the parameters.
   o *String toString()* - returns a String containing the number of steps taken so far and the current position -- The string should look something like: Steps: 12; Position: (-3,5)

2. Compile what you have so far then open the file *TestWalk.java*. This file will be used to test your RandomWalk methods. So far it prompts the user to enter a boundary, a maximum number of steps, and the x and y coordinates of a position. Add the following:
   o Declare and instantiate two RandomWalk objects -- one with boundary 5, maximum steps 10, and centered at the origin (use the two parameter constructor) and the other with the values entered by the user.
   o Print out each object. Note that you won't get any information about the boundary or maximum number of steps (think about what your toString method does), but that's ok.

   Compile and run the program to make sure everything is correct so far.

3. Next add the following method to the RandomWalk class: *void takeStep()*. This method simulates taking a single step either up, down, left, or right. To "take a step" generate a random number with 4 values (say 0, 1, 2, 3) then use a switch statement to change the position (one random value will represent going right, one left, and so on). Your method should also increment the number of steps taken.

4. Add a for loop to TestWalk.java to have each of your RandomWalk objects take 5 steps. Print out each object after each step so you can see what is going on. Compile and run the program to make sure it is correct so far.

5. Now add to RandomWalk.java the following two methods. Each should be a single return statement that returns the value of a boolean expression.
   o *boolean moreSteps()* - returns true if the number of steps taken is less than the maximum number; returns false otherwise

Chapter 6: Object-Oriented Design

o *boolean inBounds()* - returns true if the current position is on the square (include the boundary as part of the square); returns false otherwise.

6. Add to the RandomWalk class a method named *walk* that has no parameters and returns nothing. Its job is to simulate a complete random walk. That is, it should generate a sequence of steps as long the maximum number of steps has not been taken and it is still in bounds (inside the square). This should be a very simple loop (while or do... while) --- you will need to call the methods takeStep, moreSteps, and inBounds.

7. Add to TestWalk.java a statement to instantiate a RandomWalk object with a boundary of 10 and 200 as the maximum number of steps. (You may want to comment out most of the code currently in TestWalk -- especially the user input and the loop that takes five steps -- as the walk method will be easier to test on its own. The /* ... */ style of comment is useful for this. But don't delete that other code, as you'll need it later in the lab.) Then add a statement to have the object walk. Print the object after the walk. Compile and run the program. Run it more than once -- you should be able to tell by the value printed whether the object went out of bounds or whether it stopped because it reached the maximum number of steps.

8. Now write a client program in a file named *DrunkenWalk.java*. The program should simulate a drunk staggering randomly on some sort of platform (imagine a square dock in the middle of a lake). The goal of the program is to have the program simulate the walk many times (because of randomness each walk is different) and count the number of times the drunk falls off the platform (goes out of bounds). Your program should read in the boundary, the maximum number of steps, and the number of drunks to simulate. It should then have a loop (a for loop would be a good idea) that on each iteration instantiates a new RandomWalk object to represent a drunk, has the object walk, then determines whether or not the drunk fell off the platform (and updates a counter if it did). After the loop print out the number of times the drunk fell off. Compile and run your program. To see the "randomness" you should run it several times. Try input of 10 for the boundary and 200 for the number of steps first (sometimes the drunk falls off, sometimes not); try 10 for the boundary and 500 for the steps (you should see different behavior); try 50 for the boundary and 200 for the steps (again different behavior).

9. Now write a second client program in a file named *Collisions.java*. This program should simulate two particles moving in space. Its goal is to determine the number of times the two particles collide (occupy exactly the same position after the same number of steps -- the steps could be thought of as simulating time). We'll assume the particles are in a very large space so use a large number for the boundary (such as 2,000,000). Use 100,000 for the maximum number of steps. (Don't enter the commas.) Start one particle at (-3, 0) and the other at (3, 0). (You can hardcode these values into the program; no need to enter them.) Your program should contain a loop that has each particle take a step as long as the particles have not exceeded the maximum number of steps. The program then determines how often the particles have collided. Note that in order for your program to know whether or not the two different RandomWalk objects are in the same place it needs to be able to find out the position. Hence, you need to add the following two methods to the RandomWalk class.
    o *int getX()* - returns the x coordinate of the current position
    o *int getY()* - returns the y coordinate of the current position

    Compile and run your program to make sure it works. As before run it several times.

10. In your Collisions.java program the condition to determine if the points are at the same position is a bit cumbersome. This is something that would be best put in a separate method. Add a static method to Collisions.java (after the main method) with signature

    public static boolean samePosition (RandomWalk p1, RandomWalk p2)

    The method should return true if p1 and p2 are at the same position and return false otherwise. Modify your main method so it calls samePosition rather than directly testing to see if the objects are at the same position. Test the program.

11. In using random walks to simulate behavior it is often of interest to know how far away from the origin the object gets as it moves.

a. Add an instance variable *maxDistance* (type int) to the RandomWalk class. This should be set to 0 in each constructor.

b. Now the takeStep method needs to update this maximum when a step is taken. We'll add a support method to the class to do this. Add a *private* method named *max* that takes two integer parameters (say *num1* and *num2*) and returns the largest of the two.

c. Add code to takeStep to update maxDistance. This can be done in a single statement using the max method -- the new value of maxDistance should be the maximum of 1) the old value of maxDistance, and 2) the current distance to the origin. Note that if the current point is (-3, 15) the distance to the origin is 15; if the current point is (-10, 7) the distance to the origin is 10. Remember that Math.abs returns the absolute value of a number.

d. Finally add an accessor method to return that distance so a client program can access it:

    public int getMaxDistance()

e. Test the maximum by adding statements in TestWalk.java to get and print the maximum distance for each of the objects after the loop that had them take and print out 5 steps (this way you can see if the maximum is correct – each step is printed).

```
// ***********************************************************
//  TestWalk.java
//
//  Program to test methods in the RandomWalk class.
// ***********************************************************

import java.util.Scanner;

public class TestWalk
{
    public static void main (String[] args)
    {
        int maxSteps;    // maximum number of steps in a walk
        int maxCoord;    // the maximum x and y coordinate
        int x, y;        // starting x and y coordinates for a walk

        Scanner scan = new Scanner(System.in);

        System.out.println ("\nRandom Walk Test Program");
        System.out.println ();

        System.out.print ("Enter the boundary for the square: ");
        maxCoord = scan.nextInt();

        System.out.print ("Enter the maximum number of steps: ");
        maxSteps = scan.nextInt();

        System.out.print ("Enter the starting x and y coordinates with " +
                          "a space between: ");
        x = scan.nextInt();
        y = scan.nextInt();

    }
}
```

Telephone Keypad

Files *Telephone.java* and *TelephonePanel.java* contain the skeleton for a program to lay out a GUI that looks like telephone keypad with a title that says "Your Telephone!!". Save these files to your directory. Telephone.java is complete, but TelephonePanel.java is not.

1. Using the comments as a guide, add code to TelephonePanel.java to create the GUI. Some things to consider:
   a. TelephonePanel (the current object, which is a JPanel) should get a BorderLayout to make it easy to separate the title from the keypad. The title will go in the north area and the keypad will go in the center area. The other areas will be unused.
   b. You can create a JLabel containing the title and add it directly to the north section of the TelephonePanel. However, to put the keypad in the center you will first need to create a new JPanel and add the keys (each a button) to it, then add it to the center of the TelephonePanel. This new panel should have a 4x3 GridLayout.
   c. Your keypad should hold buttons containing 1 2 3, 4 5 6, 7 8 9, * 0 # in the four rows respectively. So you'll create a total of 12 buttons.

2. Compile and run Telephone.java. You should get a small keypad and title. Grow the window (just drag the corner) and see how the GUI changes – everything grows proportionately.

3. Note that the title is not centered, but it would look nicer if it were. One way to do this is to create a new JPanel , add the title label to it, then add the new JPanel to the north area of the TelephonePanel (instead of adding the label directly). This works because the default layout for a JPanel is a centered FlowLayout, and the JPanel itself will expand to fill the whole north area. Modify your program in this way so that the title is centered.

```
//*********************************************************
// Telephone.java
//
// Uses the TelephonePanel class to create a (functionless) GUI
// like a telephone keypad with a title.
// Illustrates use of BorderLayout and GridLayout.
//*********************************************************
import javax.swing.*;
public class Telephone
{
    public static void main(String[] args)
    {
        JFrame frame = new JFrame("Telephone");
        frame.setDefaultCloseOperation(JFrame.EXIT_ON_CLOSE);
        frame.getContentPane().add(new TelephonePanel());
        frame.pack();
        frame.setVisible(true);
    }
}
```

```java
//*****************************************************
// TelephonePanel.java
//
// Lays out a (functionless) GUI like a telephone keypad with a title.
// Illustrates use of BorderLayout and GridLayout.
//*****************************************************
import java.awt.*;
import javax.swing.*;

public class TelephonePanel extends JPanel
{
    public TelephonePanel()
    {
        //set BorderLayout for this panel

        //create a JLabel with "Your Telephone" title

        //add title label to north of this panel

        //create panel to hold keypad and give it a 4x3 GridLayout

        //add buttons representing keys to key panel

        //add key panel to center of this panel
    }
}
```

Chapter 6: Object-Oriented Design

Chapter 7: Arrays
Lab Exercises

Topics	Lab Exercises
One-Dimensional Arrays	Tracking Sales
	Grading Quizzes
	Reversing an Array
	Adding To and Removing From an Integer List
Arrays of Objects	A Shopping Cart
Command Line Arguments	Averaging Numbers
Variable Length Parameter Lists	Exploring Variable Length Parameter Lists
Two-Dimensional Arrays	Magic Squares
ArrayList Class	A Shopping Cart Using the ArrayList Class
Polygons & Polylines	A Polygon Person
Arrays & GUIs	An Array of Radio Buttons
Mouse Events	Drawing Circles with Mouse Clicks
	Moving Circles with the Mouse
Key Events	Moving a Stick Figure

Tracking Sales

File *Sales.java* contains a Java program that prompts for and reads in the sales for each of 5 salespeople in a company. It then prints out the id and amount of sales for each salesperson and the total sales. Study the code, then compile and run the program to see how it works. Now modify the program as follows:

1. Compute and print the average sale. (You can compute this directly from the total; no loop is necessary.)
2. Find and print the maximum sale. Print both the id of the salesperson with the max sale and the amount of the sale, e.g., "Salesperson 3 had the highest sale with $4500." Note that you don't need another loop for this; you can do it in the same loop where the values are read and the sum is computed.
3. Do the same for the minimum sale.
4. After the list, sum, average, max and min have been printed, ask the user to enter a value. Then print the id of each salesperson who exceeded that amount, and the amount of their sales. Also print the total number of salespeople whose sales exceeded the value entered.
5. The salespeople are objecting to having an id of 0—no one wants that designation. Modify your program so that the ids run from 1–5 instead of 0–4. **Do not modify the array**—just make the information for salesperson 1 reside in array location 0, and so on.
6. Instead of always reading in 5 sales amounts, at the beginning ask the user for the number of sales people and then create an array that is just the right size. The program can then proceed as before.

```
// ****************************************************************
// Sales.java
//
// Reads in and stores sales for each of 5 salespeople.  Displays
// sales entered by salesperson id and total sales for all salespeople.
//
// ****************************************************************
import java.util.Scanner;

public class Sales
{
    public static void main(String[] args)
    {
      final int SALESPEOPLE = 5;
      int[] sales = new int[SALESPEOPLE];
      int sum;

      Scanner scan = new Scanner(System.in);

      for (int i=0; i<sales.length; i++)
         {
            System.out.print("Enter sales for salesperson " + i + ": ");
            sales[i] = scan.nextInt();
         }

      System.out.println("\nSalesperson   Sales");
      System.out.println("--------------------");
      sum = 0;
      for (int i=0; i<sales.length; i++)
         {
            System.out.println("    " + i + "         " + sales[i]);
            sum += sales[i];
         }

      System.out.println("\nTotal sales: " + sum);
    }
}
```

Grading Quizzes

Write a program that grades arithmetic quizzes as follows:

1. Ask the user how many questions are in the quiz.
2. Ask the user to enter the key (that is, the correct answers). There should be one answer for each question in the quiz, and each answer should be an integer. They can be entered on a single line, e.g., 34 7 13 100 81 3 9 10 321 12 might be the key for a 10-question quiz. You will need to store the key in an array.
3. Ask the user to enter the answers for the quiz to be graded. As for the key, these can be entered on a single line. Again there needs to be one for each question. Note that these answers do not need to be stored; each answer can simply be compared to the key as it is entered.
4. When the user has entered all of the answers to be graded, print the number correct and the percent correct.

When this works, add a loop so that the user can grade any number of quizzes with a single key. After the results have been printed for each quiz, ask "Grade another quiz? (y/n)."

Reversing an Array

Write a program that prompts the user for an integer, then asks the user to enter that many values. Store these values in an array and print the array. Then reverse the array elements so that the first element becomes the last element, the second element becomes the second to last element, and so on, with the old last element now first. Do not just reverse the order in which they are printed; actually change the way they are stored in the array. Do not create a second array; just rearrange the elements within the array you have. (Hint: Swap elements that need to change places.) When the elements have been reversed, print the array again.

Adding To and Removing From an Integer List

File *IntegerList.java* contains a Java class representing a list of integers. The following public methods are provided:

- ☐ IntegerList(int size)—creates a new list of *size* elements. Elements are initialized to 0.
- ☐ void randomize()—fills the list with random integers between 1 and 100, inclusive.
- ☐ void print()—prints the array elements and indices

File *IntegerListTest.java* contains a Java program that provides menu-driven testing for the IntegerList class. Copy both files to your directory, and compile and run IntegerListTest to see how it works.

It is often necessary to add items to or remove items from a list. When the list is stored in an array, one way to do this is to create a new array of the appropriate size each time the number of elements changes, and copy the values over from the old array. However, this is rather inefficient. A more common strategy is to choose an initial size for the array and add elements until it is full, then double its size and continue adding elements until it is full, and so on. (It is also possible to decrease the size of the array if it falls under, say, half full, but we won't do that in this exercise.) The CDCollection class in Listing 7.8 of the text uses this strategy—it keeps track of the current size of the array and the number of elements already stored in it, and method *addCD* calls *increaseSize* if the array is full. Study that example.

1. Add this capability to the IntegerList class. You will need to add an *increaseSize* method plus instance variables to hold the current number of integers in the list and the current size of the array. Since you do not have any way to add elements to the list, you won't need to call *increaseSize* yet.

2. Add a method *void addElement(int newVal)* to the IntegerList class that adds an element to the list. At the beginning of *addElement*, check to see if the array is full. If so, call *increaseSize* before you do anything else.

   Add an option to the menu in IntegerListTest to test your new method.

3. Add a method *void removeFirst(int newVal)* to the IntegerList class that removes the first occurrence of a value from the list. If the value does not appear in the list, it should do nothing (but it's not an error). Removing an item should not change the size of the array, but note that the array values do need to remain contiguous, so when you remove a value you will have to shift everything after it down to fill up its space. Also remember to decrement the variable that keeps track of the number of elements.

   Add an option to the menu in IntegerListTest to test your new method.

4. Add a method *removeAll(int newVal)* to the IntegerList class that removes all occurrences of a value from the list. If the value does not appear in the list, it should do nothing (but it's not an error).

   Add an option to the menu in IntegerListTest to test your new method.

```
// ****************************************************************
// IntegerList.java
//
// Define an IntegerList class with methods to create & fill
// a list of integers.
//
// ****************************************************************

public class IntegerList
{
    int[] list; //values in the list

    //-------------------------------------------------------
    //create a list of the given size
    //-------------------------------------------------------
    public IntegerList(int size)
```

```java
    {
      list = new int[size];
    }


    //-----------------------------------------------------------
    //fill array with integers between 1 and 100, inclusive
    //-----------------------------------------------------------
    public void randomize()
    {
      for (int i=0; i<list.length; i++)
          list[i] = (int)(Math.random() * 100) + 1;
    }


    //-----------------------------------------------------------
    //print array elements with indices
    //-----------------------------------------------------------
    public void print()
    {
      for (int i=0; i<list.length; i++)
          System.out.println(i + ":\t" + list[i]);
    }
}




// ***************************************************************
// IntegerListTest.java
//
// Provide a menu-driven tester for the IntegerList class.
//
// ***************************************************************
import java.util.Scanner;

public class IntegerListTest
{
    static IntegerList list = new IntegerList(10);
    static Scanner scan = new Scanner(System.in);

    //--------------------------------------------------------
    // Create a list, then repeatedly print the menu and do what the
    // user asks until they quit
    //--------------------------------------------------------
    public static void main(String[] args)
    {
      printMenu();
      int choice = scan.nextInt();
      while (choice != 0)
          {
            dispatch(choice);
            printMenu();
            choice = scan.nextInt();
          }
    }


    //-----------------------------------
    // Do what the menu item calls for
    //-----------------------------------
    public static void dispatch(int choice)
    {
```

```java
        int loc;
        switch(choice)
            {
            case 0:
                System.out.println("Bye!");
                break;
            case 1:
                System.out.println("How big should the list be?");
                int size = scan.nextInt();
                list = new IntegerList(size);
                list.randomize();
                break;
            case 2:
                list.print();
                break;
            default:
                System.out.println("Sorry, invalid choice");
            }
    }

    //---------------------------
    // Print the user's choices
    //---------------------------
    public static void printMenu()
    {
        System.out.println("\n    Menu    ");
        System.out.println("    ====");
        System.out.println("0: Quit");
        System.out.println("1: Create a new list (** do this first!! **)");
        System.out.println("2: Print the list");
        System.out.print("\nEnter your choice: ");
    }
}
```

A Shopping Cart

In this exercise you will complete a class that implements a shopping cart as an array of items. The file *Item.java* contains the definition of a class named *Item* that models an item one would purchase. An item has a name, price, and quantity (the quantity purchased). The file *ShoppingCart.java* implements the shopping cart as an array of Item objects.

1. Complete the *ShoppingCart* class by doing the following:
   a. Declare an instance variable *cart* to be an array of Items and instantiate *cart* in the constructor to be an array holding *capacity* Items.
   b. Fill in the code for the *increaseSize* method. Your code should be similar to that in Listing 7.8 of the text but instead of doubling the size just increase it by 3 elements.
   c. Fill in the code for the *addToCart* method. This method should add the item to the cart and update the *totalPrice* instance variable (note this variable takes into account the quantity).
   d. Compile your class.

2. Write a program that simulates shopping. The program should have a loop that continues as long as the user wants to shop. Each time through the loop read in the name, price, and quantity of the item the user wants to add to the cart. After adding an item to the cart, the cart contents should be printed. After the loop print a "Please pay ..." message with the total price of the items in the cart.

```
//  ************************************************************
//    Item.java
//
//    Represents an item in a shopping cart.
//  ************************************************************

import java.text.NumberFormat;

public class Item
{
    private String name;
    private double price;
    private int quantity;

    // ------------------------------------------------------
    //  Create a new item with the given attributes.
    // ------------------------------------------------------
    public Item (String itemName, double itemPrice, int numPurchased)
    {
      name = itemName;
      price = itemPrice;
      quantity = numPurchased;
    }

    // ------------------------------------------------------
    //   Return a string with the information about the item
    // ------------------------------------------------------
    public String toString ()
    {
      NumberFormat fmt = NumberFormat.getCurrencyInstance();

      return (name + "\t" + fmt.format(price) + "\t" + quantity + "\t"
            + fmt.format(price*quantity));
    }

    // ------------------------------------------------------
    //   Returns the unit price of the item
    // ------------------------------------------------------
```

```java
    public double getPrice()
    {
      return price;
    }

    // ----------------------------------------------------
    //   Returns the name of the item
    // ----------------------------------------------------
    public String getName()
    {
      return name;
    }

    // ----------------------------------------------------
    //   Returns the quantity of the item
    // ----------------------------------------------------
    public int getQuantity()
    {
      return quantity;
    }
}




// ************************************************************************
//    ShoppingCart.java
//
//    Represents a shopping cart as an array of items
// ************************************************************************

import java.text.NumberFormat;

public class ShoppingCart
{
    private int itemCount;      // total number of items in the cart
    private double totalPrice;  // total price of items in the cart
    private int capacity;       // current cart capacity

    // ------------------------------------------------------------
    //   Creates an empty shopping cart with a capacity of 5 items.
    // ------------------------------------------------------------
    public ShoppingCart()
    {
      capacity = 5;
      itemCount = 0;
      totalPrice = 0.0;
    }

    // ------------------------------------------------------------
    //   Adds an item to the shopping cart.
    // ------------------------------------------------------------
    public void addToCart(String itemName, double price, int quantity)
    {
    }

    // ------------------------------------------------------------
    //   Returns the contents of the cart together with
    //   summary information.
```

```java
// ----------------------------------------------------------
public String toString()
{
    NumberFormat fmt = NumberFormat.getCurrencyInstance();

    String contents = "\nShopping Cart\n";
    contents += "\nItem\t\tUnit Price\tQuantity\tTotal\n";

    for (int i = 0; i < itemCount; i++)
        contents += cart[i].toString() + "\n";

    contents += "\nTotal Price: " + fmt.format(totalPrice);
    contents += "\n";

    return contents;
}

// ----------------------------------------------------------
//  Increases the capacity of the shopping cart by 3
// ----------------------------------------------------------
private void increaseSize()
{
}
}
```

Averaging Numbers

As discussed in Section 7.4 of the text book, when you run a Java program called Foo, anything typed on the command line after "java Foo" is passed to the main method in the args parameter as an array of strings.

1. Write a program Average.java that just prints the strings that it is given at the command line, one per line. If nothing is given at the command line, print "No arguments".

2. Modify your program so that it assumes the arguments given at the command line are integers. If there are no arguments, print a message. If there is at least one argument, compute and print the average of the arguments. Note that you will need to use the parseInt method of the Integer class to extract integer values from the strings that are passed in. If any non-integer values are passed in, your program will produce an error, which is unavoidable at this point.

3. Test your program thoroughly using different numbers of command line arguments.

Exploring Variable Length Parameter Lists

The file *Parameters.java* contains a program to test the variable length method *average* from Section 7.5 of the text. Note that *average* must be a static method since it is called from the static method *main*.

1. Compile and run the program. You must use the -source 1.5 option in your compile command.
2. Add a call to find the average of a single integer, say 13. Print the result of the call.
3. Add a call with an empty parameter list and print the result. Is the behavior what you expected?
4. Add an interactive part to the program. Ask the user to enter a sequence of at most 20 nonnegative integers. Your program should have a loop that reads the integers into an array and stops when a negative is entered (the negative number should not be stored). Invoke the average method to find the average of the integers in the array (send the array as the parameter). Does this work?
5. Add a method *minimum* that takes a variable number of integer parameters and returns the minimum of the parameters. Invoke your method on each of the parameter lists used for the average function.

```
//************************************************************
//   Parameters.java
//
//   Illustrates the concept of a variable parameter list.
//************************************************************

import java.util.Scanner;

public class Parameters
{
    //----------------------------------------------------
    //   Calls the average and minimum methods with
    //   different numbers of parameters.
    //----------------------------------------------------
    public static void main(String[] args)
    {
        double mean1, mean2;

        mean1 = average(42, 69, 37);
        mean2 = average(35, 43, 93, 23, 40, 21, 75);

        System.out.println ("mean1 = " + mean1);
        System.out.println ("mean2 = " + mean2);
    }

    //----------------------------------------------------
    //   Returns the average of its parameters.
    //----------------------------------------------------
    public static double average (int ... list)
    {
        double result = 0.0;

        if (list.length != 0)
            {
                int sum = 0;
                for (int num: list)
                    sum += num;
                result = (double)sum / list.length;
            }

        return result;
    }
}
```

Magic Squares

One interesting application of two-dimensional arrays is *magic squares*. A magic square is a square matrix in which the sum of every row, every column, and both diagonals is the same. Magic squares have been studied for many years, and there are some particularly famous magic squares. In this exercise you will write code to determine whether a square is magic.

File *Square.java* contains the shell for a class that represents a square matrix. It contains headers for a constructor that gives the size of the square and methods to read values into the square, print the square, find the sum of a given row, find the sum of a given column, find the sum of the main (or other) diagonal, and determine whether the square is magic. The read method is given for you; you will need to write the others. Note that the read method takes a Scanner object as a parameter.

File *SquareTest.java* contains the shell for a program that reads input for squares from a file named *magicData* and tells whether each is a magic square. Following the comments, fill in the remaining code. Note that the main method reads the size of a square, then after constructing the square of that size, it calls the *readSquare* method to read the square in. The readSquare method must be sent the Scanner object as a parameter.

You should find that the first, second, and third squares in the input are magic, and that the rest (fourth through seventh) are not. Note that the -1 at the bottom tells the test program to stop reading.

```java
// **************************************************************
// Square.java
//
// Define a Square class with methods to create and read in
// info for a square matrix and to compute the sum of a row,
// a col, either diagonal, and whether it is magic.
//
// **************************************************************

import java.util.Scanner;

public class Square
{
    int[][] square;

    //------------------------------------
    //create new square of given size
    //------------------------------------
    public Square(int size)
    {

    }

    //------------------------------------
    //return the sum of the values in the given row
    //------------------------------------
    public int sumRow(int row)
    {

    }

    //------------------------------------
    //return the sum of the values in the given column
    //------------------------------------
    public int sumCol(int col)
    {

    }

    //------------------------------------
```

```java
//return the sum of the values in the main diagonal
//------------------------------------
public int sumMainDiag()
{

}

//------------------------------------
//return the sum of the values in the other ("reverse") diagonal
//------------------------------------
public int sumOtherDiag()
{

}

//------------------------------------
//return true if the square is magic (all rows, cols, and diags have
//same sum), false otherwise
//------------------------------------
public boolean magic()
{

}

//------------------------------------
//read info into the square from the standard input.
//------------------------------------
public void readSquare(Scanner scan)
{
   for (int row = 0; row < square.length; row++)
     for (int col = 0; col < square.length; col ++)
       square[row][col] = scan.nextInt();
}

//------------------------------------
//print the contents of the square, neatly formatted
//------------------------------------
public void printSquare()
{

}

}
```

```
// ****************************************************************
// SquareTest.java
//
// Uses the Square class to read in square data and tell if
// each square is magic.
//
// ****************************************************************

import java.util.Scanner;

public class SquareTest
{
    public static void main(String[] args) throws IOException
    {
      Scanner scan = new Scanner(new File("magicData"));

        int count = 1;                  //count which square we're on
        int size = scan.nextInt();      //size of next square

        //Expecting -1 at bottom of input file
        while (size != -1)
            {

                //create a new Square of the given size

                //call its read method to read the values of the square

                System.out.println("\n******** Square " + count + " ********");
                //print the square

                //print the sums of its rows

                //print the sums of its columns

                //print the sum of the main diagonal

                //print the sum of the other diagonal

                //determine and print whether it is a magic square

                //get size of next square
                size = scan.nextInt();

            }

    }
}
```

```
3
8    1    6
3    5    7
4    9    2
7
30   39   48    1   10   19   28
38   47    7    9   18   27   29
46    6    8   17   26   35   37
5    14   16   25   34   36   45
13   15   24   33   42   44    4
21   23   32   41   43    3   12
22   31   40   49    2   11   20
4
48    9    6   39
27   18   21   36
15   30   33   24
12   45   42    3
3
6    2    7
1    5    3
2    9    4
4
3   16    2   13
6    9    7   12
10    5   11    8
15    4   14    1
5
17   24   15    8    1
23    5   16   14    7
4    6   22   13   20
10   12    3   21   19
11   18    9    2   25
7
30   39   48    1   10   28   19
38   47    7    9   18   29   27
46    6    8   17   26   37   35
5    14   16   25   34   45   36
13   15   24   33   42    4   44
21   23   32   41   43   12    3
22   31   40   49    2   20   11
-1
```

A Shopping Cart Using the ArrayList Class

In this exercise you will implement a shopping cart using the ArrayList class. The file *Item.java* contains the definition of a class named *Item* that models an item one would purchase (this class was used in an earlier lab). An item has a name, price, and quantity (the quantity purchased). The file *Shop.java* is an incomplete program that models shopping.

1. Complete Shop.java as follows:
    a. Declare and instantiate a variable *cart* to be an empty ArrayList.
    b. Fill in the statements in the loop to add an item to the cart and to print the cart contents (using the default *toString* in the ArrayList class). Comments in the code indicate where these statements go.
    c. Compile your program and run it.

2. You should have observed two problems with using the default printing for the cart object: the output doesn't look very good and the total price of the goods in the cart is not computed or printed. Modify the program to correct these problems by replacing the print statement with a loop that does the following:
    a. gets each item from the cart and prints the item
    b. computes the total price of the items in the cart (you need to use the *getPrice* and *getQuantity* methods of the Item class). The total price should be printed after the loop.

3. Compile and run your program.

```
// **************************************************************
//    Shop.java
//
//    Uses the Item class to create items and add them to a shopping
//    cart stored in an ArrayList.
// **************************************************************

import java.util.ArrayList;
import java.util.Scanner;

public class Shop
{
    public static void main (String[] args)
    {
        ArrayList<Item> cart = new ArrayList();

        Item item;
        String itemName;
        double itemPrice;
        int quantity;

        Scanner scan = new Scanner(System.in);

        String keepShopping = "y";

        do
            {
                System.out.print ("Enter the name of the item: ");
                itemName = scan.nextLine();

                System.out.print ("Enter the unit price: ");
                itemPrice = scan.nextDouble();

                System.out.print ("Enter the quantity: ");
                quantity = scan.nextInt();

                // *** create a new item and add it to the cart
```

```
            // *** print the contents of the cart object using println


        System.out.print ("Continue shopping (y/n)? ");
        keepShopping = scan.nextLine();
      }
   while (keepShopping.equals("y"));

  }
}
```

A Polygon Person

A polygon is a multisided closed figure; a polyline is a line with an arbitrary number of segments. Both polygons and polylines are defined by a set of points, and Java provides graphics methods for both that are based on arrays. Read section 7.8 in the text and study the Rocket example in Listing 7.16 & 7.17.

Files *DrawPerson.java* and *DrawPersonPanel.java* contain a program that draws a blue shirt. Copy the programs to your directory, compile DrawPerson.java, and run it to see what it does. Now modify it as follows:

1. Draw pants to go with the shirt (they should be a different color). You will need to declare pantsX and pantsY arrays like the shirtX and shirtY arrays and figure out what should go in them. Then make the paint method draw the pants as well as the shirt.
2. Draw a head. This can just be a circle (or oval), so you won't need to use the Polygon methods. Declare variables headX and headY to hold the position of the head (its upper lefthand corner), and use them when you draw the circle.
3. Draw hair on the head. This is probably best done with a polygon, so again you'll need two arrays to hold the points.
4. Draw a zigzag across the front of the shirt. Use a polyline.
5. Write a method *movePerson(int x, int y)* that moves the person by the given number of pixels in the x and y direction. This method should just go through the shirt, pants, hair and zigzag arrays and the head x and y coords and increment all of the coordinates by the x or y value as appropriate. (This isn't necessarily the cleanest way to do this, but it's very straightforward).
6. Now put a loop in your paintComponent method that draws the person three times, moving him (her?) 150 or so pixels each time (you decide how far).

```
// ****************************************************************
//   DrawPerson.java
//
//   An program that uses the Graphics draw methods to draw a person.
// ****************************************************************

import javax.swing.JPanel;

public class DrawPerson
{
    //------------------------------------------------
    //   Creates the main frame for the draw program
    //------------------------------------------------
    public static void main (String[] args)
    {
        JFrame frame = new JFrame ("Draw Person");
        frame.setDefaultCloseOperaton (JFrame.EXIT_ON_CLOSE);

        DrawPersonPanel panel = new DrawPersonPanel ();

        frame.getContentPane().add(panel);
        frame.pack();
        frame.setVisible(true);
    }
}

// ****************************************************************
//   DrawPersonPanel.java
//
//   An program that uses the Graphics draw methods to draw a person.
// ****************************************************************

import javax.swing.JPanel;
import java.awt.*;
```

```java
public class DrawPersonPanel extends JPanel
{
    private final int WIDTH = 600;
    private final int HEIGHT = 400;

    private int[] shirtX = {60,0,20,60,50,130,120,160,180,120};
    private int[] shirtY = {100,150,180,160,250,250,160,180,150,100};

    //------------------------------------
    //  Constructor: Set up the panel.
    //------------------------------------
    public DrawPersonPanel()
    {
        setPreferredSize(new Dimension(WIDTH, HEIGHT));
    }

    //------------------------------------
    //   Draw person
    //------------------------------------
    public void paintComponent (Graphics page)
    {
        page.setColor(Color.blue);
        page.fillPolygon(shirtX, shirtY, shirtX.length);

    }
}
```

An Array of Radio Buttons

File *ColorOptions.java* contains a program that will display a set of radio buttons that let the user change the background color of the GUI. The file *ColorOptionsPanel.java* contains the skeleton of the panel for this program . Open the files and study the code that is already there. You will note that in ColorOptionsPanel.java there is an array *color* containing 5 colors already defined. Your task is to add an array of radio buttons so that a click of a radio button will cause the background of the panel to change to the corresponding color in the *color* array.

1. Define *colorButton* to be an array of NUM_COLORS objects of type JRadioButton.

2. Instantiate each *colorButton* with the appropriate color as the label (for example, the first button should be labeled "Yellow"). The first button (corresponding to yellow) should be on (*true*) initially.

3. Recall that radio buttons must be grouped and that the selection of a radio button produces an action event. Hence you must have a ButtonGroup object and an ActionListener. Note that the skeleton of an ActionListener named *ColorListener* is already provided. So, you need to:
   a. Instantiate a ButtonGroup object and a ColorListener object. Comments in the code indicate where to do this.
   b. Each radio button needs to be added to your ButtonGroup object, the background color needs to be set (use white), your ColorListener needs to be added, and the button needs to be added to the panel. All of these can be done using a single for loop. So, add a for loop that goes through the radio buttons adding each to your ButtonGroup object, setting the background of each to white, adding your ColorListener to each, and adding each to the panel.

4. Fill in the body of the actionPerformed method. This method needs to go through the buttons to determine which is selected and then set the background color accordingly. A simple for loop can do this. Use the *isSelected* method to determine if a button is selected (for example, if (colorButton[i].isSelected())....). Use the *color* array to set the background color.

5. Test your program!

```java
// ********************************************************************
//   ColorOptions.java
//
//   Uses an array of radio buttons to change the background color.
// ********************************************************************

import javax.swing.*;

public class ColorOptions
{
    // -------------------------------------------------------------
    //  Creates and presents the frame for the color change panel.
    // -------------------------------------------------------------
    public static void main (String[] args)
    {
        JFrame colorFrame = new JFrame ("Color Options");
        colorFrame.setDefaultCloseOperation (JFrame.EXIT_ON_CLOSE);

        ColorOptionsPanel panel = new ColorOptionsPanel();
        colorFrame.getContentPane().add (panel);

        colorFrame.pack();
        colorFrame.setVisible(true);
    }
}
```

```
// **************************************************************
//  ColorOptionsPanel.java
//
//  Represents the user interface for the ColorOptions program that lets
//  the user change background color by selecting a radio button.
// **************************************************************

import javax.swing.*;
import java.awt.*;
import java.awt.event.*;

public class ColorOptionsPanel
{
    private final int WIDTH = 350, HEIGHT = 100, FONT_SIZE = 20;
    private final int NUM_COLORS = 5;
    private Color [] color = new Color[NUM_COLORS];
    private JLabel heading;

    // ----------------------------------------------------------------
    //  Sets up a panel with a label at the top and a set of radio buttons
    //  that control the background color of the panel.
    // ----------------------------------------------------------------
    public ColorOptionsPanel ()
    {
      // Set up heading and colors
      heading = new JLabel ("Choose the background color!");
      heading.setFont (new Font ("Helvetica", Font.BOLD, FONT_SIZE));

      color[0] = Color.yellow;
      color[1] = Color.cyan;
      color[2] = Color.red;
      color[3] = Color.green;
      color[4] = Color.magenta;

      // Instantiate a ButtonGroup object and a ColorListener object

      // Set up the panel
      add (heading);
      setBackground (Color.yellow);
      setPreferredSize (new Dimension (WIDTH, HEIGHT));

      // Group the radio buttons, add a ColorListener to each,
      // set the background color of each and add each to the panel.
    }

    // **************************************************************
    //    Represents the listener for the radio buttons.
    // **************************************************************
    private class ColorListener implements ActionListener
    {
      // ----------------------------------------------------------
      //  Updates the background color of the panel based on
      //  which radio button is selected.
      // ----------------------------------------------------------
      public void actionPerformed (ActionEvent event)
      {

      }
    }
}
```

Drawing Circles with Mouse Clicks

File *Circles.java* sets up a panel that creates and draws a circle as defined in *Circle.java* of random size and color at each mouse click. Each circle replaces the one before it. The code to handle the mouse clicks and do the drawing is in *CirclePanel.java*. Save these files to your directory, compile them and run them and experiment with the GUI. Then modify these files as described below.

1. This program creates a new circle each time—you can tell because each circle is a different color and size. Write a method *void move(Point p)* for your Circle class that takes a Point and moves the circle so its center is at that point. Now modify your CirclesListener class (defined inside CirclePanel) so that instead of creating a new circle every time the user clicks, it moves the existing circle to the clickpoint if a circle already exists. If no circle exists, a new one should be created at the clickpoint. So now a circle of the same color and size should move around the screen.

2. Write a method *boolean isInside(Point p)* for your Circle class that takes a Point and tells whether it is inside the circle. A point is inside the circle if its distance from the center is less than the radius. (Recall that the distance between two points (x1,y1) and (x2,y2) is sqrt((x2-x1)^2+(y2-y1)^2.)

3. Now modify the *mousePressed* method of CirclesListener so that the GUI behaves as follows:
    - ☐ If there is no circle (i.e., it is null) and the user clicks anywhere, a new (random) circle should be drawn at the click point.
    - ☐ If there is a circle on the screen and the user clicks inside that circle, the circle should go away. (Hint: To make the circle go away, set it to null and repaint.)
    - ☐ If there is a circle on the screen and the user clicks somewhere else, the circle should move to that point (no change from before).

    So the logic for *mousePressed* should look like this:

    ```
    if there is currently no circle
        create a new circle at the click point
    else if the click is inside the circle
        make the circle go away
    else
        move the circle to the click point

    repaint
    ```

4. Add bodies for the *mouseEntered* and *mouseExited* methods so that when the mouse enters the panel the background turns white, and when it exits the background turns blue. Remember that you can set the background color with the *setBackground* method.

```
//************************************************************
//  Circles.java
//
//  Demonstrates mouse events and drawing on a panel.
//  Derived from Dots.java in Lewis and Loftus
//************************************************************

import javax.swing.JFrame;

public class Circles
{
   //-------------------------------------------------------------
   //  Creates and displays the application frame.
   //-------------------------------------------------------------
   public static void main (String[] args)
   {
      JFrame circlesFrame = new JFrame ("Circles");
      circlesFrame.setDefaultCloseOperation (JFrame.EXIT_ON_CLOSE);

      circlesFrame.getContentPane().add (new CirclePanel());

      circlesFrame.pack();
      circlesFrame.setVisible(true);
   }
}
```

```
// ***************************************************************
// Circle.java
//
// Define a Circle class with methods to create and draw
// a circle of random size, color, and location.
//
// ***************************************************************

import java.awt.*;
import java.util.Random;

public class Circle
{
    private int centerX, centerY;
    private int radius;
    private Color color;

    static Random generator = new Random();

    //-------------------------------------------------------------
    // Creates a circle with center at point given, random radius and color
    //     -- radius 25..74
    //     -- color RGB value 0..16777215 (24-bit)
    //-------------------------------------------------------------
    public Circle(Point point)
    {
      radius = Math.abs(generator.nextInt())%50 + 25;
      color = new Color(Math.abs(generator.nextInt())% 16777216);
      centerX = point.x;
      centerY = point.y;
    }

    //-------------------------------------------------------------
    // Draws circle on the graphics object given
    //-------------------------------------------------------------
    public void draw(Graphics page)
    {
      page.setColor(color);
      page.fillOval(centerX-radius,centerY-radius,radius*2,radius*2);
    }
}
```

```
//************************************************************************
//  CirclePanel.java
//
//  Represents the primary panel for the Circles program on which the
//  circles are drawn.  Derived from the Lewis and Loftus DotsPanel class.
//************************************************************************

import javax.swing.*;
import java.awt.*;
import java.awt.event.*;
import java.util.*;

public class CirclePanel extends JPanel
{
    private final int WIDTH = 600, HEIGHT = 400;
    private Circle circle;

    //------------------------------------------------------------------
    //  Sets up this panel to listen for mouse events.
    //------------------------------------------------------------------
    public CirclePanel()
    {
        addMouseListener (new CirclesListener());
        setPreferredSize (new Dimension(WIDTH, HEIGHT));
    }

    //------------------------------------------------------------------
    //  Draws the current circle, if any.
    //------------------------------------------------------------------
    public void paintComponent (Graphics page)
    {
        super.paintComponent(page);
        if (circle != null)
          circle.draw(page);
    }

    //************************************************************************
    //  Represents the listener for mouse events.
    //************************************************************************
    private class CirclesListener implements MouseListener
    {
        //------------------------------------------------------------------
        // Creates a new circle at the current location whenever the
        // mouse button is pressed and repaints.
        //------------------------------------------------------------------
        public void mousePressed (MouseEvent event)
        {
            circle = new Circle(event.getPoint());
            repaint();
        }

        //------------------------------------------------------------------
        //  Provide empty definitions for unused event methods.
        //------------------------------------------------------------------
        public void mouseClicked (MouseEvent event) {}
        public void mouseReleased (MouseEvent event) {}
        public void mouseEntered (MouseEvent event) {}
        public void mouseExited (MouseEvent event) {}
    }
}
```

Moving Circles with the Mouse

File *Circles.java* sets up a GUI that creates and draws a circle as defined in *Circle.java* of random size and color at each mouse click. Each circle replaces the one before it. The code to handle the mouse clicks and do the drawing is in *CirclePanel.java*. (The files are from the previous exercise, Drawing Circles.) Save these files to your directory, compile them and run them and experiment with the GUI. Then modify the code in CirclePanel.java so that a circle is drawn when the user presses a mouse, but the user can drag it around as long as the mouse button is depressed. If the mouse button is released and then pressed again, a new circle is created, which can then be dragged around. You will need to make the following changes:

1. Write a method *void move(Point p)* for your Circle class that takes a Point and moves the circle so its center is at that point. (You may have already done this in a previous exercise.)

2. In the CirclePanel constructor, create a CirclesListener object and make it listen for both mouse events and mouse motion events.

3. Make the CirclesListener class implement the MouseMotionListener interface in addition to the MouseListener interface. This requires two steps:
    - Note in the header that CirclesListener implements MouseMotionListener.
    - Add bodies for the two MouseMotionListener methods, *mouseDragged* and *mouseMoved*. In *mouseDragged*, simply move the circle to the point returned by the *getPoint* method of the MouseEvent and repaint. Provide an empty body for *mouseMoved*.

Moving a Stick Figure

The file *StickFigure.java* contains a class that represents a stick figure. Study the file and note that in addition to a method to draw the stick figure there are methods to manipulate it:

☐ The method *move* repositions ("moves") the figure up or down and over (left or right) on the panel by changing the instance variables *baseX* and *baseY*.

☐ The method *grow* changes the size of the figure by a given factor by modifying the instance variable *height* and others.

☐ The method *setLegPosition* sets the position of the legs (number of pixels from vertical).

☐ The method *setArmPosition* sets the position of the arms (number of pixels from horizontal).

The file *MoveStickMan.java* contains a program that draws a single stick figure that can be moved around and modified using the keyboard. The file *MovePanel.java* represents the panel on which the stick figure is displayed. It is similar to DirectionPanel.java in Listing 7.23 of the text. Note that the constructor adds a KeyListener and contains a call to the setFocusable method. There is a partially defined inner class named *MoveListener* that implements the KeyListener interface. Currently the MoveListener listens only for two arrow keys (left and right) and the g key. The arrow keys move the stick figure left and right on the panel (the number of pixels moved is in the constant *JUMP*) and when the user presses the letter g, the figure "grows" (increases in height by 50%). Compile, and run the program. Test out the arrow keys and the g key.

Now add code to MovePanel.java to have the program respond to the following additional key events:

☐ When the up and down arrow keys are pressed the figure should move JUMP pixels up or down, respectively, on the panel.

☐ When the s key is pressed the figure should shrink by 50%.

☐ When the letter u (for up) is pressed, the stick figure should move its arms up and legs out; to make this happen add a call to *setArmPosition* to set the arm position and a call to *setLegPosition* to set the leg position. For example, when the u is pressed set the arm position to 60 and the leg position to 40 as follows:

```
stickMan.setArmPosition(60);

stickMan.setLegPosition(40);
```

☐ When the letter m (for middle) is pressed, the stick figure should place its arms horizontally with legs not quite as far out. To do this the arm position needs to be 0 (0 pixels above horizontal); a value of 20 for the leg position is good.

☐ When the letter d (down) is pressed, the figure should move its arms down and its legs closer together. (Use -60 and 10 for the arm and leg positions, respectively).

Compile and run the program. Try out all the keys it implements.

```
// ********************************************************
//     StickFigure.java
//
//     Represents a graphical stick figure
// ********************************************************

import java.awt.*;

public class StickFigure
{
    private int baseX;       // center of the figure
    private int baseY;       // bottom of the feet
    private Color color;     // color of the figure
    private int height;      // height of the figure
    private int headW;       // width of the head
    private int legLength;   // length of the legs
    private int legPosition;// # pixels the legs are up from vertical
    private int armLength;   // horizontal length of the arms
    private int armToFloor;  // distance from base to arms
```

```
private int armPosition;// # pixels arm is above/below horizontal

// ----------------------------------------------------------------
// Construct a stick figure given its four attributes
// ----------------------------------------------------------------
public StickFigure (int center, int bottom, Color shade, int size)
{
   baseX = center;
   baseY = bottom;
   color = shade;
   height = size;

   // define body positions proportional to height
   headW = height / 5;
   legLength = height / 2;
   armToFloor = 2 * height / 3;
   armLength =   height / 3;

   // set initial position of arms and legs
   armPosition = -20;
   legPosition = 15;
}

// ----------------------------------------------
// Draw the figure
// ----------------------------------------------
public void draw (Graphics page)
{
   // compute y-coordinate of top of head
   int top = baseY - height;

   page.setColor (color);

   // draw the head
   page.drawOval(baseX-headW/2, top, headW, headW);

   // draw the trunk
   page.drawLine (baseX, top+headW, baseX, baseY - legLength);

   // draw the legs
   page.drawLine(baseX, baseY-legLength, baseX-legPosition, baseY);
   page.drawLine(baseX, baseY-legLength, baseX+legPosition, baseY);

   // draw the arms
   int startY = baseY - armToFloor;
   page.drawLine(baseX, startY, baseX-armLength, startY-armPosition);
   page.drawLine(baseX, startY, baseX+armLength, startY-armPosition);
}

// -------------------------------------------------------
// Move the figure -- first parameter gives the
// number of pixels over (to right if over is positive,
// to the left if over is negative) and up or down
// (down if the parameter down is positive, up if it is
// negative)
// -------------------------------------------------------
public void move (int over, int down)
{
   baseX += over;
   baseY += down;
```

```java
    }

    // --------------------------------------------------------
    // Increase the height by the given factor (if the
    // factor is > 1 the figure will "grow" else it will
    // shrink)
    // --------------------------------------------------------
    public void grow (double factor)
    {
      height = (int) (factor * height);

      // reset body parts proportional to new height
      headW = height / 5;
      legLength = height / 2;
      armToFloor = 2 * height / 3;
      armLength = height / 3;
    }

    // ------------------------------------------------
    // set the legPosition (dist. from vertical) to
    // new value
    // ------------------------------------------------
    public void setLegPosition (int newPosition)
    {
      legPosition = newPosition;
    }

    // ------------------------------------------
    // set the arm position to the new value
    // ------------------------------------------
    public void setArmPosition (int newPos)
    {
      armPosition = newPos;
    }
}


// *****************************************************************
//   MoveStickMan.java
//
//   Uses key events to move a stick figure around.
// *****************************************************************
import javax.swing.*;

public class MoveStickMan
{
    // ---------------------------------------------
    //  Creates and displays the application frame.
    // ---------------------------------------------
    public static void main (String[] args)
    {
      JFrame frame = new JFrame ("Moving a Stick Figure");
      frame.setDefaultCloseOperation (JFrame.EXIT_ON_CLOSE);

      frame.getContentPane().add (new MovePanel());

      frame.pack();
      frame.setVisible(true);
    }
}
```

```java
// ****************************************************************
// FILE:  MovePanel.java
//
// The display panel for a key events program  -- arrow keys are used
// to move a stick figure around, the g key is used to make the figure
// grow by 50% (increase in height by 50%), the s key causes the
// figure to shrink (to half its size)
// ****************************************************************

import javax.swing.*;
import java.awt.*;
import java.awt.event.*;

public class MovePanel extends JPanel
{
    private final int WIDTH = 600;
    private final int HEIGHT = 400;

    private final int JUMP = 5;     // number of pixels moved each step

    // the following give the initial parameters for the figure
    private final int START_CENTER = WIDTH/2;
    private final int START_BOTTOM = HEIGHT - 40;
    private final int SIZE = HEIGHT / 2;

    private StickFigure stickMan;

    // ---------------------------------------
    //    Constructor:  Sets up the panel
    // ---------------------------------------
    public MovePanel ()
    {
      addKeyListener(new MoveListener());

      stickMan = new StickFigure (START_CENTER, START_BOTTOM,
                       Color.yellow, SIZE);

      setBackground (Color.black);
      setPreferredSize (new Dimension (WIDTH, HEIGHT));
      setFocusable(true);
    }

    // ---------------------------------------
    //     Draws the figure
    // ---------------------------------------
    public void paintComponent (Graphics page)
    {
      super.paintComponent (page);
      stickMan.draw (page);
    }


    // ************************************************************
    //   Represents a listener for keyboard activity.
    // ************************************************************
    private class MoveListener implements KeyListener
    {
      // ----------------------------------------------------
      // Handle a key-pressed event: arrow keys cause the
      // figure to move horizontally or vertically; the g
```

```java
// key causes the figure to "grow", the s key causes
// the figure to shrink, the u key causes arms and
// legs to go up, m puts them in the middle, and d
// down.
// --------------------------------------------------
public void keyPressed (KeyEvent event)
{
    switch (event.getKeyCode())
      {
      case KeyEvent.VK_LEFT:
          stickMan.move(-1*JUMP, 0);
          break;
      case KeyEvent.VK_RIGHT:
          stickMan.move(JUMP, 0);
          break;
      case KeyEvent.VK_G:
          stickMan.grow (1.5);
          break;
      default:
      }

    repaint();
}


// ---------------------------------------------
// Define empty bodies for key event methods
// not used
// ---------------------------------------------
public void keyTyped (KeyEvent event) {}
public void keyReleased (KeyEvent event) {}
}
}
```

Chapter 8: Inheritance
Lab Exercises

Exploring Inheritance

File *Dog.java* contains a declaration for a Dog class. Save this file to your directory and study it—notice what instance variables and methods are provided. Files *Labrador.java* and *Yorkshire.java* contain declarations for classes that extend Dog. Save and study these files as well.

File *DogTest.java* contains a simple driver program that creates a dog and makes it speak. Study DogTest.java, save it to your directory, and compile and run it to see what it does. Now modify these files as follows:

1. Add statements in DogTest.java after you create and print the dog to create and print a Yorkshire and a Labrador. Note that the Labrador constructor takes two parameters: the name and color of the labrador, both strings. Don't change any files besides DogTest.java. Now recompile DogTest.java; you should get an error saying something like

   ```
   ./Labrador.java:18: Dog(java.lang.String) in Dog cannot be applied to ()
      {
      ^
   ```

   1 error

   If you look at line 18 of Labrador.java it's just a {, and the constructor the compiler can't find (Dog()) isn't called anywhere in this file.
   a. What's going on? (Hint: What call must be made in the constructor of a subclass?)
      =>

   b. Fix the problem (which really is in Labrador) so that DogTest.java creates and makes the Dog, Labrador, and Yorkshire all speak.

2. Add code to DogTest.java to print the average breed weight for both your Labrador and your Yorkshire. Use the avgBreedWeight() method for both. What error do you get? Why?

   =>

   Fix the problem by adding the needed code to the Yorkshire class.

3. Add an abstract *int avgBreedWeight()* method to the Dog class. Remember that this means that the word *abstract* appears in the method header after *public*, and that the method does not have a body (just a semicolon after the parameter list). It makes sense for this to be abstract, since Dog has no idea what breed it is. Now any subclass of Dog must have an avgBreedWeight method; since both Yorkshire and Laborador do, you should be all set.

   Save these changes and recompile DogTest.java. You should get an error in Dog.java (unless you made more changes than described above). Figure out what's wrong and fix this error, then recompile DogTest.java. You should get another error, this time in DogTest.java. Read the error message carefully; it tells you exactly what the problem is. Fix this by changing DogTest (which will mean taking some things out).

```
// ****************************************************************
// Dog.java
//
// A class that holds a dog's name and can make it speak.
//
// ****************************************************************
public class Dog
{
    protected String name;

    // ----------------------------------------------------------
    // Constructor -- store name
    // ----------------------------------------------------------
    public Dog(String name)
    {
      this.name = name;
    }

    // ----------------------------------------------------------
    // Returns the dog's name
    // ----------------------------------------------------------
    public String getName()
    {
      return name;
    }

    // ----------------------------------------------------------
    // Returns a string with the dog's comments
    // ----------------------------------------------------------
    public String speak()
    {
      return "Woof";
    }
}
```

```java
// ***************************************************************
// Labrador.java
//
// A class derived from Dog that holds information about
// a labrador retriever.  Overrides Dog speak method and includes
// information about avg weight for this breed.
//
// ***************************************************************

public class Labrador extends Dog
{
    private String color; //black, yellow, or chocolate?
    private int breedWeight = 75;

    public Labrador(String name,  String color)
    {
      this.color = color;
    }

    // -----------------------------------------------------------
    // Big bark -- overrides speak method in Dog
    // -----------------------------------------------------------
    public String speak()
    {
      return "WOOF";
    }

    // -----------------------------------------------------------
    // Returns weight
    // -----------------------------------------------------------
    public static int avgBreedWeight()
    {
      return breedWeight;
    }
}
```

```
// ******************************************************************
// Yorkshire.java
//
// A class derived from Dog that holds information about
// a Yorkshire terrier. Overrides Dog speak method.
//
// ******************************************************************

public class Yorkshire extends Dog
{

    public Yorkshire(String name)
    {
      super(name);
    }

    // -----------------------------------------------------------
    // Small bark -- overrides speak method in Dog
    // -----------------------------------------------------------
    public String speak()
    {
      return "woof";
    }

}




// ******************************************************************
// DogTest.java
//
// A simple test class that creates a Dog and makes it speak.
//
// ******************************************************************

public class DogTest
{
    public static void main(String[] args)
    {
      Dog dog = new Dog("Spike");
      System.out.println(dog.getName() + " says " + dog.speak());

    }
}
```

A Sorted Integer List

File *IntList.java* contains code for an integer list class. Save it to your directory and study it; notice that the only things you can do are create a list of a fixed size and add an element to a list. If the list is already full, a message will be printed. File *ListTest.java* contains code for a class that creates an IntList, puts some values in it, and prints it. Save this to your directory and compile and run it to see how it works.

Now write a class SortedIntList that extends IntList. SortedIntList should be just like IntList except that its elements should always be in sorted order from smallest to largest. This means that when an element is inserted into a SortedIntList it should be put into its sorted place, not just at the end of the array. To do this you'll need to do two things when you add a new element:

- Walk down the array until you find the place where the new element should go. Since the list is already sorted you can just keep looking at elements until you find one that is at least as big as the one to be inserted.
- Move down every element that will go after the new element, that is, everything from the one you stop on to the end. This creates a slot in which you can put the new element. Be careful about the order in which you move them or you'll overwrite your data!

Now you can insert the new element in the location you originally stopped on.

All of this will go into your *add* method, which will override the *add* method for the IntList class. (Be sure to also check to see if you need to expand the array, just as in the IntList *add* method.) What other methods, if any, do you need to override?

To test your class, modify ListTest.java so that after it creates and prints the IntList, it creates and prints a SortedIntList containing the same elements (inserted in the same order). When the list is printed, they should come out in sorted order.

```java
// ****************************************************************
// IntList.java
//
// An (unsorted) integer list class with a method to add an
// integer to the list and a toString method that returns the contents
// of the list with indices.
//
// ****************************************************************
public class IntList
{

    protected int[] list;
    protected int numElements = 0;

    //-------------------------------------------------------------
    // Constructor -- creates an integer list of a given size.
    //-------------------------------------------------------------
    public IntList(int size)
    {
      list = new int[size];
    }

    //-------------------------------------------------------------
    // Adds an integer to the list.  If the list is full,
    // prints a message and does nothing.
    //-------------------------------------------------------------
    public void add(int value)
    {
      if (numElements == list.length)
          System.out.println("Can't add, list is full");
      else
          {
            list[numElements] = value;
            numElements++;
```

```
        }
    }

    //-----------------------------------------------------------
    // Returns a string containing the elements of the list with their
    // indices.
    //-----------------------------------------------------------
    public String toString()
    {
      String returnString = "";
      for (int i=0; i<numElements; i++)
          returnString += i + ": " + list[i] + "\n";
      return returnString;
    }
}




//  ****************************************************************
// ListTest.java
//
// A simple test program that creates an IntList, puts some
// ints in it, and prints the list.
//
//  ****************************************************************

public class ListTest
{
    public static void main(String[] args)
    {
      IntList myList = new IntList(10);
      myList.add(100);
      myList.add(50);
      myList.add(200);
      myList.add(25);
      System.out.println(myList);
    }
}
```

Test Questions

In this exercise you will use inheritance to read, store, and print questions for a test. First, write an abstract class TestQuestion that contains the following:

- ☐ A protected String variable that holds the test question.
- ☐ An abstract method *protected abstract void readQuestion()* to read the question.
  Now define two subclasses of TestQuestion, Essay and MultChoice. Essay will need an instance variable to store the number of blank lines needed after the question (answering space). MultChoice will not need this variable, but it will need an array of Strings to hold the choices along with the main question. Assume that the input is provided from the standard input as follows, with each item on its own line:
  - ☐ type of question (character, m=multiple choice, e=essay)
  - ☐ number of blank lines for essay, number of blank lines for multiple choice (integer)
  - ☐ choice 1 (multiple choice only)
  - ☐ choice 2 (multiple choice only) ...
  The very first item of input, before any questions, is an integer indicating how many questions will be entered. So the following input represents three questions: an essay question requiring 5 blank lines, a multiple choice question with 4 choices, and another essay question requiring 10 blank lines:

```
3
e
5
Why does the constructor of a derived class have to call the constructor
of its parent class?
m
4
Which of the following is not a legal identifier in Java?
guess2
2ndGuess
_guess2_
Guess
e
5
What does the "final" modifier do?
```

You will need to write *readQuestion* methods for the MultChoice and Essay classes that read information in this format. (Presumably the character that identifies what kind of question it is will be read by a driver.) You will also need to write *toString* methods for the MultChoice and Essay classes that return nicely formatted versions of the questions (e.g., the choices should be lined up, labeled a), b), etc, and indented in MultChioce).

Now define a class WriteTest that creates an array of TestQuestion objects. It should read the questions from the standard input as follows in the format above, first reading an integer that indicates how many questions are coming. It should create a MultChoice object for each multiple choice question and an Essay object for each essay question and store each object in the array. (Since it's an array of TestQuestion and both Essay and MultChoice are subclasses of TestQuestion, objects of both types can be stored in the array.) When all of the data has been read, it should use a loop to print the questions, numbered, in order.

Use the data in *testbank.dat* to test your program.

```
testbank.dat

5
e
5
Why does the constructor of a subclass class have to call the constructor of its
parent class?
m
4
Which of the following is not a legal identifier in Java?
```

guess2
2ndGuess
guess2
Guess
e
5
What does the "final" modifier do?
e
3
Java does not support multiple inheritance. This means that a class cannot do
what?
m
3
A JPanel has an addMouseListener method because JPanel is a subclass of
JComponent
JApplet
Object

Overriding the *equals* Method

File *Player.java* contains a class that holds information about an athlete: name, team, and uniform number. File *ComparePlayers.java* contains a skeletal program that uses the Player class to read in information about two baseball players and determine whether or not they are the same player.

1. Fill in the missing code in ComparePlayers so that it reads in two players and prints "Same player" if they are the same, "Different players" if they are different. Use the *equals* method, which Player inherits from the Object class, to determine whether two players are the same. Are the results what you expect?

2. The problem above is that as defined in the Object class, *equals* does an address comparison. It says that two objects are the same if they live at the same memory location, that is, if the variables that hold references to them are aliases. The two Player objects in this program are not aliases, so even if they contain exactly the same information they will be "not equal." To make *equals* compare the actual information in the object, you can override it with a definition specific to the class. It might make sense to say that two players are "equal" (the same player) if they are on the same team and have the same uniform number.

    ☐   Use this strategy to define an *equals* method for the Player class. Your method should take a Player object and return true if it is equal to the current object, false otherwise.

    ☐   Test your ComparePlayers program using your modified Player class. It should give the results you would expect.

```
// ************************************************************
// Player.java
//
// Defines a Player class that holds information about an athlete.
// ************************************************************

import java.util.Scanner;

public class Player
{
    private String name;
    private String team;
    private int jerseyNumber;


    //------------------------------------------------------------
    // Prompts for and reads in the player's name, team, and
    // jersey number.
    //------------------------------------------------------------

    public void readPlayer()
    {
      Scanner scan = new Scanner(System.in);
      System.out.print("Name: ");
      name = scan.nextLine();
      System.out.print("Team: ");
      team = scan.nextLine();
      System.out.print("Jersey number: ");
      jerseyNumber = Scan.nextInt();
    }

}
```

```
// ***************************************************************
// ComparePlayers
//
// Reads in two Player objects and tells whether they represent
// the same player.
// ***************************************************************
import java.util.Scanner;
public class ComparePlayers
{
    public static void main(String[] args)
    {
      Player player1 = new Player();
      Player player2 = new Player();

      Scanner scan = new Scanner();

      //Prompt for and read in information for player 1

      //Prompt for and read in information for player 2

      //Compare player1 to player 2 and print a message saying
      //whether they are equal

    }
}
```

Extending Adapter Classes

Files *Dots.java* and *DotsPanel.java* contain the code in Listings 7.18 and 7.19 of the text. This program draws dots where the user clicks and counts the number of dots that have been drawn. Save these files to your directory and compile and run Dots to see how it works.

Now study the code in DotsPanel.java. (Dots just creates an instance of DotsPanel and adds it to its content pane.) DotsPanel defines an inner class, DotsListener, that implements the MouseListener interface. Notice that it defines the *mousePressed* method to draw a dot at the click point and gives empty bodies for the rest of the MouseListener methods.

1. Modify the DotsListener class so that instead of implementing the MouseListener interface, it extends the MouseAdapter class. What other code does this let you eliminate? For now, just comment out this code. Test your modified program.

2. We have been using inner classes to define event listeners. Another common strategy is to make the panel itself be a MouseListener, eliminating the need for the inner class. Do this as follows:
    - Modify the header to the DotsPanel class to indicate that it implements the MouseListener interface (it still extends JPanel).
    - Delete the DotsListener class entirely, moving the five MouseListener methods into the DotsPanel class.
    - The DotsPanel constructor contains the following statement:

              addMouseListener (new DotsListener());

      This creates an instance of the DotsListener class and makes it listen for mouse events on the panel. This will have to change, since the DotsListener class has gone away. The listener is now the panel itself, so the argument to *addMouseListener* should change to *this*, that is, the current object. So the panel is listening for its own mouse events! Compile and run your modified program; it should behave just as before.

3. When we were using the DotsListener class we saw that it could either implement the MouseListener interface or extend the MouseAdapter class. With the new approach in #2, where the DotsPanel is also a MouseListener, can we do the same thing – that is, can DotsPanel extend MouseAdapter instead of implementing MouseListener? Why or why not? If you're not sure, try it and explain what happens.

```
//********************************************************************
//  Dots.java          Author: Lewis/Loftus
//
//  Demonstrates mouse events.
//********************************************************************

import javax.swing.JFrame;

public class Dots
{
    //-----------------------------------------------------------------
    //  Creates and displays the application frame.
    //-----------------------------------------------------------------
    public static void main (String[] args)
    {
        JFrame frame = new JFrame ("Dots");
        frame.setDefaultCloseOperation (JFrame.EXIT_ON_CLOSE);

        frame.getContentPane().add (new DotsPanel());

        frame.pack();
        frame.setVisible(true);
    }
}
```

```
//********************************************************************
//  DotsPanel.java          Author: Lewis/Loftus
//
//  Represents the primary panel for the Dots program.
//********************************************************************

import java.util.ArrayList;
import javax.swing.JPanel;
import java.awt.*;
import java.awt.event.*;

public class DotsPanel extends JPanel
{
    private final int SIZE = 6;  // radius of each dot

    private ArrayList<Point> pointList;

    //-----------------------------------------------------------------
    //  Constructor: Sets up this panel to listen for mouse events.
    //-----------------------------------------------------------------
    public DotsPanel()
    {
        pointList = new ArrayList<Point>();

        addMouseListener (new DotsListener());

        setBackground (Color.black);
        setPreferredSize (new Dimension(300, 200));
    }

    //-----------------------------------------------------------------
    //  Draws all of the dots stored in the list.
    //-----------------------------------------------------------------
    public void paintComponent (Graphics page)
    {
        super.paintComponent(page);

        page.setColor (Color.green);

        for (Point spot : pointList)
            page.fillOval (spot.x-SIZE, spot.y-SIZE, SIZE*2, SIZE*2);

        page.drawString ("Count: " + pointList.size(), 5, 15);
    }

    //********************************************************************
    //  Represents the listener for mouse events.
    //********************************************************************
    private class DotsListener implements MouseListener
    {
        //-----------------------------------------------------------------
        //  Adds the current point to the list of points and redraws
        //  the panel whenever the mouse button is pressed.
        //-----------------------------------------------------------------
        public void mousePressed (MouseEvent event)
        {
            pointList.add(event.getPoint());
            repaint();
        }
```

```
    //-------------------------------------------------------------
    //  Provide empty definitions for unused event methods.
    //-------------------------------------------------------------
    public void mouseClicked (MouseEvent event) {}
    public void mouseReleased (MouseEvent event) {}
    public void mouseEntered (MouseEvent event) {}
    public void mouseExited (MouseEvent event) {}
  }
}
```

Rebound Revisited

The files *Rebound.java* and *ReboundPanel.java* contain the program are in Listings 8.15 and 8.16 of the text. This program has an image that moves around the screen, bouncing back when it hits the sides (you can use any GIF or JPEG you like). Save these files to your directory, then open *ReboundPanel.java* in the editor and observe the following:

- ☐ The constructor instantiates a Timer object with a delay of 20 (the time, in milliseconds, between generation of action events). The Timer object is started with its *start* method.
- ☐ The constructor also gives the initial position of the ball (*x* and *y*) and the distance it will move at each interval (*moveX* and *moveY*).
- ☐ The *actionPerformed* method in the *ReboundListener* inner class "moves" the image by adding the value of *moveX* to *x* and of *moveY* to *y*. This has the effect of moving the image to the right when *moveX* is positive and to the left when *moveX* is negative, and similarly (with down and up) with *moveY*. The *actionPerformed* method then checks to see if the ball has hit one of the sides of the panel—if it hits the left side (x <= 0) or the right side (x >= WIDTH-IMAGE_SIZE) the sign of *moveX* is changed. This has the effect of changing the direction of the ball. Similarly the method checks to see if the ball hit the top or bottom.

Now do the following:

1. First experiment with the speed of the animation. This is affected by two things—the value of the DELAY constant and the amount the ball is moved each time.
   - ☐ Change DELAY to 100. Save, compile, and run the program. How does the speed compare to the original?
   - ☐ Change DELAY back to 20 and change *moveX* and *moveY* to 15. Save, compile, and run the program. Compare the motion to that in the original program.
   - ☐ Experiment with other combinations of values.
   - ☐ Change *moveX* and *moveY* back to 3. Use any value of DELAY you wish.
2. Now add a second image to the program by doing the following:
   - ☐ Declare a second ImageIcon object as an instance variable. You can use the same image as before or a new one.
   - ☐ Declare integer variables *x2* and *y2* to represent the location of the second image, and *moveX2* and *moveY2* to control the amount the second ball moves each time.
   - ☐ Initialize *moveX2* to 5 and *moveY2* to 8 (note—this image will have a different trajectory than the first—no longer a 45 degree angle).
   - ☐ In *actionPerformed*, move the second image by the amount given in the *moveX2* and *moveY2* variable, and add code to check to see if the second image has hit a side.
   - ☐ In *paintComponent*, draw the second image as well as the first.
2. Compile and run the program. Make sure it is working correctly.

```
//*******************************************************************
//  Rebound.java          Author: Lewis/Loftus
//
//  Demonstrates an animation and the use of the Timer class.
//*******************************************************************
import java.awt.*;
import java.awt.event.*;
import javax.swing.*;

public class Rebound
{
    //----------------------------------------------------------
    //  Displays the main frame of the program.
    //----------------------------------------------------------
    public static void main (String[] args)
    {
        JFrame frame = new JFrame ("Rebound");
        frame.setDefaultCloseOperation (JFrame.EXIT_ON_CLOSE);

        frame.getContentPane().add(new ReboundPanel());
        frame.pack();
        frame.setVisible(true);
    }
}
```

```java
//********************************************************************
//  ReboundPanel.java         Author: Lewis/Loftus
//
//  Represents the primary panel for the Rebound program.
//********************************************************************
import java.awt.*;
import java.awt.event.*;
import javax.swing.*;

public class ReboundPanel extends JPanel
{
    private final int WIDTH = 300, HEIGHT = 100;
    private final int DELAY = 20, IMAGE_SIZE = 35;

    private ImageIcon image;
    private Timer timer;
    private int x, y, moveX, moveY;

    //-----------------------------------------------------------------
    //  Sets up the panel, including the timer for the animation.
    //-----------------------------------------------------------------
    public ReboundPanel()
    {
        timer = new Timer(DELAY, new ReboundListener());
        image = new ImageIcon ("happyFace.gif");

        x = 0;
        y = 40;
        moveX = moveY = 3;

        setPreferredSize (new Dimension(WIDTH, HEIGHT));
        setBackground (Color.black);
        timer.start();
    }

    //-----------------------------------------------------------------
    //  Draws the image in the current location.
    //-----------------------------------------------------------------
    public void paintComponent (Graphics page)
    {
        super.paintComponent (page);
        image.paintIcon (this, page, x, y);
    }

    //********************************************************************
    //  Represents the action listener for the timer.
    //********************************************************************
    private class ReboundListener implements ActionListener
    {
        //-----------------------------------------------------------------
        //  Updates the position of the image and possibly the direction
        //  of movement whenever the timer fires an action event.
        //-----------------------------------------------------------------
        public void actionPerformed (ActionEvent event)
        {
            x += moveX;
            y += moveY;

            if (x <= 0 || x >= WIDTH-IMAGE_SIZE)
                moveX = moveX * -1;

            if (y <= 0 || y >= HEIGHT-IMAGE_SIZE)
                moveY = moveY * -1;

            repaint();
        }
    }
}
```

Count Down

Clocks are a standard thing to animate—they change at regular intervals. In this exercise, you will write an applet that displays a simple "clock" that just counts down from 10. The clock will be a DigitalDisplay object. The file *DigitalDisplay.java* contains the code for the class. The file *CountDown.java* contains the program and *CountDownPanel.java* contains a skeleton for the panel for the animation. Copy these files to your directory, compile and run the program. It should just display the clock with the number 10. Now do the following to make the clock count down, stop when it hits 0, and reset to 10 if the user clicks the mouse.

1. Add an inner class named *CountListener* that implements ActionListener. In actionPerformed,
   ☐ Decrement the clock value. To do this use the decrement method in the DigitalDisplay class. (Look at its signature to see how to use it.)
   ☐ If the display value of the clock is negative, stop the timer; otherwise repaint the panel.

2. In the constructor, set up the timer.

3. Compile and run the program to see if it works.

4. Now add code to let a mouse click have some control over the clock. In particular, if the clock is running when the mouse is clicked the clock should be stopped (stop the timer). If the clock is not running, it should be reset to 10 and started. To add the ability of the panel to respond to mouse clicks, do the following:
   ☐ Add an inner class that implements the MouseListener interface. In mouseClicked, if the timer is running, stop it; otherwise reset the clock to 10 (there is a method in the DigitalDisplay class to do this), start the timer, and repaint the applet. The bodies of the other methods in the MouseListener interface will be empty.
   ☐ Add a second parameter of type JApplet to the constructor for CountDownPanel. In your constructor, add the mouse listener to the applet.
   ☐ Modify the program CountDown.java to send the applet (*this*) as the second parameter for the CountDownPanel constructor.

5. Compile and run the program to make sure everything works right.

```
// ****************************************************
//   DigitalDisplay.java
//
//   A simple rectangular display of a single number
// ****************************************************

import java.awt.*;

public class DigitalDisplay
{
    private int displayVal;        // value to be displayed
    private int x, y;              // position
    private int width, height;     // size
    private Font displayFont;      // font for the number

    // -------------------------------------------------------
    // construct a DigitalDisplay object with the given values
    // and New Century Schoolbook font in 40 point bold
    // -------------------------------------------------------
    public DigitalDisplay(int start, int x, int y, int w, int h)
    {
        this.x = x;
        this.y = y;
        width = w;
        height = h;
        displayVal = start;
```

```java
      displayFont = new Font ("New Century Schoolbook", Font.BOLD, 40);
   }

   // --------------------------
   // decrement the display value
   // --------------------------
   public void decrement()
   {
      displayVal--;
   }

   // --------------------------
   // increment the display value
   // --------------------------
   public void increment()
   {
      displayVal++;
   }

   // --------------------------
   // return the display value
   // --------------------------
   public int getVal()
   {
      return displayVal;
   }

   // --------------------------------------------------------
   // reset the display value to that given in the parameter
   // --------------------------------------------------------
   public void reset (int val)
   {
      displayVal = val;
   }

   // ----------------
   // draw the display
   // ----------------
   public void draw (Graphics page)
   {
      // draw a black border
      page.setColor (Color.black);
      page.fillRect (x, y, width, height);

      // a white inside
      page.setColor (Color.white);
      page.fillRect (x + 5, y + 5, width - 10, height - 10);

      // display the number centered
      page.setColor (Color.black);
      page.setFont (displayFont);
      int fontHeight = page.getFontMetrics().getHeight();
      int strWidth = page.getFontMetrics().stringWidth(""+displayVal);
      page.drawString (""+displayVal, x + width/2 - strWidth/2,
                y + fontHeight/2 + height/2);
   }
}
```

```
// ************************************************************
//   CountDown.java
//
//   Draws a digital display that counts down from 10.  The
//   display can be stopped or reset with a mouse click.
// ************************************************************

import DigitalDisplay;
import java.awt.*;
import java.awt.event.*;
import javax.swing.*;

public class CountDown extends JApplet
{
    private final int DELAY = 200;
    private Timer timer;


    // ----------------------------------------------------------
    //   Initialize the applet, including the animation.
    // ----------------------------------------------------------
    public void init()
    {
      timer = new Timer (DELAY, null);

      getContentPane().add (new CountDownPanel(timer));
    }


    // ----------------------------------------------------------
    //   Start the animation when the applet is started.
    // ----------------------------------------------------------
    public void start()
    {
      timer.start();
    }

    // ----------------------------------------------------------
    //   Stop the animation when the applet is stopped.
    // ----------------------------------------------------------
    public void stop()
    {
      timer.stop();
    }


}
```

```
// ************************************************************
//   CountDownPanel.java
//
//   Panel for a digital display that counts down from 10.
//   The display can be stopped or reset with a mouse click.
// ************************************************************

import DigitalDisplay;
import java.awt.*;
import java.awt.event.*;
import javax.swing.*;

public class CountDownPanel extends JPanel
{
    private final int WIDTH = 600;
    private final int HEIGHT = 400;
    private final int DISPLAY_WIDTH = 150;
    private final int DISPLAY_HEIGHT = 100;
    private final int DELAY = 200;
    private final int COUNT_START = 10;

    private DigitalDisplay clock;
    private Timer timer;


    // ----------------------------------------------------------
    //   Set up the applet.
    // ----------------------------------------------------------
    public CountDownPanel (Timer countdown)
    {
      // Set up the timer



      setBackground (Color.blue);
      setPreferredSize (new Dimension (WIDTH, HEIGHT));


      clock = new DigitalDisplay(COUNT_START, WIDTH/2 - DISPLAY_WIDTH,
                      HEIGHT/2 - DISPLAY_HEIGHT,
                      DISPLAY_WIDTH, DISPLAY_HEIGHT);
    }


    // ----------------
    // draw the clock
    // ----------------
    public void paintComponent (Graphics page)
    {
      super.paintComponent (page);
      clock.draw(page);
    }

}
```

Chapter 9: Polymorphism
Lab Exercises

Topics	Lab Exercises
Polymorphism via Inheritance	Another Type of Employee
	Painting Shapes
Sorting & Searching	Polymorphic Sorting
	Searching and Sorting An Integer List
Comparing Searches	Timing Searching and Sorting Algorithms
Color Choosers	Coloring a Moveable Circle
Sliders	Speed Control

Another Type of Employee

The files *Firm.java, Staff.java, StaffMember.java, Volunteer.java, Employee.java, Executive.java,* and *Hourly.java* are from Listings 9.1 – 9.7 in the text. The program illustrates inheritance and polymorphism. In this exercise you will add one more employee type to the class hierarchy (see Figure 9.1 in the text). The employee will be one that is an hourly employee but also earns a commission on sales. Hence the class, which we'll name *Commission*, will be derived from the *Hourly* class.

Write a class named *Commission* with the following features:

☐ It extends the *Hourly* class.
☐ It has two instance variables (in addition to those inherited): one is the total sales the employee has made (type double) and the second is the commission rate for the employee (the commission rate will be type double and will represent the percent (in decimal form) commission the employee earns on sales (so .2 would mean the employee earns 20% commission on sales)).
☐ The constructor takes 6 parameters: the first 5 are the same as for *Hourly* (name, address, phone number, social security number, hourly pay rate) and the 6th is the commission rate for the employee. The constructor should call the constructor of the parent class with the first 5 parameters then use the 6th to set the commission rate.
☐ One additional method is needed: *public void addSales (double totalSales)* that adds the parameter to the instance variable representing total sales.
☐ The *pay* method must call the pay method of the parent class to compute the pay for hours worked then add to that the pay from commission on sales. (See the pay method in the Executive class.) The total sales should be set back to 0 (note: you don't need to set the hoursWorked back to 0—why not?).
☐ The *toString* method needs to call the *toString* method of the parent class then add the total sales to that.

To test your class, update Staff.java as follows:

☐ Increase the size of the array to 8.
☐ Add two commissioned employees to the *staffList*—make up your own names, addresses, phone numbers and social security numbers. Have one of the employees earn $6.25 per hour and 20% commission and the other one earn $9.75 per hour and 15% commission.
☐ For the first additional employee you added, put the hours worked at 35 and the total sales $400; for the second, put the hours at 40 and the sales at $950.

Compile and run the program. Make sure it is working properly.

```
//*****************************************************************
//  Firm.java          Author: Lewis/Loftus
//
//  Demonstrates polymorphism via inheritance.
//*****************************************************************

public class Firm
{
   //----------------------------------------------------------------
   //  Creates a staff of employees for a firm and pays them.
   //----------------------------------------------------------------
   public static void main (String[] args)
   {
      Staff personnel = new Staff();

      personnel.payday();
   }
}
```

```
//********************************************************************
//   Staff.java          Author: Lewis/Loftus
//
//   Represents the personnel staff of a particular business.
//********************************************************************

public class Staff
{
    StaffMember[] staffList;

    //----------------------------------------------------------------
    //  Sets up the list of staff members.
    //----------------------------------------------------------------
    public Staff ()
    {
        staffList = new StaffMember[6];

        staffList[0] = new Executive ("Sam", "123 Main Line",
            "555-0469", "123-45-6789", 2423.07);

        staffList[1] = new Employee ("Carla", "456 Off Line",
            "555-0101", "987-65-4321", 1246.15);
        staffList[2] = new Employee ("Woody", "789 Off Rocker",
            "555-0000", "010-20-3040", 1169.23);

        staffList[3] = new Hourly ("Diane", "678 Fifth Ave.",
            "555-0690", "958-47-3625", 10.55);

        staffList[4] = new Volunteer ("Norm", "987 Suds Blvd.",
            "555-8374");
        staffList[5] = new Volunteer ("Cliff", "321 Duds Lane",
            "555-7282");

        ((Executive)staffList[0]).awardBonus (500.00);

        ((Hourly)staffList[3]).addHours (40);
    }

    //----------------------------------------------------------------
    //  Pays all staff members.
    //----------------------------------------------------------------
    public void payday ()
    {
        double amount;

        for (int count=0; count < staffList.length; count++)
        {
            System.out.println (staffList[count]);

            amount = staffList[count].pay();   // polymorphic

            if (amount == 0.0)
                System.out.println ("Thanks!");
            else
                System.out.println ("Paid: " + amount);

            System.out.println ("---------------------------------");
        }
    }
}
```

```
//************************************************************
//  StaffMember.java          Author: Lewis/Loftus
//
//  Represents a generic staff member.
//************************************************************

abstract public class StaffMember
{
    protected String name;
    protected String address;
    protected String phone;

    //-----------------------------------------------------------
    //  Sets up a staff member using the specified information.
    //-----------------------------------------------------------
    public StaffMember (String eName, String eAddress, String ePhone)
    {
        name = eName;
        address = eAddress;
        phone = ePhone;
    }

    //-----------------------------------------------------------
    //  Returns a string including the basic employee information.
    //-----------------------------------------------------------
    public String toString()
    {
        String result = "Name: " + name + "\n";

        result += "Address: " + address + "\n";
        result += "Phone: " + phone;

        return result;
    }

    //-----------------------------------------------------------
    //  Derived classes must define the pay method for each type of
    //  employee.
    //-----------------------------------------------------------
    public abstract double pay();
}
```

```
//************************************************************
//  Volunteer.java          Author: Lewis/Loftus
//
//  Represents a staff member that works as a volunteer.
//************************************************************

public class Volunteer extends StaffMember
{
   //-----------------------------------------------------------------
   //  Sets up a volunteer using the specified information.
   //-----------------------------------------------------------------
   public Volunteer (String eName, String eAddress, String ePhone)
   {
      super (eName, eAddress, ePhone);
   }

   //-----------------------------------------------------------------
   //  Returns a zero pay value for this volunteer.
   //-----------------------------------------------------------------
   public double pay()
   {
      return 0.0;
   }
}
```

```
//********************************************************************
//  Employee.java         Author: Lewis/Loftus
//
//  Represents a general paid employee.
//********************************************************************

public class Employee extends StaffMember
{
    protected String socialSecurityNumber;
    protected double payRate;

    //-----------------------------------------------------------------
    //  Sets up an employee with the specified information.
    //-----------------------------------------------------------------
    public Employee (String eName, String eAddress, String ePhone,
                     String socSecNumber, double rate)
    {
        super (eName, eAddress, ePhone);

        socialSecurityNumber = socSecNumber;
        payRate = rate;
    }

    //-----------------------------------------------------------------
    //  Returns information about an employee as a string.
    //-----------------------------------------------------------------
    public String toString()
    {
        String result = super.toString();

        result += "\nSocial Security Number: " + socialSecurityNumber;

        return result;
    }

    //-----------------------------------------------------------------
    //  Returns the pay rate for this employee.
    //-----------------------------------------------------------------
    public double pay()
    {
        return payRate;
    }
}
```

```java
//************************************************************************
//  Executive.java       Author: Lewis/Loftus
//
//  Represents an executive staff member, who can earn a bonus.
//************************************************************************

public class Executive extends Employee
{
    private double bonus;

    //--------------------------------------------------------------
    //  Sets up an executive with the specified information.
    //--------------------------------------------------------------
    public Executive (String eName, String eAddress, String ePhone,
                    String socSecNumber, double rate)
    {
        super (eName, eAddress, ePhone, socSecNumber, rate);

        bonus = 0;  // bonus has yet to be awarded
    }

    //--------------------------------------------------------------
    //  Awards the specified bonus to this executive.
    //--------------------------------------------------------------
    public void awardBonus (double execBonus)
    {
        bonus = execBonus;
    }

    //--------------------------------------------------------------
    //  Computes and returns the pay for an executive, which is the
    //  regular employee payment plus a one-time bonus.
    //--------------------------------------------------------------
    public double pay()
    {
        double payment = super.pay() + bonus;

        bonus = 0;

        return payment;
    }
}
```

```java
//************************************************************************
//  Hourly.java          Author: Lewis/Loftus
//
//  Represents an employee that gets paid by the hour.
//************************************************************************

public class Hourly extends Employee
{
    private int hoursWorked;

    //---------------------------------------------------------------
    //  Sets up this hourly employee using the specified information.
    //---------------------------------------------------------------
    public Hourly (String eName, String eAddress, String ePhone,
                   String socSecNumber, double rate)
    {
        super (eName, eAddress, ePhone, socSecNumber, rate);

        hoursWorked = 0;
    }

    //---------------------------------------------------------------
    //  Adds the specified number of hours to this employee's
    //  accumulated hours.
    //---------------------------------------------------------------
    public void addHours (int moreHours)
    {
        hoursWorked += moreHours;
    }

    //---------------------------------------------------------------
    //  Computes and returns the pay for this hourly employee.
    //---------------------------------------------------------------
    public double pay()
    {
        double payment = payRate * hoursWorked;

        hoursWorked = 0;

        return payment;
    }

    //---------------------------------------------------------------
    //  Returns information about this hourly employee as a string.
    //---------------------------------------------------------------
    public String toString()
    {
        String result = super.toString();

        result += "\nCurrent hours: " + hoursWorked;

        return result;
    }
}
```

Painting Shapes

In this lab exercise you will develop a class hierarchy of shapes and write a program that computes the amount of paint needed to paint different objects. The hierarchy will consist of a parent class Shape with three derived classes - Sphere, Rectangle, and Cylinder. For the purposes of this exercise, the only attribute a shape will have is a name and the method of interest will be one that computes the area of the shape (surface area in the case of three-dimensional shapes). Do the following.

1. Write an abstract class Shape with the following properties:
    - An instance variable shapeName of type String
    - An abstract method area()
    - A toString method that returns the name of the shape

2. The file *Sphere.java* contains a class for a sphere which is a descendant of Shape. A sphere has a radius and its area (surface area) is given by the formula 4*PI*radius^2. Define similar classes for a rectangle and a cylinder. Both the Rectangle class and the Cylinder class are descendants of the Shape class. A rectangle is defined by its length and width and its area is length times width. A cylinder is defined by a radius and height and its area (surface area) is PI*radius^2*height. Define the toString method in a way similar to that for the Sphere class.

3. The file *Paint.java* contains a class for a type of paint (which has a "coverage" and a method to compute the amount of paint needed to paint a shape). Correct the return statement in the amount method so the correct amount will be returned. Use the fact that the amount of paint needed is the area of the shape divided by the coverage for the paint. (NOTE: Leave the print statement - it is there for illustration purposes, so you can see the method operating on different types of Shape objects.)

4. The file *PaintThings.java* contains a program that computes the amount of paint needed to paint various shapes. A paint object has been instantiated. Add the following to complete the program:
    - Instantiate the three shape objects: deck to be a 20 by 35 foot rectangle, bigBall to be a sphere of radius 15, and tank to be a cylinder of radius 10 and height 30.
    - Make the appropriate method calls to assign the correct values to the three amount variables.
    - Run the program and test it. You should see polymorphism in action as the amount method computes the amount of paint for various shapes.

```
//*****************************************
//   Sphere.java
//
//   Represents a sphere.
//*****************************************
public class Sphere extends Shape
{
    private double radius;   //radius in feet

    //-----------------------------------
    //   Constructor: Sets up the sphere.
    //-----------------------------------
    public Sphere(double r)
    {
        super("Sphere");
        radius = r;
    }

    //-------------------------------------------
    //   Returns the surface area of the sphere.
    //-------------------------------------------
    public double area()
    {
        return 4*Math.PI*radius*radius;
    }
```

```
    //--------------------------------
    //  Returns the sphere as a String.
    //--------------------------------
    public String toString()
    {
        return super.toString() + " of radius " + radius;
    }

}



//****************************************************
//    Paint.java
//
//    Represents a type of paint that has a fixed area
//    covered by a gallon. All measurements are in feet.
//****************************************************

public class Paint
{
    private double coverage;   //number of square feet per gallon

    //-------------------------------------------
    //  Constructor:  Sets up the paint object.
    //-------------------------------------------
    public Paint(double c)
    {
        coverage = c;
    }

    //-------------------------------------------------
    //  Returns the amount of paint (number of gallons)
    //  needed to paint the shape given as the parameter.
    //-------------------------------------------------
    public double amount(Shape s)
    {
        System.out.println ("Computing amount for " + s);
        return 0;
    }

}
```

```
//************************************************************
//   PaintThings.java
//
//   Computes the amount of paint needed to paint various
//   things. Uses the amount method of the paint class which
//   takes any Shape as a parameter.
//************************************************************

import java.text.DecimalFormat;

public class PaintThings
{
    //-----------------------------------------
    // Creates some shapes and a Paint object
    // and prints the amount of paint needed
    // to paint each shape.
    //-----------------------------------------
    public static void main (String[] args)
    {
        final double COVERAGE = 350;
        Paint paint = new Paint(COVERAGE);

        Rectangle deck;
        Sphere bigBall;
        Cylinder tank;

        double deckAmt, ballAmt, tankAmt;

        // Instantiate the three shapes to paint

        // Compute the amount of paint needed for each shape


        // Print the amount of paint for each.
        DecimalFormat fmt = new DecimalFormat("0.#");
        System.out.println ("\nNumber of gallons of paint needed...");
        System.out.println ("Deck " + fmt.format(deckAmt));
        System.out.println ("Big Ball " + fmt.format(ballAmt));
        System.out.println ("Tank " + fmt.format(tankAmt));
    }
}
```

Polymorphic Sorting

The file *Sorting.java* contains the Sorting class from Listing 9.9 in the text. This class implements both the selection sort and the insertion sort algorithms for sorting any array of Comparable objects in ascending order. In this exercise, you will use the Sorting class to sort several different types of objects.

1. The file Numbers.java reads in an array of integers, invokes the selection sort algorithm to sort them, and then prints the sorted array. Save Sorting.java and Numbers.java to your directory. Numbers.java won't compile in its current form. Study it to see if you can figure out why.

2. Try to compile Numbers.java and see what the error message is. The problem involves the difference between primitive data and objects. Change the program so it will work correctly (note: you don't need to make many changes - the autoboxing feature of Java 1.5 will take care of most conversions from int to Integer).

3. Write a program Strings.java, similar to Numbers.java, that reads in an array of String objects and sorts them. You may just copy and edit Numbers.java.

4. Modify the insertionSort algorithm so that it sorts in descending order rather than ascending order. Change Numbers.java and Strings.java to call insertionSort rather than selectionSort. Run both to make sure the sorting is correct.

5. The file Salesperson.java partially defines a class that represents a sales person. This is very similar to the Contact class in Listing 9.10. However, a sales person has a first name, last name, and a total number of sales (an int) rather than a first name, last name, and phone number. Complete the compareTo method in the Salesperson class. The comparison should be based on total sales; that is, return a negative number if the executing object has total sales less than the other object and return a positive number if the sales are greater. Use the name of the sales person to break a tie (alphabetical order).

6. The file WeeklySales.java contains a driver for testing the compareTo method and the sorting (this is similar to Listing 9.8 in the text). Compile and run it. Make sure your compareTo method is correct. The sales staff should be listed in order of sales from most to least with the four people having the same number of sales in reverse alphabetical order.

7. OPTIONAL: Modify WeeklySales.java so the salespeople are read in rather than hardcoded in the program.

```
//********************************************************************
//  Sorting.java        Author: Lewis/Loftus
//
//  Demonstrates the selection sort and insertion sort algorithms.
//********************************************************************

public class Sorting
{
    //-----------------------------------------------------------------
    //  Sorts the specified array of objects using the selection
    //  sort algorithm.
    //-----------------------------------------------------------------
    public static void selectionSort (Comparable[] list)
    {
        int min;
        Comparable temp;

        for (int index = 0; index < list.length-1; index++)
        {
            min = index;
            for (int scan = index+1; scan < list.length; scan++)
                if (list[scan].compareTo(list[min]) < 0)
```

```
                    min = scan;

                // Swap the values
                temp = list[min];
                list[min] = list[index];
                list[index] = temp;
            }
    }

    //---------------------------------------------------------------
    //   Sorts the specified array of objects using the insertion
    //   sort algorithm.
    //---------------------------------------------------------------
    public static void insertionSort (Comparable[] list)
    {
        for (int index = 1; index < list.length; index++)
        {
            Comparable key = list[index];
            int position = index;

            //   Shift larger values to the right
            while (position > 0 && key.compareTo(list[position-1]) < 0)
            {
                list[position] = list[position-1];
                position--;
            }

            list[position] = key;
        }
    }
}




//   ******************************************************
//      Numbers.java
//
//      Demonstrates selectionSort on an array of integers.
//   ******************************************************

import java.util.Scanner;

public class Numbers
{
    //   ---------------------------------------------
    //   Reads in an array of integers, sorts them,
    //   then prints them in sorted order.
    //   ---------------------------------------------
    public static void main (String[] args)
    {
        int[] intList;
        int size;

        Scanner scan = new Scanner(System.in);

        System.out.print ("\nHow many integers do you want to sort? ");
        size = scan.nextInt();
        intList = new int[size];

        System.out.println ("\nEnter the numbers...");
        for (int i = 0; i < size; i++)
            intList[i] = scan.nextInt();

        Sorting.selectionSort(intList);
```

```java
        System.out.println ("\nYour numbers in sorted order...");
        for (int i = 0; i < size; i++)
            System.out.print(intList[i] + "   ");
        System.out.println ();
    }
}


// *******************************************************
//    Salesperson.java
//
//    Represents a sales person who has a first name, last
//    name, and total number of sales.
// *******************************************************
public class Salesperson implements Comparable
{
    private String firstName, lastName;
    private int totalSales;

    //---------------------------------------------------------
    //   Constructor:  Sets up the sales person object with
    //                 the given data.
    //---------------------------------------------------------
    public Salesperson (String first, String last, int sales)
    {
        firstName = first;
        lastName = last;
        totalSales = sales;
    }

    //---------------------------------------------
    //   Returns the sales person as a string.
    //---------------------------------------------
    public String toString()
    {
        return lastName + ", " + firstName + ": \t" + totalSales;
    }


    //---------------------------------------------
    //   Returns true if the sales people have
    //   the same name.
    //---------------------------------------------
    public boolean equals (Object other)
    {
        return (lastName.equals(((Salesperson)other).getLastName()) &&
                firstName.equals(((Salesperson)other).getFirstName()));
    }

    //-----------------------------------------------------
    //   Order is based on total sales with the name
    //   (last, then first) breaking a tie.
    //-----------------------------------------------------
    public int compareTo(Object other)
    {
        int result;

        return result;
    }


    //-----------------------
    //   First name accessor.
    //-----------------------
    public String getFirstName()
    {
```

```java
            return firstName;
        }

        //------------------------
        //   Last name accessor.
        //------------------------
        public String getLastName()
        {
            return lastName;
        }

        //------------------------
        //   Total sales accessor.
        //------------------------
        public int getSales()
        {
            return totalSales;
        }
    }




// ***************************************************************
//     WeeklySales.java
//
//     Sorts the sales staff in descending order by sales.
// ***************************************************************

public class WeeklySales
{
    public static void main(String[] args)
    {
        Salesperson[] salesStaff = new Salesperson[10];

        salesStaff[0] = new Salesperson("Jane", "Jones", 3000);
        salesStaff[1] = new Salesperson("Daffy", "Duck", 4935);
        salesStaff[2] = new Salesperson("James", "Jones", 3000);
        salesStaff[3] = new Salesperson("Dick", "Walter", 2800);
        salesStaff[4] = new Salesperson("Don", "Trump", 1570);
        salesStaff[5] = new Salesperson("Jane", "Black", 3000);
        salesStaff[6] = new Salesperson("Harry", "Taylor", 7300);
        salesStaff[7] = new Salesperson("Andy", "Adams", 5000);
        salesStaff[8] = new Salesperson("Jim", "Doe", 2850);
        salesStaff[9] = new Salesperson("Walt", "Smith", 3000);

        Sorting.insertionSort(salesStaff);

        System.out.println ("\nRanking of Sales for the Week\n");

        for (Salesperson s : salesStaff)
            System.out.println (s);
    }
}
```

Searching and Sorting In An Integer List

File *IntegerList.java* contains a Java class representing a list of integers. The following public methods are provided:

- ☐ IntegerList(int size)—creates a new list of *size* elements. Elements are initialized to 0.
- ☐ void randomize()—fills the list with random integers between 1 and 100, inclusive.
- ☐ void print()—prints the array elements and indices
- ☐ int search(int target)—looks for value *target* in the list using a linear (also called sequential) search algorithm. Returns the index where it first appears if it is found, -1 otherwise.
- ☐ void selectionSort()—sorts the lists into ascending order using the selection sort algorithm.

File *IntegerListTest.java* contains a Java program that provides menu-driven testing for the IntegerList class. Copy both files to your directory, and compile and run IntegerListTest to see how it works. For example, create a list, print it, and search for an element in the list. Does it return the correct index? Now look for an element that is not in the list. Now sort the list and print it to verify that it is in sorted order.

Modify the code in these files as follows:

1. Add a method *void replaceFirst(int oldVal, int newVal)* to the IntegerList class that replaces the first occurrence of oldVal in the list with newVal. If oldVal does not appear in the list, it should do nothing (but it's not an error). If oldVal appears multiple times, only the first occurrence should be replaced. Note that you already have a method to find oldVal in the list; use it!

    Add an option to the menu in IntegerListTest to test your new method.

2. Add a method *void replaceAll(int oldVal, int newVal)* to the IntegerList class that replaces all occurrences of oldVal in the list with newVal. If oldVal does not appear in the list, it should do nothing (but it's not an error). Does it still make sense to use the search method like you did for *replaceFirst*, or should you do your own searching here? Think about this.

    Add an option to the menu in IntegerListTest to test your new method.

3. Add a method *void sortDecreasing()* to the IntegerList class that sorts the list into decreasing (instead of increasing) order. Use the selection sort algorithm, but modify it to sort the other way. Be sure you change the variable names so they make sense!

    Add an option to the menu in IntegerListTest to test your new method.

4.   Add a method *int binarySearchD (int target)* to the IntegerList class that uses a binary search to find the target <u>assuming the list is sorted in decreasing order.</u>   Your algorithm will be a modification of the binary search algorithm in listing 9.12 of the text.

    Add an option to the menu in IntegerListTest to test your new method. In testing, make sure your method works on a list sorted in descending order then see what the method does if the list is not sorted (it shouldn't be able to find some things that are in the list).

```
// ***************************************************************
// IntegerList.java
//
// Define an IntegerList class with methods to create, fill,
// sort, and search in a list of integers.
//
// ***************************************************************

import java.util.Scanner;
```

```java
public class IntegerList
{
    int[] list; //values in the list

    //-----------------------------------------------------------
    //create a list of the given size
    //-----------------------------------------------------------
    public IntegerList(int size)
    {
        list = new int[size];
    }


    //-----------------------------------------------------------
    //fill array with integers between 1 and 100, inclusive
    //-----------------------------------------------------------
    public void randomize()
    {
        for (int i=0; i<list.length; i++)
            list[i] = (int)(Math.random() * 100) + 1;
    }

    //-----------------------------------------------------------
    //print array elements with indices
    //-----------------------------------------------------------
    public void print()
    {
        for (int i=0; i<list.length; i++)
            System.out.println(i + ":\t" + list[i]);
    }

    //-----------------------------------------------------------
    //return the index of the first occurrence of target in the list.
    //return -1 if target does not appear in the list
    //-----------------------------------------------------------
    public int search(int target)
    {
        int location = -1;
        for (int i=0; i<list.length && location == -1; i++)
            if (list[i] == target)
                location = i;
        return location;
    }

    //-----------------------------------------------------------
    //sort the list into ascending order using the selection sort algorithm
    //-----------------------------------------------------------
    public void selectionSort()
    {
        int minIndex;
        for (int i=0; i < list.length-1; i++)
            {
                //find smallest element in list starting at location i
                minIndex = i;
                for (int j = i+1; j < list.length; j++)
                    if (list[j] < list[minIndex])
                        minIndex = j;

                //swap list[i] with smallest element
                int temp = list[i];
```

```
                list[i] = list[minIndex];
                list[minIndex] = temp;
            }
    }
}




// ****************************************************************
// IntegerListTest.java
//
// Provide a menu-driven tester for the IntegerList class.
//
// ****************************************************************
import java.util.Scanner;

public class IntegerListTest
{
    static IntegerList list = new IntegerList(10);
    static Scanner scan = new Scanner(System.in);

    //-------------------------------------------------------
    // Create a list, then repeatedly print the menu and do what the
    // user asks until they quit
    //-------------------------------------------------------
    public static void main(String[] args)
    {
      printMenu();
      int choice = scan.nextInt();
      while (choice != 0)
          {
            dispatch(choice);
            printMenu();
            choice = scan.nextInt();
          }
    }

    //-------------------------------------------------------
    // Do what the menu item calls for
    //-------------------------------------------------------
    public static void dispatch(int choice)
    {
      int loc;
      switch(choice)
          {
          case 0:
            System.out.println("Bye!");
            break;
          case 1:
            System.out.println("How big should the list be?");
            int size = scan.nextInt();
            list = new IntegerList(size);
            list.randomize();
            break;
          case 2:
            list.selectionSort();
            break;
          case 3:
            System.out.print("Enter the value to look for: ");
            loc = list.search(scan.nextInt());
```

```java
                if (loc != -1)
                    System.out.println("Found at location " + loc);
                else
                    System.out.println("Not in list");
                break;
            case 4:
                list.print();
                break;
            default:
                System.out.println("Sorry, invalid choice");
        }
    }


    //---------------------------------------------------
    // Print the user's choices
    //---------------------------------------------------
    public static void printMenu()
    {
        System.out.println("\n   Menu    ");
        System.out.println("   ====");
        System.out.println("0: Quit");
        System.out.println("1: Create a new list (** do this first!! **)");
        System.out.println("2: Sort the list using selection sort");
        System.out.println("3: Find an element in the list using linear search");
        System.out.println("4: Print the list");
        System.out.print("\nEnter your choice: ");
    }
}
```

Timing Searching and Sorting Algorithms

Chapter 9 has a brief discussion comparing sorting alorithms (page 506) and searching algorithms (page 513). In this exercise you will use an IntegerList class (in the file *IntegerList.java*) and a driver (in the file *IntegerListTest.java*) to examine the runtimes of the searching and sorting algorithms. The IntegerListTest class has several options for creating a list of a given size, filling the list with random integers or with already sorted integers, and searching or sorting the list. (NOTE: You may have used a version of these classes in the last lab.) Save these files to your directory and run IntegerListTest a few times to explore the options.

The runtimes of the sorting and searching algorithms can be examined using the Java method *System.currentTimeMillis()*, which returns the current system time in milliseconds. (Note that it returns a long, not an int.) You will have to import java.util.* to have access to this method. In IntegerListTest, just get the system time immediately before and immediately after you perform any of the searches or sorts. Then subtract the first from the second, and you have the time required for the operation in milliseconds. WARNING: Be sure you are not including any input or output in your timed operations; these are very expensive and will swamp your algorithm times!

Add appropriate calls to System.currentTimeMillis() to your program, run it and fill out the tables below. Note that you will use much larger arrays for the search algorithms than for the sort algorithms; do you see why? Also note that the first couple of times you run a method you might get longer runtimes as it loads the code for that method. Ignore these times and use the "steady-state" times you get on subsequent runs. On a separate sheet, explain the times you see in terms of the known complexities of the algorithms. Remember that the most interesting thing is not the absolute time required by the algorithms, but how the time changes as the size of the input increases (doubles here).

Array Size	Selection Sort (random array)	Selection Sort (sorted array)	Insertion Sort (random array)	Selection Sort (sorted array)
10,000				
20,000				
40,000				
80,000				

Array Size	Linear Search (unsuccessful)	Binary Search (unsuccessful)
100,000		
200,000		
400,000		
800,000		
1,600,000		

```java
// ****************************************************************
// FILE:    IntegerList.java
//
// Purpose: Define an IntegerList class with methods to create, fill,
//          sort, and search in a list of integers.
//
// ****************************************************************

import java.util.Scanner;

public class IntegerList
{
    int[] list; //values in the list

    //---------------------------------------------------------------
    // Constructor -- takes an integer and creates a list of that
    // size.  All elements default to value 0.
    //---------------------------------------------------------------
    public IntegerList(int size)
    {
        list = new int[size];
    }


    //---------------------------------------------------------------
    // randomize -- fills the array with randomly generated integers
    // between 1 and 100, inclusive
    //---------------------------------------------------------------
    public void randomize()
    {
        int max = list.length;
        for (int i=0; i<list.length; i++)
            list[i] = (int)(Math.random() * max) + 1;
    }


    //---------------------------------------------------------------
    // fillSorted -- fills the array with sorted values
    //---------------------------------------------------------------
    public void fillSorted()
    {
        for (int i=0; i<list.length; i++)
            list[i] = i + 2;
    }


    //---------------------------------------------------------------
    // print -- prints array elements with indices, one per line
    //---------------------------------------------------------------
    public String toString()
    {
        String s = "";
        for (int i=0; i<list.length; i++)
            s += i + ":\t" + list[i] + "\n";
        return s;
    }


    //---------------------------------------------------------------
    // linearSearch -- takes a target value and returns the index
    // of the first occurrence of target in the list.  Returns -1
    // if target does not appear in the list
    //---------------------------------------------------------------
    public int linearSearch(int target)
    {
        int location = -1;
        for (int i=0; i<list.length && location == -1; i++)
            if (list[i] == target)
```

```
                    location = i;
            return location;
    }


    //-------------------------------------------------------------
    // sortIncreasing  -- uses selection sort
    //-------------------------------------------------------------
    public void sortIncreasing()
    {
        for (int i=0; i<list.length-1; i++)
            {
                int minIndex = minIndex(list, i);
                swap(list, i, minIndex);
            }
    }



// *****************************************************************
// FILE:   IntegerListTest.java
//
// Purpose: Provide a menu-driven tester for the IntegerList class.
//
// *****************************************************************
import java.util.Scanner;

public class IntegerListTest
{
    static IntegerList list = new IntegerList(10);
    static Scanner scan = new Scanner(System.in);

    //------------------------------------------------------
    // main -- creates an initial list, then repeatedly prints
    // the menu and does what the user asks until they quit
    //------------------------------------------------------
    public static void main(String[] args)
    {
        printMenu();
        int choice = scan.nextInt();
        while (choice != 0)
            {
                dispatch(choice);
                printMenu();
                choice = scan.nextInt();
            }
    }

    //------------------------------------------------------
    // dispatch -- takes a choice and does what needs doing
    //------------------------------------------------------
    public static void dispatch(int choice)
    {
        int loc;
        int val;
        long time1, time2;
        switch(choice)
            {
            case 0:
                System.out.println("Bye!");
                break;
            case 1:
                System.out.println(list);
                break;
            case 2:
                System.out.println("How big should the list be?");
                list = new IntegerList(scan.nextInt());
                System.out.println("List is created.");
```

```
                break;
            case 3:
                list.randomize();
                System.out.println("List is filled with random elements.");
                break;
            case 4:
                list.fillSorted();
                System.out.println("List is filled with sorted elements.");
                break;
            case 5:
                System.out.print("Enter the value to look for: ");
                val = scan.nextInt();
                loc = list.linearSearch(val);
                if (loc != -1)
                    System.out.println("Found at location " + loc);
                else
                    System.out.println("Not in list");
                break;
            case 6:
                System.out.print("Enter the value to look for: ");
                val = scan.nextInt();
                loc = list.binarySearch(val);
                if (loc != -1)
                    System.out.println("Found at location " + loc);
                else
                    System.out.println("Not in list");
                break;
            case 7:
                list.sortIncreasing();
                System.out.println("List has been sorted.");
                break;
            case 8:
                list.sortDecreasing();
                System.out.println("List has been sorted.");
                break;
            default:
                System.out.println("Sorry, invalid choice");
        }
    }


    //----------------------------------------------------------
    // printMenu -- prints the user's choices
    //----------------------------------------------------------
    public static void printMenu()
    {
        System.out.println("\n   Menu    ");
        System.out.println("   ====");
        System.out.println("0: Quit");
        System.out.println("1: Print the list");
        System.out.println("2: Create a new list of a given size");
        System.out.println("3: Fill the list with random ints in range 1-length");
        System.out.println("4: Fill the list with already sorted elements");
        System.out.println("5: Use linear search to find an element");
        System.out.println("6: Use binary search to find an element " +
                "(list must be sorted in increasing order)");
        System.out.println("7: Use selection sort to sort the list into " +
                " increasing order");
        System.out.println("8: Use insertion sort to sort the list into " +
                " decreasing order");
        System.out.print("\nEnter your choice: ");
    }
```

Coloring a Movable Circle

File *MoveCircle.java* contains a program that uses *CirclePanel.java* to draw a circle and let the user move it by pressing buttons. Save these files to your directory and compile and run MoveCircle to see how it works. Then study the code, noting the following:

☐ CirclePanel uses a BorderLayout so that the buttons can go on the bottom. But the buttons are not added directly to the south of the main panel—if they were they would all be on top of each other, and only the last one would show. Instead, a new panel *buttonPanel* is created and the buttons are added to it. *buttonPanel* uses a flow layout (the default panel layout), so the buttons will appear next to each other and centered. This panel is added to the south of the main panel.

☐ The listeners for the buttons are all instances of the MoveListener class, which is also defined here. The parameters to the constructor tell how how many pixels in the x and y directions the circle should move when the button is pressed.

☐ The circle is not drawn in the constructor, as it is not a component. It is drawn in paintComponent, which provides a graphics context for drawing on CirclePanel.

☐ In MoveCircle the frame size is explicitly set so there will be room to move the circle around.

Modify the program as follows.

1. Modify CirclePanel so that in addition to moving the circle, the user can press a button to change its color. The color buttons should be on the top of the panel; have four color choices. You will need to do the following:

   ☐ Create a button for each color you want to provide, and label them appropriately.
   ☐ Write a new listener class ColorListener whose constructor takes the color the circle should change to. When the button is pressed, just change the circle's color and repaint.
   ☐ Create a new ColorListener for each color button, and add the listeners to the buttons.
   ☐ Create a panel for the color buttons to go on, and add them to it.
   ☐ Add the color panel to the north part of the main panel.

   You do not need to make any changes to MoveCircle.

2. Set the background or text (you choose) of each button to be the color that it represents.

3. Add another button to the top that says "Choose Color." Place the button in the middle of your other color buttons. When pressed, this button should bring up a JColorChooser, and the circle color should become the color that the user chooses. You can use the same ColorListener class that you used for the other buttons; just pass *null* for the color when the user wants to choose their own, and in the *actionPerformed* method bring up a JColorChooser if the color is *null*. Remember that the easiest way to use a JColorChooser is to call its static *showDialog* method, passing three parameters: the component to add it to (the "Choose Color" button), a string to title the chooser window, and a default color (the current circle color). Note that the "Choose Color" button will have to be an instance variable (instead of being local to the CirclePanel constructor like the other buttons) to be visible in the listener.

```
// ****************************************************************
//    MoveCircle.java
//
//    Uses CirclePanel to display a GUI that lets the user move
//    a circle by pressing buttons.
// ****************************************************************

import java.awt.*;
import javax.swing.*;

public class MoveCircle
{
    //---------------------------------
    //  Set up a frame for the GUI.
    //---------------------------------
    public static void main(String[] args)
    {
      JFrame frame = new JFrame ("MoveCircle");
      frame.setDefaultCloseOperation(JFrame.EXIT_ON_CLOSE);
      frame.setPreferredSize(new Dimension(400,300));

      frame.getContentPane().add(new CirclePanel(400,300));

      frame.pack();
      frame.setVisible(true);
    }
}
```

```java
// *****************************************************************
//    CirclePanel.java
//
//    A panel with a circle drawn in the center and buttons on the
//    bottom that move the circle.
// *****************************************************************
import java.awt.*;
import javax.swing.*;
import java.awt.event.*;

public class CirclePanel extends JPanel
{
    private final int CIRCLE_SIZE = 50;
    private int x,y;
    private Color c;

    //------------------------------------------------------------------
    // Set up circle and buttons to move it.
    //------------------------------------------------------------------
    public CirclePanel(int width, int height)
    {
      // Set coordinates so circle starts in middle
      x = (width/2)-(CIRCLE_SIZE/2);
      y = (height/2)-(CIRCLE_SIZE/2);

      c = Color.green;

      // Need a border layout to get the buttons on the bottom
      this.setLayout(new BorderLayout());

      // Create buttons to move the circle
      JButton left = new JButton("Left");
      JButton right = new JButton("Right");
      JButton up = new JButton("Up");
      JButton down = new JButton("Down");

      // Add listeners to the buttons
      left.addActionListener(new MoveListener(-20,0));
      right.addActionListener(new MoveListener(20,0));
      up.addActionListener(new MoveListener(0,-20));
      down.addActionListener(new MoveListener(0,20));

      // Need a panel to put the buttons on or they'll be on
      // top of each other.
      JPanel buttonPanel = new JPanel();
      buttonPanel.add(left);
      buttonPanel.add(right);
      buttonPanel.add(up);
      buttonPanel.add(down);

      // Add the button panel to the bottom of the main panel
      this.add(buttonPanel, "South");

    }

    //------------------------------------------------------------------
    // Draw circle on CirclePanel
    //------------------------------------------------------------------
    public void paintComponent(Graphics page)
    {
```

```
      super.paintComponent(page);

      page.setColor(c);
      page.fillOval(x,y,CIRCLE_SIZE,CIRCLE_SIZE);
   }

   //-----------------------------------------------------------------
   // Class to listen for button clicks that move circle.
   //-----------------------------------------------------------------
   private class MoveListener implements ActionListener
   {
      private int dx;
      private int dy;

      //-----------------------------------------------------------------
      // Parameters tell how to move circle at click.
      //-----------------------------------------------------------------
      public MoveListener(int dx, int dy)
      {
          this.dx = dx;
          this.dy = dy;
      }

      //-----------------------------------------------------------------
      // Change x and y coordinates and repaint.
      //-----------------------------------------------------------------
      public void actionPerformed(ActionEvent e)
      {
          x += dx;
          y += dy;
          repaint();
      }
   }
}
```

Speed Control

The files *SpeedControl.java* and *SpeedControlPanel.java* contain a program (and its associated panel) with a circle that moves on the panel and rebounds from the edges. (NOTE: the program is derived from Listing 8.15 and 8.16 in the text. That program uses an image rather than a circle. You may have used it in an earlier lab on animation.) The Circle class is in the file *Circle.java*. Save the program to your directory and run it to see how it works.

In this lab exercise you will add to the panel a slider that controls the speed of the animation. Study the code in SlideColorPanel.java (Listing 9.16 in the text) to help understand the steps below.

1. Set up a JSlider object. You need to
    - Declare it.
    - Instantiate it to be a JSlider that is horizontal with values ranging from 0 to 200, initially set to 30.
    - Set the major tick spacing to 40 and the minor tick spacing to 10.
    - Set paint ticks and paint labels to true and the X alignment to left.

2. Set up the change listener for the slider. A skeleton of a class named *SlideListener* is already in SpeedControlPanel.java. You need to
    - Complete the body of the statedChanged function. This function must determine the value of the slider, then set the timer delay to that value. The timer delay can be set with the method *setDelay (int delay)* in the Timer class.
    - Add the change listener to the JSlider object.

3. Create a label ("Timer Delay") for the slider and align it to the left.

4. Create a JPanel object and add the label and slider to it then add your panel to the SOUTH of the main panel (note that it has already been set up to use a border layout).

5. Compile and run the program. Make sure the speed is changing when the slider is moved. (NOTE: Larger delay means slower!)

6. You should have noticed one problem with the program. The ball (circle) goes down behind the panel the slider is on. To fix this problem do the following:
    - In actionPerformed, declare a variable *slidePanelHt* (type int). Use the getSize() method to get the size (which is a Dimension object) of the panel you put the slider on. Assign *slidePanelHt* to be the height of the Dimension object. For example, if your panel is named *slidePanel* the following assignment statement is what you need:

        ```
        slidePanelHt = slidePanel.getSize().height;
        ```

    - Now use this height to adjust the condition that tests to see if the ball hits the bottom of the panel.
    - Test your program to make sure it is correct.

```
// ******************************************************************
//   SpeedControl.java
//
//   Demonstrates animation -- balls bouncing off the sides of a panel -
//   with speed controlled by a slider.
// ******************************************************************

import java.awt.*;
import java.awt.event.*;
import javax.swing.*;

public class SpeedControl
{
    // ------------------------------------
    //  Sets up the frame for the animation.
    // ------------------------------------
    public void static main (String[] args)
    {
      JFrame frame = new JFrame ("Bouncing Balls");
      frame.setDefaultCloseOperation (JFrame.EXIT_ON_CLOSE);

      frame.getContentPane.add(new SpeedControlPanel ());
      frame.pack();
      frame.setVisible(true);
    }
}
```

```
// ***********************************************************
//    SpeedControlPanel.java
//
//    The panel for the bouncing ball.  Similar to
//    ReboundPanel.java in Listing 8.16 in the text, except a circle
//    rather than a happy face is rebounding off the edges of the
//    window.
// ***********************************************************

import java.awt.*;
import java.awt.event.*;
import javax.swing.*;
import javax.swing.event.*;

public class SpeedControlPanel extends JPanel
{
    private final int WIDTH = 600;
    private final int HEIGHT = 400;
    private final int BALL_SIZE = 50;

    private Circle bouncingBall;    // the object that moves
    private Timer timer;
    private int moveX, moveY;       // increment to move each time

    // ---------------------------------------------
    //  Sets up the panel, including the timer
    //  for the animation
    // ---------------------------------------------
    public SpeedControlPanel ()
    {
      timer = new Timer(30, new ReboundListener());

      this.setLayout (new BorderLayout());

      bouncingBall = new Circle(BALL_SIZE);

      moveX = moveY = 5;

      // Set up a slider object here

      setPreferredSize (new Dimension (WIDTH, HEIGHT));
      setBackground(Color.black);
      timer.start();
    }

    // -------------------
    // Draw the ball
    // -------------------
    public void paintComponent (Graphics page)
    {
        super.paintComponent (page);
        bouncingBall.draw(page);
    }

    // *******************************************************
    //    An action listener for the timer
    // *******************************************************
    public class ReboundListener implements ActionListener
    {
      // -----------------------------------------------------
```

```java
      // actionPerformed is called by the timer -- it updates
      // the position of the bouncing ball
      // ---------------------------------------------------
      public void actionPerformed(ActionEvent action)
      {
          bouncingBall.move(moveX, moveY);

          // change direction if ball hits a side
          int x = bouncingBall.getX();
          int y = bouncingBall.getY();
          if (x < 0 || x >= WIDTH - BALL_SIZE)
            moveX = moveX * -1;

          if (y <= 0 || y >= HEIGHT - BALL_SIZE)
            moveY = moveY * -1;
          repaint();
      }
   }


   // ****************************************************
   //   A change listener for the slider.
   // ****************************************************
   private class SlideListener implements ChangeListener
   {
      // ---------------------------------------------------
      //  Called when the state of the slider has changed;
      //  resets the delay on the timer.
      // ---------------------------------------------------
      public void stateChanged (ChangeEvent event)
      {


      }
   }
}
```

```
// ****************************************************************
// FILE:  Circle.java
//
// Purpose: Define a Circle class with methods to create and draw
//          a circle of random size, color, and location.
// ****************************************************************

import java.awt.*;
import java.util.Random;

public class Circle
{
    private int x, y;        // coordinates of the corner
    private int radius;      // radius of the circle
    private Color color;     // color of the circle

    static Random generator = new Random();

    //----------------------------------------------------------
    // Creates a random circle with properties in ranges given:
    //     -- radius 25..74
    //     -- color RGB value 0..16777215 (24-bit)
    //     -- x-coord of upper left-hand corner 0..599
    //     -- y-coord of upper left-hand corner 0..399
    //----------------------------------------------------------
    public Circle()
    {
        radius = Math.abs(generator.nextInt())%50 + 25;
        color = new Color(Math.abs(generator.nextInt())% 16777216);
        x = Math.abs(generator.nextInt())%600;
        y = Math.abs(generator.nextInt())%400;
    }


    //-----------------------------------------------------------
    // Creates a circle of a given size (diameter).  Other
    // attributes are random (as described above)
    //-----------------------------------------------------------
    public Circle(int size)
    {
        radius = Math.abs(size/2);
        color = new Color(Math.abs(generator.nextInt())% 16777216);
        x = Math.abs(generator.nextInt())%600;
        y = Math.abs(generator.nextInt())%400;
    }



    //-----------------------------------------------------------
    // Draws circle on graphics object given
    //-----------------------------------------------------------
    public void draw(Graphics page)
    {
        page.setColor(color);
        page.fillOval(x,y,radius*2,radius*2);
    }


    //-----------------------------------------------------------
    // Shifts the circle's position -- "over" is the number of
    // pixels to move horizontally (positive is to the right;
```

```java
    // negative to the left); "down" is the number of pixels
    // to move vertically (positive is down; negative is up)
    //----------------------------------------------------------
    public void move (int over, int down)
    {
        x = x + over;
        y = y + down;
    }

    // ------------------------------------------------
    // Return the x coordinate of the circle corner
    // ------------------------------------------------
    public int getX()
    {
        return x;
    }

    // ------------------------------------------------
    // Return the y coordinate of the circle corner
    // ------------------------------------------------
    public int getY()
    {
        return y;
    }
}
```

Chapter 10: Exceptions
Lab Exercises

Topics	Lab Exercises
Exceptions	Exceptions Aren't Always Errors
	Placing Exception Handlers
	Throwing Exceptions
File Input and Output	Copying a File
	Reading from and Writing to Text Files
Mnemonics	A Movable Circle
Tooltips	
Disabling Buttons	
Combo Boxes	A Currency Converter
Scroll Panes	Listing Prime Numbers

Exceptions Aren't Always Errors

File *CountLetters.java* contains a program that reads a word from the user and prints the number of occurrences of each letter in the word. Save it to your directory and study it, then compile and run it to see how it works. In reading the code, note that the word is converted to all upper case first, then each letter is translated to a number in the range 0..25 (by subtracting 'A') for use as an index. No test is done to ensure that the characters are in fact letters.

1. Run CountLetters and enter a phrase, that is, more than one word with spaces or other punctuation in between. It should throw an ArrayIndexOutOfBoundsException, because a non-letter will generate an index that is not between 0 and 25. It might be desirable to allow non-letter characters, but not count them. Of course, you could explicitly test the value of the character to see if it is between 'A' and 'Z'. However, an alternative is to go ahead and use the translated character as an index, and catch an ArrayIndexOutOfBoundsException if it occurs. Since you want don't want to do anything when a non-letter occurs, the handler will be empty. Modify this method to do this as follows:
   - ☐ Put the body of the first for loop in a try.
   - ☐ Add a catch that catches the exception, but don't do anything with it.
   Compile and run your program.

2. Now modify the body of the catch so that it prints a useful message (e.g., "Not a letter") followed by the exception. Compile and run the program. Although it's useful to print the exception for debugging, when you're trying to smoothly handle a condition that you don't consider erroneous you often don't want to. In your print statement, replace the exception with the character that created the out of bounds index. Run the program again; much nicer!

```
//  ****************************************************************
//  CountLetters.java
//
//  Reads a words from the standard input and prints the number of
//  occurrences of each letter in that word.
//
//  ****************************************************************
import java.util.Scanner;
public class CountLetters
{
    public static void main(String[] args)
    {
      int[] counts = new int[26];
      Scanner scan = new Scanner(System.in);

      //get word from user
      System.out.print("Enter a single word (letters only, please): ");
      String word = scan.nextLine();

      //convert to all upper case
      word = word.toUpperCase();

      //count frequency of each letter in string
      for (int i=0; i < word.length(); i++)
          counts[word.charAt(i)-'A']++;

      //print frequencies
      System.out.println();
      for (int i=0; i < counts.length; i++)
          if (counts[i] != 0)
            System.out.println((char)(i +'A') + ": " + counts[i]);

    }

}
```

Placing Exception Handlers

File *ParseInts.java* contains a program that does the following:

- ☐ Prompts for and reads in a line of input
- ☐ Uses a second Scanner to take the input line one token at a time and parses an integer from each token as it is extracted.
- ☐ Sums the integers.
- ☐ Prints the sum.

Save ParseInts to your directory and compile and run it. If you give it the input

```
10 20 30 40
```

it should print

```
The sum of the integers on the line is 100.
```

Try some other inputs as well. Now try a line that contains both integers and other values, e.g.,

```
We have 2 dogs and 1 cat.
```

You should get a NumberFormatException when it tries to call *Integer.parseInt* on "We", which is not an integer. One way around this is to put the loop that reads inside a *try* and catch the NumberFormatException but not do anything with it. This way if it's not an integer it doesn't cause an error; it goes to the exception handler, which does nothing. Do this as follows:

- ☐ Modify the program to add a try statement that encompasses the entire *while* loop. The *try* and opening { should go before the *while*, and the *catch* after the loop body. Catch a NumberFormatException and have an empty body for the catch.
- ☐ Compile and run the program and enter a line with mixed integers and other values. You should find that it stops summing at the first non-integer, so the line above will produce a sum of 0, and the line "1 fish 2 fish" will produce a sum of 1. This is because the entire loop is inside the *try*, so when an exception is thrown the loop is terminated. To make it continue, move the *try* and *catch* inside the loop. Now when an exception is thrown, the next statement is the next iteration of the loop, so the entire line is processed. The dogs-and-cats input should now give a sum of 3, as should the fish input.

```
// ****************************************************************
// ParseInts.java
//
// Reads a line of text and prints the integers in the line.
//
// ****************************************************************

import java.util.Scanner;

public class ParseInts
{
    public static void main(String[] args)
    {
      int val, sum=0;
      Scanner scan = new Scanner(System.in);
      String line;

      System.out.println("Enter a line of text");
      Scanner scanLine = new Scanner(scan.nextLine());

      while (scanLine.hasNext())
          {
            val = Integer.parseInt(scanLine.next());
            sum += val;
          }
      System.out.println("The sum of the integers on this line is " + sum);
    }

}
```

Throwing Exceptions

File *Factorials.java* contains a program that calls the *factorial* method of the *MathUtils* class to compute the factorials of integers entered by the user. Save these files to your directory and study the code in both, then compile and run Factorials to see how it works. Try several positive integers, then try a negative number. You should find that it works for small positive integers (values < 17), but that it returns a large negative value for larger integers and that it always returns 1 for negative integers.

1. Returning 1 as the factorial of any negative integer is not correct—mathematically, the factorial function is not defined for negative integers. To correct this, you could modify your *factorial* method to check if the argument is negative, but then what? The method must return a value, and even if it prints an error message, whatever value is returned could be misconstrued. Instead it should throw an exception indicating that something went wrong so it could not complete its calculation. You could define your own exception class, but there is already an exception appropriate for this situation— IllegalArgumentException, which extends RuntimeException. Modify your program as follows:
   - [ ] Modify the header of the *factorial* method to indicate that *factorial* can throw an IllegalArgumentException.
   - [ ] Modify the body of *factorial* to check the value of the argument and, if it is negative, throw an IllegalArgumentException. Note that what you pass to *throw* is actually an instance of the IllegalArgumentException class, and that the constructor takes a String parameter. Use this parameter to be specific about what the problem is.
   - [ ] Compile and run your Factorials program after making these changes. Now when you enter a negative number an exception will be thrown, terminating the program. The program ends because the exception is not caught, so it is thrown by the main method, causing a runtime error.
   - [ ] Modify the main method in your Factorials class to catch the exception thrown by factorial and print an appropriate message, but then continue with the loop. Think carefully about where you will need to put the *try* and *catch*.

2. Returning a negative number for values over 16 also is not correct. The problem is arithmetic overflow—the factorial is bigger than can be represented by an int. This can also be thought of as an IllegalArgumentException—this *factorial* method is only defined for arguments up to 16. Modify your code in *factorial* to check for an argument over 16 as well as for a negative argument. You should throw an IllegalArgumentException in either case, but pass different messages to the constructor so that the problem is clear.

```
// ****************************************************************
// Factorials.java
//
// Reads integers from the user and prints the factorial of each.
//
// ****************************************************************
import java.util.Scanner;

public class Factorials
{
    public static void main(String[] args)
    {
        String keepGoing = "y";
        Scanner scan = new Scanner(System.in);

        while (keepGoing.equals("y") || keepGoing.equals("Y"))
        {
            System.out.print("Enter an integer: ");
            int val = scan.nextInt();
            System.out.println("Factorial(" + val + ") = "
                            + MathUtils.factorial(val));
            System.out.print("Another factorial? (y/n) ");
            keepGoing = scan.next();
        }
    }
}
```

```
// ****************************************************************
// MathUtils.java
//
// Provides static mathematical utility functions.
//
// ****************************************************************
public class MathUtils
{
    //-----------------------------------------------------------
    // Returns the factorial of the argument given
    //-----------------------------------------------------------
    public static int factorial(int n)
    {
      int fac = 1;
      for (int i=n; i>0; i--)
          fac *= i;
      return fac;
    }
}
```

Copying a File

Write a program that prompts the user for a filename, then opens a Scanner to the file and copies it, a line at a time, to the standard output. If the user enters the name of a file that does not exist, ask for another name until you get one that refers to a valid file. Some things to consider:

- Remember that you can create a Scanner from a File object, which you can create from the String representing the filename.
- The Scanner constructor that takes a File may throw a FileNotFoundException -- this is how you will know if the file does not exist. Think carefully about how to use the try/catch structure in combination with a loop that asks for a new filename if the current file does not exist.
- Remember that the scope of a variable declared inside a try is the try itself -- it does not extend to the following code. Furthermore, the compiler knows that an initialization that occurs inside a try may or may not get executed, as the try may be thrown out of first. So any variable that you will want to use both in and after the try must be declared and initialized before the try.

Reading from and Writing to Text Files

Write a program that will read in a file of student academic credit data and create a list of students on academic warning. The list of students on warning will be written to a file. Each line of the input file will contain the student name (a single String with no spaces), the number of semester hours earned (an integer), the total quality points earned (a double). The following shows part of a typical data file:

```
Smith 27  83.7
Jones 21  28.35
Walker 96 182.4
Doe 60 150
```

The program should compute the GPA (grade point or quality point average) for each student (the total quality points divided by the number of semester hours) then write the student information to the output file if that student should be put on academic warning. A student will be on warning if he/she has a GPA less than 1.5 for students with fewer than 30 semester hours credit, 1.75 for students with fewer than 60 semester hours credit, and 2.0 for all other students. The file *Warning.java* contains a skeleton of the program. Do the following:

1. Set up a Scanner object *scan* from the input file and a PrintWriter *outFile* to the output file inside the try clause (see the comments in the program). Note that you'll have to create the PrintWriter from a FileWriter, but you can still do it in a single statement.
2. Inside the while loop add code to read and parse the input—get the name, the number of credit hours, and the number of quality points. Compute the GPA, determine if the student is on academic warning, and if so write the name, credit hours, and GPA (separated by spaces) to the output file.
3. After the loop close the PrintWriter.
4. Think about the exceptions that could be thrown by this program:
   - A FileNotFoundException if the input file does not exist
   - A NumberFormatException if it can't parse an int or double when it tries to – this indicates an error in the input file format
   - An IOException if something else goes wrong with the input or output stream

   Add a catch for each of these situations, and in each case give as specific a message as you can. The program will terminate if any of these exceptions is thrown, but at least you can supply the user with useful information.
5. Test the program. Test data is in the file *students.dat*. Be sure to test each of the exceptions as well.

```java
// ******************************************************************
//    Warning.java
//
//    Reads student data from a text file and writes data to another text file.
// ******************************************************************

import java.util.Scanner;
import java.io.*;

public class Warning
{
    // -----------------------------------------------------------------
    //    Reads student data (name, semester hours, quality points) from a
    //    text file, computes the GPA, then writes data to another file
    //    if the student is placed on academic warning.
    // -----------------------------------------------------------------
    public static void main (String[] args)
    {
        int creditHrs;          // number of semester hours earned
        double qualityPts;      // number of quality points earned
        double gpa;             // grade point (quality point) average

        String line, name, inputName = "students.dat";
        String outputName = "warning.dat";
```

```
    try
        {
            // Set up scanner to input file

            // Set up the output file stream

            // Print a header to the output file
            outFile.println ();
            outFile.println ("Students on Academic Warning");
            outFile.println ();

            // Process the input file, one token at a time

            while ()
                {
                    // Get the credit hours and quality points and
                    // determine if the student is on warning. If so,
                    // write the student data to the output file.


                }

            // Close output file
        }
    catch (FileNotFoundException exception)
        {
            System.out.println ("The file " + inputName + " was not found.");
        }
    catch (IOException exception)
        {
            System.out.println (exception);
        }
    catch (NumberFormatException e)
        {
            System.out.println ("Format error in input file: " + e);
        }

    }
}
```

students.dat

```
Smith 27   83.7
Jones 21   28.35
Walker 96 182.4
Doe 60 150
Wood 100 400
Street 33 57.4
Taylor 83 190
Davis 110 198
Smart 75 292.5
Bird 84 168
Summers 52 83.2
```

Enhancing a Movable Circle

File *MoveCircle.java* contains a program that uses *CirclePanel.java* to draw a circle and let the user move it by pressing buttons. Save these files to your directory and compile and run MoveCircle to see how it works. Then modify the code in CirclePanel as follows:

1. Add mnemonics to the buttons so that the user can move the circle by pressing the ALT-l, ALT-r, ALT-u, or ALT-d keys.
2. Add tooltips to the buttons that indicate what happens when the button is pressed, including how far it is moved.
3. When the circle gets all the way to an edge, disable the corresponding button. When it moves back in, enable the button again. Note that you will need instance variables (instead of local variables in the constructor) to hold the buttons and the panel size to make them visible to the listener. Bonus: In most cases the circle won't hit the edge exactly; check for this (e.g., x<0) and adjust the coordinates so it does.

```
// ************************************************************
//    MoveCircle.java
//
//    Uses CirclePanel to display a GUI that lets the user move
//    a circle by pressing buttons.
// ************************************************************

import java.awt.*;
import javax.swing.*;

public class MoveCircle
{
    public static void main(String[] args)
    {
      JFrame frame = new JFrame ("MoveCircle");
      frame.setDefaultCloseOperation(JFrame.EXIT_ON_CLOSE);
      frame.setSize(400,300);

      frame.getContentPane().add(new CirclePanel(400,300));
      frame.setVisible(true);
    }
}
```

```
// ****************************************************************
//   CirclePanel.java
//
//   A panel with a circle drawn in the center and buttons on the
//   bottom that move the circle.
// ****************************************************************
import java.awt.*;
import javax.swing.*;
import java.awt.event.*;

public class CirclePanel extends JPanel
{
    private final int CIRCLE_SIZE = 50;
    private int x,y;
    private Color c;

    //----------------------------------------------------------------
    // Set up circle and buttons to move it.
    //----------------------------------------------------------------
    public CirclePanel(int width, int height)
    {
      // Set coordinates so circle starts in middle
      x = (width/2)-(CIRCLE_SIZE/2);
      y = (height/2)-(CIRCLE_SIZE/2);

      c = Color.green;

      // Need a border layout to get the buttons on the bottom
      this.setLayout(new BorderLayout());

      // Create buttons to move the circle
      JButton left = new JButton("Left");
      JButton right = new JButton("Right");
      JButton up = new JButton("Up");
      JButton down = new JButton("Down");

      // Add listeners to the buttons
      left.addActionListener(new MoveListener(-20,0));
      right.addActionListener(new MoveListener(20,0));
      up.addActionListener(new MoveListener(0,-20));
      down.addActionListener(new MoveListener(0,20));

      // Need a panel to put the buttons on or they'll be on
      // top of each other.
      JPanel buttonPanel = new JPanel();
      buttonPanel.add(left);
      buttonPanel.add(right);
      buttonPanel.add(up);
      buttonPanel.add(down);

      // Add the button panel to the bottom of the main panel
      this.add(buttonPanel, "South");

    }

    //----------------------------------------------------------------
    // Draw circle on CirclePanel
    //----------------------------------------------------------------
    public void paintComponent(Graphics page)
    {
```

```
      super.paintComponent(page);

      page.setColor(c);
      page.fillOval(x,y,CIRCLE_SIZE,CIRCLE_SIZE);
   }

   //----------------------------------------------------------------
   // Class to listen for button clicks that move circle.
   //----------------------------------------------------------------
   private class MoveListener implements ActionListener
   {
      private int dx;
      private int dy;

      //-------------------------------------------------------------
      // Parameters tell how to move circle at click.
      //-------------------------------------------------------------
      public MoveListener(int dx, int dy)
      {
         this.dx = dx;
         this.dy = dy;
      }

      //-------------------------------------------------------------
      // Change x and y coordinates and repaint.
      //-------------------------------------------------------------
      public void actionPerformed(ActionEvent e)
      {
         x += dx;
         y += dy;
         repaint();
      }
   }
}
```

A Currency Converter

Your are headed off on a world-wide trip and need a program to help figure out how much things in other countries cost in dollars. You plan to visit Canada, several countries in Europe, Japan, Australia, India, and Mexico so your program must work for the currencies in those countries. The files *CurrencyConverter.java* and *RatePanel.java* contain a skeleton of a program to do this conversion. Complete it as follows:

1. CurrencyPanel currently contains only two components—a JLabel for the title and a JLabel to display the result of the calculations. It also contains two parallel arrays—one is an array of currency names (an array of strings) and the other an array of corresponding exchange rates (the value of one unit of the currency in U.S. Dollars). Compile and run the program to see what it looks like (not much!!).
2. Add a combo box to let the user select the currency. The argument to the constructor should be the array of names of the currencies. Note that the first currency name is actually an instruction to the user so there is no need to have an additional label.
3. Modify actionPerformed in ComboListener so that *index* is set to be the index of the selected item.
4. Test what you have so far. It should show what one unit of the given currency is in U.S. dollars.
5. Now add a text field (and label) so the user can enter the cost of an item in the selected currency. You need to update the ComboListener so that it gets this value from the textfield and computes and displays the equivalent amount in dollars.
6. Test your program.
7. Modify the layout to create a more attractive GUI.

```
// *****************************************************************
//    CurrencyConverter.java
//
//    Computes the dollar value of the cost of an item in another currency.
// *****************************************************************

import java.awt.*;
import javax.swing.*;

public class CurrencyConverter
{
    public static void main (String[] args)
    {
        JFrame frame = new JFrame ("Currency Converter");
        frame.setDefaultCloseOperation (JFrame.EXIT_ON_CLOSE);

        RatePanel ratePanel = new RatePanel ();
        frame.getContentPane().add(ratePanel);
        frame.pack();
        frame.setVisible(true);
    }
}


// *****************************************************************
//    RatePanel.java
//
//    Panel for a program that converts different currencies to
//    U.S. Dollars
// *****************************************************************

import java.awt.*;
import java.awt.event.*;
import javax.swing.*;

public class RatePanel extends JPanel
{
```

```
   private double[] rate;            // exchange rates
   private String[] currencyName;
   private JLabel result;

   // ----------------------------------------------------------
   //   Sets up a panel to convert cost from one of 6 currencies
   //   into U.S. Dollars. The panel contains a heading, a text
   //   field for the cost of the item, a combo box for selecting
   //   the currency, and a label to display the result.
   // ----------------------------------------------------------
   public RatePanel ()
   {
      JLabel title = new JLabel ("How much is that in dollars?");
      title.setAlignmentX (Component.CENTER_ALIGNMENT);
      title.setFont (new Font ("Helvetica", Font.BOLD, 20));

      // Set up the arrays for the currency conversions
      currencyName = new String[] {"Select the currency..",
                          "European Euro", "Canadian Dollar",
                          "Japanese Yen", "Australian Dollar",
                          "Indian Rupee", "Mexican Peso"};
      rate = new double [] {0.0, 1.2103, 0.7351,
                      0.0091, 0.6969,
                      0.0222, 0.0880};


      result = new JLabel (" ------------ ");

      add (title);

      add (result);

   }


   // ****************************************************
   //   Represents an action listener for the combo box.
   // ****************************************************
   private class ComboListener implements ActionListener
   {
      // --------------------------------------------------
      //   Determines which currency has been selected and
      //   the value in that currency then computes and
      //   displays the value in U.S. Dollars.
      // --------------------------------------------------
      public void actionPerformed (ActionEvent event)
      {
         int index = 0;
         result.setText ("1 " + currencyName[index] +
                  " = " + rate[index] + " U.S. Dollars");
      }
   }
}
```

A List of Prime Numbers

The file *Primes.java* contains a program to compute and list all prime numbers up to and including a number input by the user. Most of the work is done in the file *PrimePanel.java* that defines the panel. The GUI contains a text field for the user to enter the integer, a button for the user to click to get a list of primes, and a text area to display the primes. However, if the user puts in a large integer the primes do not all fit in the text area. The main goal of this exercise is to add scrolling capabilities to the text area.

Proceed as follows:

1. Compile and run the program as it is. You should see a GUI that contains the components listed above but nothing happens when you click on the button. Fix this.
2. Modify PrimePanel.java so that the text area for displaying the primes is in a scroll pane. To do this, keep your JTextArea but create a JScrollPane from it, and add the scroll pane to the panel. (If you look at the JScrollPane documentation on p. 834-835 you'll see that one of the constructors takes a Component, in this case your JTextArea.) Test your modification.
3. You should see that the scrollbars don't appear unless the output is longer than the text area. The default is for the scrollbars to appear only as needed. This can be changed by setting the scroll bar policy of the JScrollPane object. Use the *setVerticalScrollBarPolicy* method of the JScrollPane class to specify that the vertical scroll bar should always be displayed. The method takes an integer argument that represents the policy. The ScrollPaneConstants class has several static integer constants for the policies. These include VERTICAL_SCROLLBAR_ALWAYS, VERTICAL_SCROLLBAR_AS_NEEDED, VERTICAL_SCROLLBAR_NEVER. It should be clear which of these to use as the parameter. Remember how to access static members of a class!
4. The code to generate the list of primes could be improved some. Two things that should be done are:
    □   A exception should be caught if the user enters non-integer data. An appropriate message should be displayed in the text area.
    □   The loop that looks for divisors of the integer i should not go all the way up to i. Instead it should stop at the square root of i (if a divisor hasn't been found by then there isn't one).
    Make these modifications.

```
//  ****************************************************************
//   Primes.java
//
//   Generates a list of primes less than or equal to the integer
//   input by the user.
//  ****************************************************************

import java.awt.*;
import javax.swing.*;

public class Primes
{
    public static void main (String[] args)
    {
      JFrame frame = new JFrame ("Primes");
      frame.setDefaultCloseOperation (JFrame.EXIT_ON_CLOSE);

      PrimePanel primePanel = new PrimePanel ();
      frame.getContentPane().add(primePanel);
      frame.pack();
      frame.setVisible(true);
    }
}
```

```
// ***********************************************************
//    PrimePanel.java
//
//    Represents the panel for a program that displays all primes
//    up to a number input by the user.
// ***********************************************************

import java.awt.*;
import java.awt.event.*;
import javax.swing.*;

public class PrimePanel extends JPanel
{
    private JTextField number;
    private JButton computeButton;
    private JTextArea primeList;

    // -----------------------------------------------------
    //    Sets up a panel with a heading, a labeled text field
    //    for the user to enter an integer, a button to trigger
    //    the calculation, and a text area to display the list
    //    of primes.
    // -----------------------------------------------------
    public PrimePanel ()
    {
      JLabel heading = new JLabel ("Prime Number Listing");
      heading.setFont (new Font("Helvetica", Font.BOLD, 30));

      JLabel inputLabel = new JLabel ("Enter a number: ");
      number = new JTextField (8);
      computeButton = new JButton ("Click to see all primes up to your number!");
      primeList = new JTextArea (10, 30);

      computeButton.addActionListener(new ButtonListener());

      // Add the components to the panel
      add (heading);
      add (inputLabel);
      add (number);
      add (computeButton);
      add (primeList);

      setPreferredSize (new Dimension (400, 320));
      setBackground (Color.yellow);
    }

    // ***********************************************************
    //    Represents a listener for the click of the button.
    // ***********************************************************
    public class ButtonListener implements ActionListener
    {
      // -----------------------------------------------------
      //    Generates and displays a list of primes when the
      //    button is clicked.
      // -----------------------------------------------------
      public void actionPerformed (ActionEvent event)
      {
          String textNum = number.getText ();
          int num = Integer.parseInt (textNum);
          String ans = "";
```

```java
    int count = 0;
    if (num < 2)
      ans = "There no primes less than " + num;
    else
      {
          ans = "   " + 2;
          count++;
          for (int i = 3; i <= num; i += 2)
            {
                boolean foundDivisor = false;
                int j = 3;
                while (j < i && !foundDivisor)
                  {
                      if (i % j == 0)
                        foundDivisor = true;
                      else
                        j++;
                  }

                // Add i to the list if it is prime
                if (j == i)
                  {
                      ans += "   " + i;
                      count++;
                      if (count % 10 == 0)
                        ans += "\n";
                  }
            }
      }

    primeList.setText (ans);
}
```

Chapter 11: Recursion
Lab Exercises

Topics	Lab Exercises
Basic Recursion	Computing Powers
	Counting and Summing Digits
	Base Conversion
	Efficient Computation of Fibonacci Numbers
Recursion on Strings	Palindromes
	Printing a String Backwards
Recursion on Arrays	Recursive Linear Search
	Recursive Binary Search
	A List of Employees
Fractals	Sierpinski Triangles
	Modifying the Koch Snowflake

Computing Powers

Computing a positive integer power of a number is easily seen as a recursive process. Consider a^n:

☐ If $n = 0$, a^n is 1 (by definition)
☐ If $n > 0$, a^n is $a * a^{n-1}$

File *Power.java* contains a main program that reads in integers *base* and *exp* and calls method *power* to compute $base^{exp}$. Fill in the code for *power* to make it a recursive method to do the power computation. The comments provide guidance.

```java
// ****************************************************************
//   Power.java
//
//   Reads in two integers and uses a recursive power method
//   to compute the first raised to the second power.
// ****************************************************************

import java.util.Scanner;

public class Power
{
    public static void main(String[] args)
    {
        int base, exp;
        int answer;

        Scanner scan = new Scanner(System.in);

        System.out.print("Welcome to the power program! ");
        System.out.println("Please use integers only.");

        //get base
        System.out.print("Enter the base you would like raised to a power: ");
        base = scan.nextInt();

        //get exponent
        System.out.print("Enter the power you would like it raised to: ");
        exp = scan.nextInt();

        answer = power(base,exp);
        System.out.println(base + " raised to the " + exp + " is " + answer);
    }

    // -------------------------------------------------
    //    Computes and returns base^exp
    // -------------------------------------------------
    public static int power(int base, int exp)
    {
        int pow;

        //if the exponent is 0, set pow to 1

        //otherwise set pow to base*base^(exp-1)

        //return pow

    }
}
```

Counting and Summing Digits

The problem of counting the digits in a positive integer or summing those digits can be solved recursively. For example, to count the number of digits think as follows:

- If the integer is less than 10 there is only one digit (the base case).
- Otherwise, the number of digits is 1 (for the units digit) plus the number of digits in the rest of the integer (what's left after the units digit is taken off). For example, the number of digits in 3278 is 1 + the number of digits in 327.

The following is the recursive algorithm implemented in Java.

```
public int numDigits (int num)
{
    if (num < 10)
        return (1);    // a number < 10  has only one digit
    else
        return (1 + numDigits (num / 10));
}
```

Note that in the recursive step, the value returned is 1 (counts the units digit) + the result of the call to determine the number of digits in *num / 10*. Recall that *num/10* is the quotient when *num* is divided by 10 so it would be all the digits except the units digit.

The file *DigitPlay.java* contains the recursive method *numDigits* (note that the method is static—it must be since it is called by the static method main). Copy this file to your directory, compile it, and run it several times to see how it works. Modify the program as follows:

1. Add a static method named *sumDigits* that finds the *sum* of the digits in a positive integer. Also add code to main to test your method. The algorithm for *sumDigits* is very similar to *numDigits*; you only have to change two lines!

2. Most identification numbers, such as the ISBN number on books or the Universal Product Code (UPC) on grocery products or the identification number on a traveller's check, have at least one digit in the number that is a *check digit*. The check digit is used to detect errors in the number. The simplest check digit scheme is to add one digit to the identification number so that the sum of all the digits, including the check digit, is evenly divisible by some particular integer. For example, American Express Traveller's checks add a check digit so that the sum of the digits in the id number is evenly divisible by 9. United Parcel Service adds a check digit to its pick up numbers so that a weighted sum of the digits (some of the digits in the number are multiplied by numbers other than 1) is divisible by 7. Modify the main method that tests your sumDigits method to do the following: input an identification number (a positive integer), then determine if the sum of the digits in the identification number is divisible by 7 (use your sumDigits method but don't change it—the only changes should be in main). If the sum is not divisible by 7 print a message indicating the id number is in error; otherwise print an ok message. (FYI: If the sum is divisible by 7, the identification number could still be incorrect. For example, two digits could be transposed.) Test your program on the following input:
   - 3429072 --- error
   - 1800237 --- ok
   - 88231256 --- ok
   - 3180012 --- error

```java
// ****************************************************************
//   DigitPlay.java
//
//   Finds the number of digits in a positive integer.
// ****************************************************************

import java.util.Scanner;

public class DigitPlay
{

    public static void main (String[] args)
    {
      int num;       //a number

      Scanner scan = new Scanner(System.in);

      System.out.println ();
      System.out.print ("Please enter a positive integer: ");
      num = scan.nextInt ();

      if (num <= 0)
          System.out.println ( num + " isn't positive -- start over!!");
      else
          {
            // Call numDigits to find the number of digits in the number
            // Print the number returned from numDigits
            System.out.println ("\nThe number " + num + " contains " +
                            + numDigits(num) + " digits.");
            System.out.println ();
          }
    }

    // -----------------------------------------------------------
    //   Recursively counts the digits in a positive integer
    // -----------------------------------------------------------
    public static int numDigits(int num)
    {
      if (num < 10)
          return (1);
      else
          return (1 + numDigits(num/10));
    }
}
```

Base Conversion

One algorithm for converting a base 10 number to base b involves repeated division by the base b. Initially one divides the number by b. The remainder from this division is the units digit (the rightmost digit) in the base b representation of the number (it is the part of the number that contains no powers of b). The quotient is then divided by b on the next iteration. The remainder from this division gives the next base b digit from the right. The quotient from this division is used in the next iteration. The algorithm stops when the quotient is 0. Note that at each iteration the remainder from the division is the next base b digit from the right—that is, this algorithm finds the digits for the base b number in reverse order.

Here is an example for converting 30 to base 4:

```
                quotient        remainder
                --------        ---------
    30/4  =        7               2
    7/4   =        1               3
    1/4   =        0               1
```

The answer is read bottom to top in the remainder column, so 30 (base 10) = 132 (base 4).

Think about how this is recursive in nature: If you want to convert x (30 in our example) to base b (4 in our example), the rightmost digit is the remainder x % b. To get the rest of the digits, you perform the same process on what is left; that is, you convert the quotient x / b to base b. If x / b is 0, there is no rest; x is a single base b digit and that digit is x % b (which also is just x).

The file *BaseConversion.java* contains the shell of a method *convert* to do the base conversion and a main method to test the conversion. The convert method returns a string representing the base b number, hence for example in the base case when the remainder is what is to be returned it must be converted to a String object. This is done by concatenating the remainder with a null string. The outline of the convert method is as follows:

```
public static String convert (int num, int b)
{
    int quotient;  // the quotient when num is divided by base b
    int remainder; // the remainder when num is divided by base b

    quotient = _____;

    remainder = _____;

    if ( _____ )  //fill in base case
    {
        return ("" + _____ );
    }
    else
    {
      // Recursive step: the number is the base b representation of
         // the quotient concatenated with the remainder

    return ( _____ );

    }
}
```

Fill in the blanks above (for now don't worry about bases greater than 10), then in BaseConversion.java complete the method and main. Main currently asks the user for the number and the base and reads these in. Add a statement to print the string returned by convert (appropriately labeled).

Test your function on the following input:

☐   Number: 89 Base: 2 ---> should print 1011001

Chapter 11: Recursion   **225**

□ Number: 347 Base: 5 ---> should print 2342
□ Number: 3289 Base: 8 ---> should print 6331

Improving the program: Currently the program doesn't print the correct digits for bases greater than 10. Add code to your convert method so the digits are correct for bases up to and including 16.

```java
// ****************************************************************
//   BaseConversion.java
//
//   Recursively converts an integer from base 10 to another base
// ****************************************************************

import java.util.Scanner;

public class BaseConversion
{
    public static void main (String[] args)
    {
      int base10Num;
      int base;

      Scanner scan = new Scanner(System.in);

      System.out.println ();
      System.out.println ("Base Conversion Program");
      System.out.print ("Enter an integer: ");
      base10Num = scan.nextInt();
      System.out.print ("Enter the base: ");
      base = scan.nextInt();

      // Call convert and print the answer

    }
    // -------------------------------------------------
    //   Converts a base 10 number to another base.
    // -------------------------------------------------
    public static String convert (int num, int b)
    {
      int quotient;  // the quotient when num is divided by base b
      int remainder; // the remainder when num is divided by base b
    }

}
```

Efficient Computation of Fibonacci Numbers

The *Fibonacci* sequence is a well-known mathematical sequence in which each term is the sum of the two previous terms. More specifically, if fib(n) is the nth term of the sequence, then the sequence can be defined as follows:

```
fib(0) = 0
fib(1) = 1
fib(n) = fib(n-1) + fib(n-2)   n>1
```

1. Because the Fibonacci sequence is defined recursively, it is natural to write a recursive method to determine the nth number in the sequence. File *Fib.java* contains the skeleton for a class containing a method to compute Fibonacci numbers. Save this file to your directory. Following the specification above, fill in the code for method *fib1* so that it recursively computes and returns the nth number in the sequence.

2. File *TestFib.java* contains a simple driver that asks the user for an integer and uses the *fib1* method to compute that element in the Fibonacci sequence. Save this file to your directory and use it to test your *fib1* method. First try small integers, then larger ones. You'll notice that the number doesn't have to get very big before the calculation takes a very long time. The problem is that the *fib1* method is making lots and lots of recursive calls. To see this, add a print statement at the beginning of your *fib1* method that indicates what call is being computed, e.g., "In fib1(3)" if the parameter is 3. Now run TestFib again and enter 5—you should get a number of messages from your print statement. Examine these messages and figure out the sequence of calls that generated them. (This is easiest if you first draw the call tree on paper.) . Since fib(5) is fib(4) + fib(3),you should not be surprised to find calls to fib(4) and fib(3) in the printout. But why are there two calls to fib(3)? Because both fib(4) and fib(5) need fib(3), so they both compute it—very inefficient. Run the program again with a slightly larger number and again note the repetition in the calls.

3. The fundamental source of the inefficiency is not the fact that recursive calls are being made, but that values are being recomputed. One way around this is to compute the values from the beginning of the sequence instead of from the end, saving them in an array as you go. Although this could be done recursively, it is more natural to do it iteratively. Proceed as follows:
   a. Add a method *fib2* to your Fib class. Like *fib1*, *fib2* should be static and should take an integer and return an integer.
   b. Inside *fib2*, create an array of integers the size of the value passed in.
   c. Initialize the first two elements of the array to 0 and 1, corresponding to the first two elements of the Fibonacci sequence. Then loop through the integers up to the value passed in, computing each element of the array as the sum of the two previous elements. When the array is full, its last element is the element requested. Return this value.
   d. Modify your TestFib class so that it calls *fib2* (first) and prints the result, then calls *fib1* and prints that result. You should get the same answers, but very different computation times.

```
// *****************************************************************
//    Fib.java
//
//    A utility class that provide methods to compute elements of the
//    Fibonacci sequence.
// *****************************************************************
public class Fib
{

    //----------------------------------------------------------------
    // Recursively computes fib(n)
    //----------------------------------------------------------------
    public static int fib1(int n)
    {
        //Fill in code -- this should look very much like the
        //mathematical specification
    }

}
```

```
// ***********************************************************************
//    TestFib.java
//
//    A simple driver that uses the Fib class to compute the
//    nth element of the Fibonacci sequence.
// ***********************************************************************

import java.util.Scanner;

public class TestFib
{
    public static void main(String[] args)
    {
      int n, fib;

      Scanner scan = new Scanner(System.in);

      System.out.print("Enter an integer: ");
      n = scan.nextInt();

      fib = Fib.fib1(n);
      System.out.println("Fib(" + n + ") is " + fib);
    }
}
```

Palindromes

A *palindrome* is a string that is the same forward and backward. In Chapter 5 you saw a program that uses a loop to determine whether a string is a palindrome. However, it is also easy to define a palindrome recursively as follows:

☐ A string containing fewer than 2 letters is always a palindrome.
☐ A string containing 2 or more letters is a palindrome if
   ☐ its first and last letters are the same, and
   ☐ the rest of the string (without the first and last letters) is also a palindrome.

Write a program that prompts for and reads in a string, then prints a message saying whether it is a palindrome. Your main method should read the string and call a recursive (static) method *palindrome* that takes a string and returns true if the string is a palindrome, false otherwise. Recall that for a string s in Java,

☐ *s.length()* returns the number of charaters in s
☐ *s.charAt(i)* returns the ith character of s, 0-based
☐ *s.substring(i,j)* returns the substring that starts with the ith character of s and ends with the $j-1^{st}$ character of s (not the jth), both 0-based.

So if s="happy", *s.length*=5, *s.charAt(1)*=a, and *s.substring(2,4)* = "pp".

Printing a String Backwards

Printing a string backwards can be done iteratively or recursively. To do it recursively, think of the following specification:

If *s* contains any characters (i.e., is not the empty string)

☐   print the last character in *s*
☐   print *s'* backwards, where *s'* is *s* without its last character

File *Backwards.java* contains a program that prompts the user for a string, then calls method *printBackwards* to print the string backwards. Save this file to your directory and fill in the code for *printBackwards* using the recursive strategy outlined above.

```java
// *****************************************************************
//   Backwards.java
//
//   Uses a recursive method to print a string backwards.
// *****************************************************************
import java.util.Scanner;

public class Backwards
{

    //----------------------------------------------------------
    // Reads a string from the user and prints it backwards.
    //----------------------------------------------------------
    public static void main(String[] args)
    {
        String msg;
        Scanner scan = new Scanner(System.in);

        System.out.print("Enter a string: ");
        msg = scan.nextLine();

        System.out.print("\nThe string backwards: ");
        printBackwards(msg);
        System.out.println();
    }

    //----------------------------------------------------------
    // Takes a string and recursively prints it backwards.
    //----------------------------------------------------------
    public static void printBackwards(String s)
    {

        // Fill in code

    }
}
```

Recursive Linear Search

File *IntegerListS.java* contains a class IntegerListS that represents a list of integers (you may have used a version of this in an earlier lab); *IntegerListSTest.java* contains a simple menu-driven test program that lets the user create, sort, and print a list and search for an element using a linear search.

Many list processing tasks, including searching, can be done recursively. The base case typically involves doing something with a limited number of elements in the list (say the first element), then the recursive step involves doing the task on the rest of the list. Think about how linear search can be viewed recursively; if you are looking for an item in a list starting at index i:

- If i exceeds the last index in the list, the item is not found (return -1).
- If the item is at list[i], return i.
- If the is not at list[i], do a linear search starting at index i+1.

Fill in the body of the method *linearSearchR* in the IntegerList class. The method should do a recursive linear search of a list starting with a given index (parameter *lo*). Note that the IntegerList class contains another method linearSearchRec that does nothing but call your method (linearSearchR). This is done because the recursive method (*linearSearchR*) needs more information (the index to start at) than you want to pass to the top-level search routine (*linearSearchRec*), which just needs the thing to look for.

Now change IntegerListTest.java so that it calls linearSearchRec instead of linearSearch when the user asks for a linear search. Thoroughly test the program.

```
// ****************************************************************
//    IntegerListS.java
//
//    Defines an IntegerListS class with methods to create, fill,
//    sort, and search in a list of integers. (Version S -
//    for use in the linear search exercise.)
//
// ****************************************************************

public class IntegerListS
{
    int[] list; //values in the list

    // -----------------------------------
    //    Creates a list of the given size
    // -----------------------------------
    public IntegerListS (int size)
    {
      list = new int[size];
    }

    // -----------------------------------------------------------
    //    Fills the array with integers between 1 and 100, inclusive
    // -----------------------------------------------------------
    public void randomize()
    {
      for (int i=0; i< list.length; i++)
          list[i] = (int)(Math.random() * 100) + 1;
    }

    // -------------------------------------
    //    Prints array elements with indices
    // -------------------------------------
    public void print()
```

```java
{
  for (int i=0; i<list.length; i++)
      System.out.println(i + ":\t" + list[i]);
}

//  -------------------------------------------------------------------
//    Returns the index of the first occurrence of target in the list.
//    Returns -1 if target does not appear in the list.
//  -------------------------------------------------------------------
public int linearSearch(int target)
{
  int location = -1;
  for (int i=0; i<list.length && location == -1; i++)
      if (list[i] == target)
        location = i;
  return location;
}

//  -------------------------------------------------------------------
//    Returns the index of an occurrence of target in the list, -1
//    if target does not appear in the list.
//  -------------------------------------------------------------------
public int linearSearchRec(int target)
{
  return linearSearchR (target, 0);
}

//  -------------------------------------------------------------------
//    Recursive implementation of the linear search - searches
//    for target starting at index lo.
//  -------------------------------------------------------------------
private int linearSearchR (int target, int lo)
{
  return -1;
}

//  -------------------------------------------------------------------
//   Sorts the list into ascending order using the selection sort algorithm.
//  -------------------------------------------------------------------
public void selectionSort()
{
  int minIndex;
  for (int i=0; i < list.length-1; i++)
     {
       //find smallest element in list starting at location i
       minIndex = i;
       for (int j = i+1; j < list.length; j++)
           if (list[j] < list[minIndex])
                 minIndex = j;

       //swap list[i] with smallest element
       int temp = list[i];
       list[i] = list[minIndex];
       list[minIndex] = temp;
     }
  }
}
```

```
// ***************************************************************
//      IntegerListSTest.java
//
//      Provide a menu-driven tester for the IntegerList class.
//      (Version S - for use in the linear search lab exercise).
//
// ***************************************************************
import java.util.Scanner;

public class IntegerListSTest
{
    static IntegerListS list = new IntegerListS (10);
    static Scanner scan = new Scanner(System.in);

    // ------------------------------------------------------------------
    //    Creates a list, then repeatedly print the menu and do what the
    //    user asks until they quit.
    // ------------------------------------------------------------------
    public static void main(String[] args)
    {
      printMenu();
      int choice = scan.nextInt();
      while (choice != 0)
          {
            dispatch(choice);
            printMenu();
            choice = scan.nextInt();
          }
    }

    // ------------------------------------
    //   Does what the menu item calls for.
    // ------------------------------------
    public static void dispatch(int choice)
    {
      int loc;
      switch(choice)
          {
          case 0:
            System.out.println("Bye!");
            break;
          case 1:
            System.out.println("How big should the list be?");
            int size = scan.nextInt();
            list = new IntegerListS(size);
            list.randomize();
            break;
          case 2:
            list.selectionSort();
            break;
          case 3:
            System.out.print("Enter the value to look for: ");
            loc = list.linearSearch(scan.nextInt());
            if (loc != -1)
                System.out.println("Found at location " + loc);
            else
                System.out.println("Not in list");
            break;
          case 4:
            list.print();
```

```
          break;
        default:
          System.out.println("Sorry, invalid choice");
      }
  }


  // ------------------------------------
  //    Prints the menu of user's choices.
  // ------------------------------------
  public static void printMenu()
  {
    System.out.println("\n   Menu    ");
    System.out.println("    ====");
    System.out.println("0: Quit");
    System.out.println("1: Create new list elements (** do this first!! **)");
    System.out.println("2: Sort the list using selection sort");
    System.out.println("3: Find an element in the list using linear search");
    System.out.println("4: Print the list");
    System.out.print("\nEnter your choice: ");
  }

}
```

Recursive Binary Search

The binary search algorithm from Chapter 9 is a very efficient algorithm for searching an ordered list. The algorithm (in pseudocode) is as follows:

```
highIndex - the maximum index of the part of the list being searched
lowIndex - the minimum index of the part of the list being searched
target -- the item being searched for

//look in the middle
middleIndex = (highIndex + lowIndex) / 2
if the list element at the middleIndex is the target
   return the middleIndex
else
   if the list element in the middle is greater than the target
      search the first half of the list
   else
      search the second half of the list
```

Notice the recursive nature of the algorithm. It is easily implemented recursively. Note that three parameters are needed—the target and the indices of the first and last elements in the part of the list to be searched. To "search the first half of the list" the algorithm must be called with the high and low index parameters representing the first half of the list. Similarly, to search the second half the algorithm must be called with the high and low index parameters representing the second half of the list. The file *IntegerListB.java* contains a class representing a list of integers (the same class that has been used in a few other labs); the file *IntegerListBTest.java* contains a simple menu-driven test program that lets the user create, sort, and print a list and search for an item in the list using a linear search or a binary search. Your job is to complete the binary search algorithm (method binarySearchR). The basic algorithm is given above but it leaves out one thing: what happens if the target is not in the list? What condition will let the program know that the target has not been found? If the low and high indices are changed each time so that the middle item is NOT examined again (see the diagram of indices below) then the list is guaranteed to shrink each time and the indices "cross"—that is, the high index becomes less than the low index. That is the condition that indicates the target was not found.

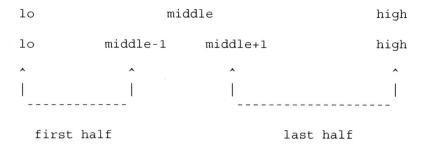

Fill in the blanks below, then type your code in. Remember when you test the search to first sort the list.

```
private int binarySearchR (int target, int lo, int hi)
{
  int index;
  if ( _____ ) // fill in the "not found" condition
      index = -1;
  else
      {
        int mid = (lo + hi)/2;
        if ( _____ ) // found it!
            index = mid;
        else if (target < list[mid])
                // fill in the recursive call to search the first half
                // of the list
              index = _____ ;
        else
```

```
                    // search the last half of the list
                index = _____ ;
            }
        return index;
    }
```

Optional: The binary search algorithm "works" (as in does something) even on a list that is not in order. Use the algorithm on an unsorted list and show that it may not find an item that is in the list. Hand trace the algorithm to understand why.

```
// ****************************************************************
//    IntegerListB.java
//
//    Defines an IntegerList class with methods to create, fill,
//    sort, and search in a list of integers. (Version B - for use
//    in the binary search lab exercise)
//
// ****************************************************************

public class IntegerListB
{
    int[] list; //values in the list

    // -----------------------------------
    //    Creates a list of the given size
    // -----------------------------------
    public IntegerListB (int size)
    {
      list = new int[size];
    }

    // ------------------------------------------------------------
    //    Fills the array with integers between 1 and 100, inclusive
    // ------------------------------------------------------------
    public void randomize()
    {
      for (int i=0; i<list.length; i++)
          list[i] = (int)(Math.random() * 100) + 1;
    }

    // ---------------------------------------
    //    Prints array elements with indices
    // ---------------------------------------
    public void print()
    {
      for (int i=0; i<list.length; i++)
          System.out.println(i + ":\t" + list[i]);
    }

    // ----------------------------------------------------------------
    //    Returns the index of the first occurrence of target in the list.
    //    Returns -1 if target does not appear in the list.
    // ----------------------------------------------------------------
    public int linearSearch(int target)
    {
      int location = -1;
      for (int i=0; i<list.length && location == -1; i++)
          if (list[i] == target)
              location = i;
      return location;
    }
```

```
//  ------------------------------------------------------------------
//    Returns the index of an occurrence of target in the list, -1
//    if target does not appear in the list.
//  ------------------------------------------------------------------
public int binarySearchRec(int target)
{
   return binarySearchR (target, 0, list.length-1);
}


//  ------------------------------------------------------------------
//    Recursive implementation of the binary search algorithm.
//    If the list is sorted the index of an occurrence of the
//    target is returned (or -1 if the target is not in the list).
//  ------------------------------------------------------------------
private int binarySearchR (int target, int lo, int hi)
{
   int index;

   // fill in code for the search

   return index;
}


//  ------------------------------------------------------------------------
//  Sorts the list into ascending order using the selection sort algorithm.
//  ------------------------------------------------------------------------
public void selectionSort()
{
   int minIndex;
   for (int i=0; i < list.length-1; i++)
      {
         //find smallest element in list starting at location i
         minIndex = i;
         for (int j = i+1; j < list.length; j++)
             if (list[j] < list[minIndex])
                    minIndex = j;

         //swap list[i] with smallest element
         int temp = list[i];
         list[i] = list[minIndex];
         list[minIndex] = temp;
      }
}

}
```

```
// ****************************************************************
//    IntegerListBTest.java
//
//    Provides a menu-driven tester for the IntegerList class.
//    (Version B - for use with the binary search lab exerice)
//
// ****************************************************************
import java.util.Scanner;

public class IntegerListBTest
{
    static IntegerListB list = new IntegerListB (10);
    static Scanner scan = new Scanner(System.in);

    // ------------------------------------------------------------
    //   Create a list, then repeatedly print the menu and do what the
    //   user asks until they quit.
    // ------------------------------------------------------------
    public static void main(String[] args)
    {
      printMenu();
      int choice = scan.nextInt();
      while  (choice != 0)
          {
             dispatch(choice);
             printMenu();
             choice = scan.nextInt();
          }
    }


    // ---------------------------------------------------
    //   Does what the menu item calls for.
    // ---------------------------------------------------
    public static void dispatch(int choice)
    {
      int loc;
      switch(choice)
          {
          case 0:
             System.out.println("Bye!");
             break;
          case 1:
             System.out.println("How big should the list be?");
             int size = scan.nextInt();
             list = new IntegerListB(size);
             list.randomize();
             break;
          case 2:
             list.selectionSort();
             break;
          case 3:
             System.out.print("Enter the value to look for: ");
             loc = list.linearSearch(scan.nextInt());
             if (loc != -1)
                 System.out.println("Found at location " + loc);
             else
                 System.out.println("Not in list");
             break;
          case 4:
             System.out.print("Enter the value to look for: ");
```

```
            loc = list.binarySearchRec(scan.nextInt());
            if (loc != -1)
                System.out.println("Found at location " + loc);
            else
                System.out.println("Not in list");
            break;
          case 5:
            list.print();
            break;
          default:
            System.out.println("Sorry, invalid choice");
        }
    }

    // --------------------------
    //  Prints the user's choices.
    // --------------------------
    public static void printMenu()
    {
      System.out.println("\n   Menu    ");
      System.out.println("   ====");
      System.out.println("0: Quit");
      System.out.println("1: Create new list elements (** do this first!! **)");
      System.out.println("2: Sort the list using selection sort");
      System.out.println("3: Find an element in the list using linear search");
      System.out.println("4: Find an element in the list using binary search");
      System.out.println("5: Print the list");
      System.out.print("\nEnter your choice: ");
    }

}
```

A List of Employees

The files *Employee.java* and *Payroll.java* contain a definition of a simple list of hourly wage employees. An employee has a name, number of hours worked, and an hourly pay rate. The Payroll class is the list of employees. Currently there is a method in the class, *public void readPayrollInfo(String file)*, that reads in the employee information from a file and sets up the employee list. Your job is to add a recursive method that determines the number of employees who worked overtime (more than 40 hours). The method *numOvertime* is already defined. It is the public method that would be used by a program. It calls your method *int overtime (int start)* which will do all the work.

1. Complete the overtime method. The parameter *start* is the index of the first element in the part of the array being processed. Recall that to recursively process the elements in an array in sequential order the strategy is to "process" the first element (in this case count it if the number of hours worked is greater than 40), then call the method recursively to process the rest of the array. Don't forget the base case.

2. Complete the test program *Overtime.java* to test your method. The program currently has code to read in the name of the file that contains employee data. You need to add code to instantiate a Payroll object, read the data in, then call the *numOvertime* method to determine how many employees worked overtime.

3. Run the program at least twice using the files *payroll.dat* and *payroll2.dat* as input.

```
// ***********************************************************
//    Employee.java
//
//    Represents an hourly wage worker.
// ***********************************************************

public class Employee
{
    String name;
    int hours;        // hours worked
    double rate;      // hourly pay rate

    // ------------------------------------------------
    //   Sets up the Employee object with the given data.
    // ------------------------------------------------
    public Employee (String name, int hours, double rate)
    {
      this.name = name;
      this.hours = hours;
      this.rate = rate;
    }

    // ------------------------------------------------
    //   Returns the number of hours worked.
    // ------------------------------------------------
    public int getHours ()
    {
      return hours;
    }
}
```

```
// **********************************************************
//   Payroll.java
//
//   Represents a list of employees.
// **********************************************************

import java.util.Scanner;
import java.util.*;
import java.io.*;

public class Payroll
{
    final int MAX = 30;
    Employee[] payroll = new Employee[MAX];
    int numEmployees = 0;

    // ------------------------------------------------------
    //   Reads the list of employee wage data from the given
    //   file.
    // ------------------------------------------------------
    public void readPayrollInfo(String file)
    {
        String line;        // a line in the file
        String name;        // name of an employee
        int hours;          // hours worked
        double rate;        // hourly pay rate

        Scanner fileScan, lineScan;

        try
            {
                fileScan = new Scanner (new File(file));

                while (fileScan.hasNext())
                    {
                        line = fileScan.nextLine();

                        lineScan = new Scanner(line);
                        name = lineScan.next ();

                        try
                            {
                                hours = lineScan.nextInt();
                                rate = lineScan.nextDouble();
                                payroll[numEmployees] = new Employee (name, hours, rate);
                                numEmployees++;
                            }
                        catch (InputMismatchException exception)
                            {
                                System.out.println ("Error in input. Line ignored.");
                                System.out.println (line);
                            }
                        catch {ArrayIndexOutOfBoundsException exception)
                            {
                                System.out.println ("Too many employees!");
                            }
                    }
                fileScan.close();

            }
```

```java
         catch (FileNotFoundException exception)
            {
               System.out.println ("The file " + file + " was not found.");
            }
         catch (IOException exception)
            {
               System.out.println (exception);
            }
      }


   // -------------------------------------------
   //    Returns the number of employees who
   //    worked over 40 hours; the helper method
   //    overtime is called to do all the work.
   // -------------------------------------------
   public int numOvertime ()
   {
      return overtime (0);
   }


   // -------------------------------------------------
   //    Returns the number of employees in the part
   //    of the list from index start to the end who
   //    worked more than 40 hours.
   // -------------------------------------------------
   private int overtime (int start)
   {

   }
}



// *****************************************************************
//    Overtime.java
//
//    Reads a file of employee payroll information and determines
//    how many employees worked more than 40 hours.
// *****************************************************************

import java.util.Scanner;

public class Overtime
{
   public static void main (String[] args)
   {
      String fileName;    // Name of the file containing employee data
      Scanner scan = new Scanner(System.in);

      System.out.println ("\nPayroll Program");
      System.out.print ("Enter the name of the file containing payroll data: ");
      fileName = scan.nextLine();

      // Instantiate a Payroll object and read in the data from the file


      // Print the number of workers who worked overtime.

   }
}
```

payroll.dat

```
Smith 45 13.50
Jones 39 23.75
Doe 40 17.80
Moe 30 21.90
Walker 41 14.60
Walton 57 8.95
Taylor 40 16.75
Lewis 40 35.50
Abbott 43 12.70
Who 39 33.95
Herrod 21 19.90
James 49 13.50
Summers 40 20.00
Winter 40 18.75
Farthington 38 24.50
Walsh 42 45.70
```

payroll2.dat

```
Jones 40 9.75
Ricardo 35 13.69
Smith 40 20.00
Smythe 40 17.80
```

Sierpinski Triangles

A Sierpinski triangle is a geometric figure that may be constructed as follows:

1. Draw a triangle.
2. Draw a new triangle by connecting the midpoints of the three sides of your original triangle. This should split your triangle into four smaller triangles, one in the center and three around the outside.
3. Repeat (2) for each of the outside triangles (not the center one). Each of them will split into four yet smaller triangles. Repeat for each of their outside triangles.. and for each of the new ones.. and so on, forever. Draw a few rounds of this on paper to see how it works. Check out the demo at http://cs.roanoke.edu/labs4e/demo.html to see how the program works on screen.

Your job is to write an applet that draws a Sierpinski triangle. Think about the following:

- A Sierpinski triangle is a recursively defined structure, since each of the three outer triangles formed by joining the midpoints is itself a Sierpinski triangle.
- In practice you don't want to go on with the process "forever" as suggested above, so we'll limit how deep it goes. Define the *depth* of a Sierpinski triangle as the number of directly nested triangles at the deepest point. So a Sierpinski triangle consisting of a single triangle has depth 0; when a triangle is drawn inside of it, the resulting Sierpinski triangle has depth 1; when the three outside triangles have triangles drawn inside of them, the resulting triangle is depth 2, and so on. A depth of 10 or 11 gives a nice looking triangle in a reasonable amount of time. (The demo uses depth 10.) Smaller depths are interesting in that you can see more of the construction; higher depths generally take too long for casual viewing.
- A triangle is a polygon, so you'll use the drawPolygon method. Remember that it takes an array containing the x coordinates, an array containing the y coordinates, and an integer indicating how many points should be drawn (3 for a triangle). Refer to Chapter 7 or the appendix (the Graphics class) to refresh your memory on this.
- Your initial triangle should look like the one in the demo—one point at the top center of the applet and one point in each lower corner.
- Your overall program is quite simple. The paint method will just call a recursive method sierpinski, passing it the Graphics object, the points of the initial triangle to be drawn, and the initial depth (0). Make the variables that hold the initial points instance variables and initialize them in the init method. The sierpinski method will then check to see if the desired depth has been exceeded (the depth can be a constant), and if not, draw the triangle, then call itself recursively to drawn the three Sierpinski triangles that will be embedded. Note that it will have to figure out what points to pass to each of these, and that each recursive call increases the depth by one.

When this works (that is, when your triangle looks like the one in the demo), modify it so that when the user clicks a new, random Sierpinski triangle is drawn. (The demo does this too.) This just means choosing three random points and repainting—nothing will change in your paint or sierpinski methods (if you followed the guidelines above). For fun you can choose a random color each time as well, as the demo does.

Modifying the Koch Snowflake

The Koch snowflake is a fractal generated by starting with 3 line sements forming an equilateral triangle (a Koch fractal of order 1). The algorithm for generating higher order Koch fractals involves splitting each line segment into three equal segments then replacing the middle segment by two line segments that protrude outward. The same algorithm is then recursively applied to each of the 4 new line segments. In the basic Koch snowflake the two protruding line segments meet at a 60 degree angle. These line segments form an equilateral triangle with the middle segment that is removed. (See the discussion in Chapter 11 for more details.) Files *KochSnowflake.java* and *KochPanel.java* contain slight modifications to the program from the text that generates Koch snowflakes (Listings 11.6 and 11.7). Copy these files to your directory, compile them, and run the program in the appletviewer to see how it works (you may use the file *Koch.html* to run the program). In this exercise you will generalize the pattern to allow for triangles other than equilateral ones to be built on the middle third segment. In the drawFractal method this involves changing the calculation of x3 and y3, the coordinates of the protrusion point. The following calculations are equivalent to those currently in the program:

```
x3 = (int) (x2 + (cosine * deltaX - sine * deltaY)/3);
y3 = (int) (y2 + (cosine * deltaY + sine * deltaX)/3);
```

where cosine is the cosine of 60 degrees (which is 1/2) and sine is the sine of 60 degrees (which is the square root of 3 over 2). These equations are generalizable to angles other than 60. In this exercise you will generalize the program to work for angles other than 60. The angle will be controlled by increase and decrease buttons in the same way that the order is currently controlled. Do the following:

1. In KochPanel.java,
   - Add instance variables *angle*, *sine*, and *cosine*. Angle will be an integer and sine and cosine type double.
   - In the constructor, set angle to 60 (this will be the default), and set sine to Math.sin (Math.PI / 3) and cosine to Math.cos (Math.PI / 3).
   - In drawFractal, replace the current calculations for x3 and y3 with those given above.

2. Compile and run the program. It should behave just as before.

3. To add controls to allow the angle to change, do the following:
   - In KochPanel, add two public methods *getAngle()* that returns the angle (type int), and *setAngle (int newAngle)* that sets the angle to be the value of *newAngle* and sets *sine* and *cosine* of that angle. Remember that the sin and cos methods in the Math class must have arguments that are in radians not degrees so you need to multiply the angle (which is in degrees) by Math.PI divided by 180 (pi/180 is the degree to radian conversion factor).
   - In KochSnowflake.java, add a new "tools" panel for the buttons to increase and decrease the angle. This panel will contain two buttons and a label giving the current angle. A horizontal box layout should be used. The applet should be added as a listener for the buttons.
   - The new tools panel should be added to the appletPanel. To accomodate it change APPLET_HEIGHT to 480.
   - The method actionPerformed must be modified to take action if the event source was one of the new buttons. If the source was the button to increase the angle, increase the angle by 10 degrees (you can get the current angle using the method you added to KochPanel); if the source was the button to decrease the angle, decrease it by 10 degrees. The new angle should be between 10 and 170 (inclusive)—you should add constants (similar to MIN and MAX) for the minimum and maximum angles.

4. Compile and run the program. Play with the angles and order to see what fractal patterns are generated.

```
// ******************************************************************
//  KochSnowflake.java              Author:  Lewis/Loftus
//
//  Demonstrates the use of recursion in graphics.
// ******************************************************************

import java.awt.*;
import java.awt.event.*;
import javax.swing.*;

public class KochSnowflake extends JApplet implements ActionListener
{
    private final int APPLET_WIDTH = 400;
    private final int APPLET_HEIGHT = 440;

    private final int MIN = 1, MAX = 9;

    private JButton increase, decrease;
    private JLabel titleLabel, orderLabel;
    private KochPanel drawing;
    private JPanel appletPanel, tools;

    // ---------------------------------------------------------
    //   Sets up the components for the applet.
    // ---------------------------------------------------------
    public void init()
    {
      tools = new JPanel ();
      tools.setLayout (new BoxLayout (tools, BoxLayout.X_AXIS));
      tools.setPreferredSize (new Dimension (APPLET_WIDTH, 40));
      tools.setBackground (Color.yellow);
      tools.setOpaque (true);

      titleLabel = new JLabel ("The Koch Snowflake");
      titleLabel.setForeground (Color.black);

      increase = new JButton ("Increase");
      increase.setMargin (new Insets (0, 0, 0, 0));
      increase.addActionListener (this);

      decrease = new JButton ("Decrease");
      decrease.setMargin (new Insets (0, 0, 0, 0));
      decrease.addActionListener (this);

      orderLabel = new JLabel ("Order: 1");
      orderLabel.setForeground (Color.black);

      tools.add (titleLabel);
      tools.add (Box.createHorizontalStrut (40));
      tools.add (decrease);
      tools.add (increase);
      tools.add (Box.createHorizontalStrut (20));
      tools.add (orderLabel);

      drawing = new KochPanel (1);

      appletPanel = new JPanel ();
      appletPanel.add (tools);
      appletPanel.add (drawing);
```

```
      getContentPane().add (appletPanel);

      setSize (APPLET_WIDTH, APPLET_HEIGHT);
   }

   // ---------------------------------------------------------
   //  Determines which button was pushed, and sets the new order
   //  if it is in range.
   // ---------------------------------------------------------
   public void actionPerformed (ActionEvent event)
   {
      int order = drawing.getOrder ();

      if (event.getSource() == increase)
         order++;
      else
         order--;

      if (order >= MIN && order <= MAX)
         {
            orderLabel.setText ("Order: " + order);
            drawing.setOrder (order);
            repaint ();
         }
   }
}
```

```
// ************************************************************************
//   KochPanel.java              Author:   Lewis/Loftus
//
//   Represents a drawing surface on which to paint a Koch Snowflake.
// ************************************************************************

import java.awt.*;
import javax.swing.JPanel;

public class KochPanel extends JPanel
{
    private final int PANEL_WIDTH = 400;
    private final int PANEL_HEIGHT = 400;

    private final double SQ = Math.sqrt (3.0) / 6;

    private final int TOPX = 200, TOPY = 20;
    private final int LEFTX = 60, LEFTY = 300;
    private final int RIGHTX = 340, RIGHTY = 300;

    private int current;       // current order

    // ----------------------------------------------------------------
    //   Sets the initial fractal order to the value specified.
    // ----------------------------------------------------------------
    public KochPanel (int currentOrder)
    {
      current = currentOrder;
      setBackground (Color.black);
      setPreferredSize (new Dimension (PANEL_WIDTH, PANEL_HEIGHT));
    }

    // ----------------------------------------------------------------
    //   Draws the fractal recursively.  The base case is order 1 for
    //   which a simple straight line is drawn.  Otherwise three
    //   intermediate points arae computed, and each line segment is
    //   drawn as a fractal.
    // ----------------------------------------------------------------
    public void drawFractal (int order, int x1, int y1, int x5, int y5,
                   Graphics page)
    {
      int deltaX, deltaY, x2, y2, x3, y3, x4, y4;

      if (order ==1)
          page.drawLine (x1, y1, x5, y5);
      else
          {
            deltaX = x5 - x1;      // distance between end points
            deltaY = y5 - y1;

            x2 = x1 + deltaX /3;
            y2 = y1 + deltaY / 3;

            x3 = (int) ((x1 + x5)/2 + SQ * (y1 - y5));
            y3 = (int) ((y1 + y5)/2 + SQ * (x5 - x1));

            x4 = x1 + deltaX * 2 / 3;
            y4 = y1 + deltaY * 2 / 3;

            drawFractal (order - 1, x1, y1, x2, y2, page);
```

```java
            drawFractal (order - 1, x2, y2, x3, y3, page);
            drawFractal (order - 1, x3, y3, x4, y4, page);
            drawFractal (order - 1, x4, y4, x5, y5, page);
         }
      }

   // ----------------------------------------------------------------
   //  Performs the initial calls to the drawFractal method.
   // ----------------------------------------------------------------
   public void paintComponent (Graphics page)
   {
      super.paintComponent (page);

      page.setColor (Color.green);

      drawFractal (current, TOPX, TOPY, LEFTX, LEFTY, page);
      drawFractal (current, LEFTX, LEFTY, RIGHTX, RIGHTY, page);
      drawFractal (current, RIGHTX, RIGHTY, TOPX, TOPY, page);
   }

   // ----------------------------------------------------------------
   //  Sets the fractal order to the specified value.
   // ----------------------------------------------------------------
   public void setOrder (int order)
   {
      current = order;
   }

   // ----------------------------------------------------------------
   //  Returns the current order.
   // ----------------------------------------------------------------
   public int getOrder ()
   {
      return current;
   }
}
```

koch.html

```html
<html>
<title>Koch Snowflake</title>
<applet CODE="KochSnowflake.class" HEIGHT=400 WIDTH=440>
</applet>
</html>
```

Chapter 12: Collections
Lab Exercises

Topic	Lab Exercises
Linked Lists	Linked List of Integers
	Recursive Processing of Linked List
	Linked List of Objects
	Doubly Linked Lists
Queues	An Array Queue Implementation
	A Linked Queue Implementation
	Queue Manipulation
Stacks	An Array Stack Implementation
	A Linked Stack Implementation
	Stack Manipulation
	Matching Parentheses

A Linked List of Integers

File *IntList.java* contains definitions for a linked list of integers. The class contains an inner class *IntNode* that holds information for a single node in the list (a node has a value and a reference to the next node) and the following *IntList* methods:

- ☐ public IntList()—constructor; creates an empty list of integers
- ☐ public void addToFront(int val)—takes an integer and puts it on the front of the list
- ☐ public void addToEnd(int val)—takes an integer and puts it on the end of the list
- ☐ public void removeFirst()—removes the first value from the list
- ☐ public void print()—prints the elements in the list from first to last

File *IntListTest.java* contains a driver that allows you to experiment with these methods. Save both of these files to your directory, compile and run IntListTest, and play around with it to see how it works. Then add the following methods to the IntList class. For each, add an option to the driver to test it.

1. public int length()—returns the number of elements in the list
2. public String toString()—returns a String containing the print value of the list.
3. public void removeLast()—removes the last element of the list. If the list is empty, does nothing.
4. public void replace(int oldVal, int newVal)—replaces all occurrences of oldVal in the list with newVal. Note that you can still use the old nodes; just replace the values stored in those nodes.

```java
// ****************************************************************
// FILE:   IntList.java
//
// Purpose: Defines a class that represents a list of integers
//
// ****************************************************************
public class IntList
{
    private IntNode front;        //first node in list

    //-----------------------------------------
    //  Constructor.  Initially list is empty.
    //-----------------------------------------
    public IntList()
    {
      front = null;
    }

    //-----------------------------------------
    //   Adds given integer to front of list.
    //-----------------------------------------
    public void addToFront(int val)
    {
      front = new IntNode(val,front);
    }

    //-----------------------------------------
    //   Adds given integer to end of list.
    //-----------------------------------------
    public void addToEnd(int val)
    {
      IntNode newnode = new IntNode(val,null);

      //if list is empty, this will be the only node in it
      if (front == null)
          front = newnode;
```

```java
        else
            {
                //make temp point to last thing in list
                IntNode temp = front;
                while (temp.next != null)
                    temp = temp.next;
                //link new node into list
                temp.next = newnode;
            }
    }

    //--------------------------------------------
    //    Removes the first node from the list.
    //    If the list is empty, does nothing.
    //--------------------------------------------
    public void removeFirst()
    {
        if (front != null)
            front = front.next;
    }

    //--------------------------------------------------
    //    Prints the list elements from first to last.
    //--------------------------------------------------
    public void print()
    {
        System.out.println("--------------------");
        System.out.print("List elements: ");

        IntNode temp = front;

        while (temp != null)
            {
                System.out.print(temp.val + " ");
                temp = temp.next;
            }
        System.out.println("\n--------------------\n");
    }

    //*************************************************************
    // An inner class that represents a node in the integer list.
    // The public variables are accessed by the IntList class.
    //*************************************************************
    private class IntNode
    {
        public int val;          //value stored in node
        public IntNode next;     //link to next node in list

        //----------------------------------------------------------------
        // Constructor; sets up the node given a value and IntNode reference
        //----------------------------------------------------------------
        public IntNode(int val, IntNode next)
        {
            this.val = val;
            this.next = next;
        }
    }
}
```

```
// ************************************************************
//    IntListTest.java
//
//    Driver to test IntList methods.
// ************************************************************

import java.util.Scanner;

public class IntListTest
{
    private static Scanner scan;
    private static IntList list = new IntList();

    //-------------------------------------------------------------
    // Creates a list, then repeatedly prints the menu and does what
    // the user asks until they quit.
    //-------------------------------------------------------------
    public static void main(String[] args)
    {
      scan = new Scanner(System.in);
      printMenu();
      int choice = scan.nextInt();
      while (choice != 0)
          {
            dispatch(choice);
            printMenu();
            choice = scan.nextInt();

          }
    }

    //-----------------------------------------
    //  Does what the menu item calls for.
    //-----------------------------------------
    public static void dispatch(int choice)
    {
      int newVal;
      switch(choice)
          {
          case 0:
            System.out.println("Bye!");
            break;

          case 1:    //add to front
            System.out.println("Enter integer to add to front");
            newVal = scan.nextInt();
            list.addToFront(newVal);
            break;

          case 2:    //add to end
            System.out.println("Enter integer to add to end");
            newVal = scan.nextInt();
            list.addToEnd(newVal);
            break;

          case 3:  //remove first element
            list.removeFirst();
            break;

          case 4:  //print
```

```
            list.print();
            break;
          default:
            System.out.println("Sorry, invalid choice");
        }
    }

    //----------------------------------------
    //  Prints the user's choices
    //----------------------------------------
    public static void printMenu()
    {
      System.out.println("\n   Menu   ");
      System.out.println("   ====");
      System.out.println("0: Quit");
      System.out.println("1: Add an integer to the front of the list");
      System.out.println("2: Add an integer to the end of the list");
      System.out.println("3: Remove an integer from the front of the list");
      System.out.println("4: Print the list");

      System.out.print("\nEnter your choice: ");
    }
}
```

Recursive Processing of Linked Lists

File *IntList.java* contains definitions for a linked list of integers (see previous exercise). The class contains an inner class *IntNode*, which holds information for a single node in the list (a node has a value and a reference to the next node) and the following *IntList* methods:

- ☐ public IntList()—constructor; creates an empty list of integers
- ☐ public void addToFront(int val)—takes an integer and puts it on the front of the list
- ☐ public void addToEnd(int val)—takes an integer and puts it on the end of the list
- ☐ public void removeFirst()—removes the first value from the list
- ☐ public void print()—prints the elements in the list from first to last

File *IntListTest.java* contains a driver that allows you to experiment with these methods. Save both of these files to your directory. If you have not already worked with these files in a previous exercise, compile and run IntListTest and play around with it to see how it works. Then add the following methods to the IntList class. For each, add an option in the driver to test the method.

1. public void printRec()—prints the list from first to last using recursion. **Hint:** The basic idea is that you print the first item in the list then do a recursive call to print the rest of the list. This means you need to keep track of what hasn't been printed yet (the "rest" of the list). In particular, your recursive method needs to know where the first item is. Note that printRec() has no parameter so you need to use a helper method that does most of the work. It should have a parameter that lets it know where the part of the list to be printed starts.

2. public void printRecBackwards()—prints the list from last to first using recursion. **Hint:** Printing backward recursively is just like printing forward recursively except you print the rest of the list *before* printing this element. Simple!

A Linked List of Objects

Listing 12.2 in the text is an example of a linked list of objects of type Magazine; the file IntList.java contains an example of a linked list of integers (see previous exercise). A list of objects is a lot like a list of integers or a particular type of object such as a Magazine, except the value stored is an Object, not an int or Magazine. Write a class ObjList that contains arbitrary objects and that has the following methods:

- public void addToFront (Object obj)—puts the object on the front of the list
- public void addToEnd (Object obj)—puts the object on the end of the list
- public void removeFirst()—removes the first value from the list
- public void removeLast()—removes the last value from the list
- public void print()—prints the elements of the list from first to last

These methods are similar to those in IntList. Note that you won't have to write all of these again; you can just make very minor modifications to the IntList methods.

Also write an ObjListTest class that creates an ObjList and puts various different kinds of objects in it (String, array, etc) and then prints it.

Doubly Linked Lists

Sometimes it is convenient to maintain references to both the next node and the previous node in a linked list. This is called a *doubly linked list* and is illustrated in Figure 12.4 of the text. File *DoubleLinked.java* contains definitions for a doubly linked list of integers. This class contains an inner class *IntNode* that holds information for a single node in the list (its value and references to the next and previous nodes). The DoubleLinked class also contains the following methods:

- □   public DoubleLinked()—constructor; creates an empty list of integers
- □   public void addToFront(int val)—takes an integer and puts it on the front of the list
- □   public void print()—prints the elements in the list from first to last

File *DoubleLinkedTest.java* contains a driver that allows you to experiment with these methods. Save both of these files to your directory, compile and run DoubleLinkedTest, and play around with it to see how it works. Then add the following methods to the DoubleLinked class. For each, add an option to the driver to test it.

1.   public void addToEnd(int val)—takes an integer and puts it on the end of the list
2.   public void removeFirst()—removes the first value from the list. If the list is empty, does nothing.
3.   public void removeLast()—removes the last element of the list. If the list is empty, does nothing.
4.   public void remove(int oldVal)—removes the first occurrence of oldVal in the list.

```
// ****************************************************************
//    DoubleLinked.java
//
//    A class using a doubly linked list to represent a list of integers.
//
// ****************************************************************
public class DoubleLinked
{
    private IntNode list;

    // --------------------------------------------------
    // Constructor -- initializes list
    // --------------------------------------------------
    public DoubleLinked()
    {
      list = null;
    }

    // --------------------------------------------------
    // Prints the list elements
    // --------------------------------------------------
    public void print()
    {
      for (IntNode temp = list; temp != null; temp = temp.next)
          System.out.println(temp.val);
    }

    // --------------------------------------------------
    // Adds new element to front of list
    // --------------------------------------------------
    public void addToFront(int val)
    {
      IntNode newNode = new IntNode(val);
      newNode.next = list;
      if (list != null)
            list.prev = newNode;
      list = newNode;
    }
```

```java
//**********************************************************
// An inner class that represents a list element.
//**********************************************************

    private class IntNode
    {
        public int val;
        public IntNode next;
        public IntNode prev;

        public IntNode(int val)
        {
          this.val = val;
          this.next = null;
          this.prev = null;
        }
    }
}


// ***********************************************************
//   DoubleLinkedTest.java
//
//   Driver to test DoubleLinked methods.
// ***********************************************************

import java.util.Scanner;

public class DoubleLinkedTest
{
    private static Scanner scan;
    private static DoubleLinked list = new DoubleLinked();

    //-------------------------------------------------------------
    // Creates a list, then repeatedly prints the menu and does what
    // the user asks until they quit.
    //-------------------------------------------------------------
    public static void main(String[] args)
    {
      scan = new Scanner(System.in);
      printMenu();
      int choice = scan.nextInt();
      while (choice != 0)
          {
            dispatch(choice);
            printMenu();
            choice = scan.nextInt();

          }
    }

    //-----------------------------------------
    //  Does what the menu item calls for.
    //-----------------------------------------
    public static void dispatch(int choice)
    {
      int newVal;
      switch(choice)
          {
          case 0:
```

```java
            System.out.println("Bye!");
            break;

          case 1:   //print
            System.out.println("** List elements **");
            list.print();
            break;

          case 2:      //add to front
            System.out.println("Enter integer to add to front");
            newVal = scan.nextInt();
            list.addToFront(newVal);
            break;

          default:
            System.out.println("Sorry, invalid choice");
          }
      }

    //-------------------------------------
    //  Prints the user's choices
    //-------------------------------------
    public static void printMenu()
    {
      System.out.println("\n   Menu    ");
      System.out.println("    ====");
      System.out.println("0: Quit");
      System.out.println("1: Print list");
      System.out.println("2: Add an integer to the front of the list");
      System.out.print("\nEnter your choice: ");
    }
}
```

An Array Queue Implementation

File *QueueADT.java* contains a Java interface representing a queue ADT. In addition to *enqueue(), dequeue(),* and *isEmpty(),* this interface contains two methods that are not described in the book – *isFull ()* and *size().* File *ArrayQueue.java* contains a skeleton for an array-based implementation of this interface; it also includes a *toString()* method that returns a string containing the queue elements, one per line. File *TestQueue.java* contains a simple test program.

Complete the method definitions in *ArrayQueue.java.* Some things to think about:

- A queue has activity at both ends -- elements are enqueued at one end and dequeued from the other end. In an array implementation this means that repeated enqueues and dequeues will shift the queue elements from the beginning to the end of the array, so the array may appear full (in that the last element is in the last slot) when there are actually spaces available at the beginning. To address this the next element can simply be placed in the first element of the array, so that the queue "wraps around" the array. This is called a *circular* array implementation, and is used because it allows the enqueue and dequeue methods to be implemented efficiently in both space and time.
- You'll need to use integers to keep track of the indices of the front and back of the queue. Think carefully about what initial values these variables (*front* and *back*) should get in the constructor and how they should be incremented given the circular nature of the implementation.
- The easiest way to implement the *size()* method is to keep track of the number of elements as you go with the *numElements* variable -- just increment this variable when you enqueue an element and decrement it when you dequeue an element.
- An easy way to tell if a queue is full in an array implementation is to check how many elements it contains (stored in *numElements*). If it's equal to the size of the array, the queue is full. You can also use *numElements* to check if the queue is empty.
- The test program given tries to enqueue more elements than will fit in default size of the queue. Be sure that you check if the queue is full before enqueueing, and if it is full just do nothing. It's safest to do this in the enqueue() method.

Study the code in *TestQueue.java* so you know what it is doing, then compile and run it. Correct any problems in your Linked Queue class.

```
//*********************************************************
// QueueADT.java
// The classic FIFO queue interface.
//*********************************************************
public interface QueueADT
{
    //---------------------------------------------
    // Puts item on end of queue.
    //---------------------------------------------
    public void enqueue(Object item);

    //---------------------------------------------
    // Removes and returns object from front of queue.
    //---------------------------------------------
    public Object dequeue();

    //---------------------------------------------
    // Returns true if queue is empty.
    //---------------------------------------------
    public boolean isEmpty();

    //---------------------------------------------
    // Returns true if queue is full.
    //---------------------------------------------
    public boolean isFull();
```

```java
        //--------------------------------------------------
        // Returns the number of elements in the queue.
        //--------------------------------------------------
        public int size();
}


//**********************************************************
// ArrayQueue.java
// An array-based implementation of the classic FIFO queue interface.
//**********************************************************

public class ArrayQueue implements QueueADT
{
        private final int DEFAULT_SIZE = 5;
        private Object[] elements;
        private int numElements;
        private int front, back;

        //--------------------------------------------------
        // Constructor; creates array of default size.
        //--------------------------------------------------
        public ArrayQueue()
        {
        }


        //--------------------------------------------------
        // Puts item on end of queue.
        //--------------------------------------------------
        public void enqueue(Object item)
        {
        }


        //--------------------------------------------------
        // Removes and returns object from front of queue.
        //--------------------------------------------------
        public Object dequeue()
        {
        }


        //--------------------------------------------------
        // Returns true if queue is empty.
        //--------------------------------------------------
        public boolean isEmpty()
        {
        }


        //--------------------------------------------------
        // Returns true if queue is full, but it never is.
        //--------------------------------------------------
        public boolean isFull()
        {
        }


        //--------------------------------------------------
```

```
    // Returns the number of elements in the queue.
    //-----------------------------------------------
    public int size()
    {
    }


    //-----------------------------------------------
    // Returns a string containing the elements of the queue
    // from first to last
    //-----------------------------------------------
    public String toString()
    {
      String result = "\n";
      for (int i = front, count=0; count < numElements;
                        i=(i+1)%elements.length,count++)
          result = result elements[i]+ "\n";
      return result;

    }
}



//*************************************************************
// TestQueue
// A driver to test the methods of the QueueADT implementations.
//*************************************************************
public class TestQueue
{
    public static void main(String[] args)
    {
      QueueADT q = new ArrayQueue();

      System.out.println("\nEnqueuing chocolate, cake, pie, truffles:");
      q.enqueue("chocolate");
      q.enqueue("cake");
      q.enqueue("pie");
      q.enqueue("truffles");

      System.out.println("\nHere's the queue: " + q);
      System.out.println("It contains " + q.size() + " items.");

      System.out.println("\nDequeuing two...");
      System.out.println(q.dequeue());
      System.out.println(q.dequeue());

      System.out.println("\nEnqueuing cookies, profiteroles, mousse, cheesecake,
ice cream:");
      q.enqueue("cookies");
      q.enqueue("profiteroles");
      q.enqueue("mousse");
      q.enqueue("cheesecake");
      q.enqueue("ice cream");

      System.out.println("\nHere's the queue again: " + q);
      System.out.println("Now it contains "  + q.size() + " items.");

      System.out.println("\nDequeuing everything in queue");
      while (!q.isEmpty())
```

```
            System.out.println(q.dequeue());

        System.out.println("\nNow it contains "  + q.size() + " items.");
        if (q.isEmpty())
            System.out.println("Queue is empty!");
        else
            System.out.println("Queue is not empty -- why not??!!");
    }
}
```

A Linked Queue Implementation

File *QueueADT.java* contains a Java interface representing a queue ADT. In addition to *enqueue()*, *dequeue()*, and *isEmpty()*, this interface contains two methods that are not described in the book – *isFull ()* and *size()*. File *LinkedQueue.java* contains a skeleton for a linked implementation of this interface; it also includes a *toString()* method that returns a string containing the queue elements, one per line. It depends on the Node class in *Node.java*. (This could also be defined as an inner class.) File *TestQueue.java* contains a simple test program.

Complete the method definitions in *LinkedQueue.java*. Some things to think about:
- In *enqueue()* and *dequeue()* you have to maintain both the front and back pointers – this takes a little thought. In particular, in *enqueue* be careful of the case where the queue is empty and you are putting the first item in. This case requires special treatment (think about why).
- The easiest way to implement the *size()* method is to keep track of the number of elements as you go with the *numElements* variable -- just increment this variable when you enqueue an element and decrement it when you dequeue an element.
- A linked queue is never full, so *isFull()* always returns false. Easy!

Study the code in *TestQueue.java* so you know what it is doing, then compile and run it. Correct any problems in your Linked Queue class.

```
//***********************************************************
// QueueADT.java
// The classic FIFO queue interface.
//***********************************************************
public interface QueueADT
{
    //---------------------------------------------
    // Puts item on end of queue.
    //---------------------------------------------
    public void enqueue(Object item);

    //---------------------------------------------
    // Removes and returns object from front of queue.
    //---------------------------------------------
    public Object dequeue();

    //---------------------------------------------
    // Returns true if queue is empty.
    //---------------------------------------------
    public boolean isEmpty();

    //---------------------------------------------
    // Returns true if queue is full.
    //---------------------------------------------
    public boolean isFull();

    //---------------------------------------------
    // Returns the number of elements in the queue.
    //---------------------------------------------
    public int size();
}

//***********************************************************
// LinkedQueue.java
// A linked-list implementation of the classic FIFO queue interface.
//***********************************************************
public class LinkedQueue implements QueueADT
```

```
{
    private Node front, back;
    private int numElements;

    //------------------------------------------------
    // Constructor; initializes the front and back pointers
    // and the number of elements.
    //------------------------------------------------
    public LinkedQueue()
    {
    }

    //------------------------------------------------
    // Puts item on end of queue.
    //------------------------------------------------
    public void enqueue(Object item)
    {
    }

    //------------------------------------------------
    // Removes and returns object from front of queue.
    //------------------------------------------------
    public Object dequeue()
    {
        Object item = null;
    }

    //------------------------------------------------
    // Returns true if queue is empty.
    //------------------------------------------------
    public boolean isEmpty()
    {
    }

    //------------------------------------------------
    // Returns true if queue is full, but it never is.
    //------------------------------------------------
    public boolean isFull()
    {
    }

    //------------------------------------------------
    // Returns the number of elements in the queue.
    //------------------------------------------------
    public int size()
    {
    }

    //------------------------------------------------
    // Returns a string containing the elements of the queue
    // from first to last
    //------------------------------------------------
    public String toString()
    {
        String result = "\n";
        Node temp = front;
        while (temp != null)
        {
            result += temp.getElement() + "\n";
            temp = temp.getNext();
```

```
        }
        return result;
    }
}


//*************************************************************
//   Node.java
//   A general node for a singly linked list of objects.
//*************************************************************
public class Node
{
    private Node next;
    private Object element;

    //-------------------------------------------------------
    // Creates an empty node
    //-------------------------------------------------------
    public Node()
    {
      next = null;
      element = null;
    }

    //-------------------------------------------------------
    // Creates a node storing a specified element
    //-------------------------------------------------------
    public Node(Object element)
    {
      next = null;
      this.element = element;
    }

    //-------------------------------------------------------
    // Returns the node that follows this one
    //-------------------------------------------------------
    public Node getNext()
    {
      return next;
    }

    //-------------------------------------------------------
    // Sets the node that follows this one
    //-------------------------------------------------------
    public void setNext(Node node)
    {
      next = node;
    }

    //-------------------------------------------------------
    // Returns the element stored in this node
    //-------------------------------------------------------
    public Object getElement()
    {
      return element;
    }

    //-------------------------------------------------------
    // Sets the element stored in this node
    //-------------------------------------------------------
```

```java
      public void setElement(Object element)
      {
        this.element = element;
      }
}


//*************************************************************
// TestQueue
// A driver to test the methods of the QueueADT implementations.
//*************************************************************
public class TestQueue
{
    public static void main(String[] args)
    {
      QueueADT q = new LinkedQueue();

      System.out.println("\nEnqueuing chocolate, cake, pie, truffles:");
      q.enqueue("chocolate");
      q.enqueue("cake");
      q.enqueue("pie");
      q.enqueue("truffles");

      System.out.println("\nHere's the queue: " + q);
      System.out.println("It contains " + q.size() + " items.");

      System.out.println("\nDequeuing two...");
      System.out.println(q.dequeue());
      System.out.println(q.dequeue());

      System.out.println("\nEnqueuing cookies, profiteroles, mousse, cheesecake,
ice cream:");
      q.enqueue("cookies");
      q.enqueue("profiteroles");
      q.enqueue("mousse");
      q.enqueue("cheesecake");
      q.enqueue("ice cream");

      System.out.println("\nHere's the queue again: " + q);
      System.out.println("Now it contains "  + q.size() + " items.");

      System.out.println("\nDequeuing everything in queue");
      while (!q.isEmpty())
          System.out.println(q.dequeue());

      System.out.println("\nNow it contains "  + q.size() + " items.");
      if (q.isEmpty())
          System.out.println("Queue is empty!");
      else
          System.out.println("Queue is not empty -- why not??!!");
    }
}
```

Queue Manipulation

The file *QueueTest.java* contains a printQueue method that takes an object of type QueueADT and prints its contents, restoring the queue before it returns. It uses a temporary queue that actually holds the same information as the original queue. If you know the number of elements in the queue, you can write a printQueue method that prints the queue and restores it to its original form without using an auxiliary data structure (stack, queue, etc.). Think about how, then do it! That is, modify the printQueue method in QueueTest so that it behaves exactly as it does now but does not require an auxiliary data structure. Note that this code uses a LinkedQueue implementation for the QueueADT (see previous exercises), but you could substitute an ArrayQueue if you like.

```java
// ****************************************************************
//    QueueTest.java
//
//    A simple driver to manipulate a queue.
//
// ****************************************************************

public class QueueTest
{
    public static void main(String[] args)
    {

        QueueADT queue = new LinkedQueue();

        //put some stuff in the queue: 0,2,4,..,14
        for (int i=0; i<8; i++)
            queue.enqueue(i*2);
        System.out.println("\n\n** Initial queue **");
        printQueue(queue);

        //dequeue 4 items
        for (int i=0; i<4; i++)
            queue.dequeue();
        System.out.println("\n\n** After dequeueing 4 items **");
        printQueue(queue);

        //enqueue 7 more: 1,2,..,7
        for (int i=0; i<7; i++)
            queue.enqueue(i+1);
        System.out.println("\n\n** After enqueueing 7 more items **");
        printQueue(queue);

    }

    //-----------------------------------------------------------
    // Prints elements of queue, restoring it before returning
    //-----------------------------------------------------------
    public static void printQueue(QueueADT queue)
    {
        QueueADT temp = new LinkedQueue();

        //print everything in the queue, putting elements
        //back into a temporary queue
        while (!queue.isEmpty())
            {
                int val = queue.dequeue();
                temp.enqueue(val);
                System.out.print(val + " ");
```

```
            }
        System.out.println ();

        //restore the original queue
        while (!temp.isEmpty())
            {
                int val = temp.dequeue();
                queue.enqueue(val);
            }
    }

}
```

An Array Stack Implementation

Java has a Stack class that holds elements of type Object. However, many languages do not provide stack types, so it is useful to be able to define your own. File *StackADT.java* contains an interface representing the ADT for a stack of objects and *ArrayStack.java* contains a skeleton for a class that uses an array to implement this interface. Fill in code for the following public methods:

- ☐ void push(Object val)
- ☐ int pop()
- ☐ boolean isEmpty()
- ☐ boolean isFull()

In writing your methods, keep in mind the following:
- ☐ The bottom of an array-based stack is always the first element in the array. In the skeleton given, variable *top* holds the index of the location where the next value pushed will go. So when the stack is empty, *top* is 0; when it contains one element (in location 0 of the array), *top* is 1, and so on.
- ☐ Make *push* check to see if the array is full first, and do nothing if it is. Similarly, make *pop* check to see if the array is empty first, and return null if it is.
- ☐ Popping an element removes it from the stack, but not from the array—only the value of *top* changes.

File *StackTest.java* contains a simple driver to test your stack. Save it to your directory, compile it, and make sure it works. Note that it tries to push more things than will fit on the stack, but your *push* method should deal with this.

```
// ****************************************************************
//    StackADT.java
//    The classic Stack interface.
// ****************************************************************
public interface StackADT
{
    // -------------------------------------------------
    // Adds a new element to the top of the stack.
    // -------------------------------------------------
    public void push(Object val);

    // -------------------------------------------------
    // Removes and returns the element at the top of the stack.
    // -------------------------------------------------
    public Object pop();

    // -------------------------------------------------
    // Returns true if stack is empty, false otherwise.
    // -------------------------------------------------
    public boolean isEmpty();

    // -------------------------------------------------
    // Returns true if stack is full, false otherwise.
    // -------------------------------------------------
    public boolean isFull();
}


// ****************************************************************
//    ArrayStack.java
//
//    An array-based Object stack class with operations push,
//    pop, and isEmpty and isFull.
//
// ****************************************************************
```

```java
public class ArrayStack implements StackADT
{
    private int stackSize = 5;    // capacity of stack
    private int top;              // index of slot for next element
    private Object[] elements;

    // -----------------------------------------------
    // Constructor -- initializes top and creates array
    // -----------------------------------------------
    public ArrayStack()
    {

    }

    // -----------------------------------------------
    // Adds element to top of stack if it's not full, else
    // does nothing.
    // -----------------------------------------------
    public void push(Object val)
    {

    }

    // -----------------------------------------------
    // Removes and returns value at top of stack.  If stack
    // is empty returns null.
    // -----------------------------------------------
    public Object pop()
    {

    }

    // -----------------------------------------------
    // Returns true if stack is empty, false otherwise.
    // -----------------------------------------------
    public boolean isEmpty()
    {

    }

    // -----------------------------------------------
    // Returns true if stack is full, false otherwise.
    // -----------------------------------------------
    public boolean isFull()
    {

    }

}
```

```
// ************************************************************
// StackTest.java
//
// A simple driver that exercises push, pop, isFull and isEmpty.
// Thanks to autoboxing, we can push integers onto a stack of Objects.
//
// ************************************************************

public class StackTest
{
    public static void main(String[] args)
    {
      StackADT stack = new ArrayStack();

      //push some stuff on the stack
      for (int i=0; i<6; i++)
          stack.push(i*2);

      //pop and print
      //should print 8 6 4 2 0
      while (!stack.isEmpty())
          System.out.print(stack.pop() + " ");
      System.out.println();


      //push a few more things
      for (int i=1; i<=6; i++)
          stack.push(i);

      //should print 5 4 3 2 1
      while (!stack.isEmpty())
          System.out.print(stack.pop() + " ");
      System.out.println();

    }
}
```

A Linked Stack Implementation

Java has a Stack class that holds elements of type Object. However, many languages do not provide stack types, so it is useful to be able to define your own. File *StackADT.java* contains an interface representing the ADT for a stack of objects and *LinkedStack.java* contains a skeleton for a class that uses a linked list to implement this interface. It depends on the Node class in *Node.java*. (This could also be defined as an inner class.) Fill in code for the following public methods:

- ☐ void push(Object val)
- ☐ int pop()
- ☐ boolean isEmpty()
- ☐ boolean isFull()

In writing your methods, keep in mind that in a linked implementation of a stack, the top of stack is always at the front of the list. This makes it easy to add (push) and remove (pop) elements.

File *StackTest.java* contains a simple driver to test your stack. Save it to your directory, compile it, and make sure it works.

```
// *******************************************************************
//    StackADT.java
//    The classic Stack interface.
// *******************************************************************
public interface StackADT
{
    // ---------------------------------------------------
    // Adds a new element to the top of the stack.
    // ---------------------------------------------------
    public void push(Object val);

    // ---------------------------------------------------
    // Removes and returns the element at the top of the stack.
    // ---------------------------------------------------
    public Object pop();

    // ---------------------------------------------------
    // Returns true if stack is empty, false otherwise.
    // ---------------------------------------------------
    public boolean isEmpty();

    // ---------------------------------------------------
    // Returns true if stack is full, false otherwise.
    // ---------------------------------------------------
    public boolean isFull();
}




// *******************************************************************
//    LinkedStack.java
//
//    An linked implementation of an Object stack class with operations push,
//    pop, and isEmpty and isFull.
//
// *******************************************************************
public class LinkedStack implements StackADT
{
    private Node top;                   // reference to top of stack

    // ---------------------------------------------------
```

```java
        // Constructor -- initializes top
        // ---------------------------------------------------
        public LinkedStack()
        {
        }


        // ---------------------------------------------------
        // Adds element to top of stack if it's not full, else
        // does nothing.
        // ---------------------------------------------------
        public void push(Object val)
        {
        }


        // ---------------------------------------------------
        // Removes and returns value at top of stack.  If stack
        // is empty returns null.
        // ---------------------------------------------------
        public Object pop()
        {
        }


        // ---------------------------------------------------
        // Returns true if stack is empty, false otherwise.
        // ---------------------------------------------------
        public boolean isEmpty()
        {
        }

        // ---------------------------------------------------
        // Returns true if stack is full, false otherwise.
        // ---------------------------------------------------
        public boolean isFull()
        {
        }
}


//************************************************************
// Node.java
// A general node for a singly linked list of objects.
//************************************************************
public class Node
{
    private Node next;
    private Object element;

    //---------------------------------------------------------
    // Creates an empty node
    //---------------------------------------------------------
    public Node()
    {
      next = null;
      element = null;
    }

    //---------------------------------------------------------
    // Creates a node storing a specified element
    //---------------------------------------------------------
    public Node(Object element)
```

```
  {
    next = null;
    this.element = element;
  }

  //---------------------------------------------------
  // Returns the node that follows this one
  //---------------------------------------------------
  public Node getNext()
  {
    return next;
  }

  //---------------------------------------------------
  // Sets the node that follows this one
  //---------------------------------------------------
  public void setNext(Node node)
  {
    next = node;
  }

  //---------------------------------------------------
  // Returns the element stored in this node
  //---------------------------------------------------
  public Object getElement()
  {
    return element;
  }

  //---------------------------------------------------
  // Sets the element stored in this node
  //---------------------------------------------------
  public void setElement(Object element)
  {
    this.element = element;
  }
}


// ********************************************************
// StackTest.java
//
// A simple driver that exercises push, pop, isFull and isEmpty.
// Thanks to autoboxing, we can push integers onto a stack of Objects.
//
// ********************************************************

public class StackTest
{
    public static void main(String[] args)
    {
      StackADT stack = new LinkedStack();

      //push some stuff on the stack
      for (int i=0; i<10; i++)
          stack.push(i*2);

      //pop and print
      //should print 18 16 14 12 10 8 6 4 2 0
      while (!stack.isEmpty())
```

```java
            System.out.print(stack.pop() + " ");
        System.out.println();


        //push a few more things
        for (int i=1; i<=6; i++)
            stack.push(i);

        //should print 5 4 3 2 1
        while (!stack.isEmpty())
            System.out.print(stack.pop() + " ");
        System.out.println();

    }
}
```

Stack Manipulation

Sometimes it's useful to define operations on an ADT without changing the type definition itself. For example, you might want to print the elements in a stack without actually adding a method to the Stack ADT (you may not even have access to it). To explore this, use either the Stack class provided by Java (in java.util) or one of the stack classes that you wrote in an earlier lab exercise and the test program *StackTest.java*. Add the following static methods to the StackTest class (the signature for these methods and the declaration in StackTest assumes you are using a stack class named Stack—modify them to use the name of your class):

☐ void printStack(Stack s)—prints the elements in stack s from top to bottom. When printStack returns, s should be unchanged.
☐ Stack reverseStack(Stack s)—returns a new stack whose elements are backwards from those in s. Again, s is unchanged.
☐ Stack removeElement(Stack s, int val)—returns a new stack whose elements are the same as those in s (and in the same order) except that all occurrences of val have been removed. Again, s is unchanged.

Modify the main method to test these methods. Be sure you print enough information to see if they're working!

```
//  ******************************************************************
//    StackTest.java
//
//    A simple driver to test a stack.
//
//  ******************************************************************
import java.util.Stack;
public class StackTest
{
    public static void main(String[] args)
    {
      // Declare and instantiate a stack
      Stack stack = new Stack();

      //push some stuff on the stack
      for (int i=0; i<10; i++)
          stack.push(i);
      stack.push(5);

      // call printStack to print the stack

      // call reverseStack to reverse the stack

      // call printStack to print the stack again

      // call removeElement to remove all occurrences of the value 5 - save the
      // stack returned from this call

      // call printStack to print the original stack and the new stack.

    }
}
```

Matching Parentheses

One application of stacks is to keep track of things that must match up such as parentheses in an expression or braces in a program. In the case of parentheses when a left parenthesis is encountered it is pushed on the stack and when a right parenthesis is encountered its matching left parenthesis is popped from the stack. If the stack has no left parenthesis, that means the parentheses don't match—there is an extra right parenthesis. If the expression ends with at least one left parenthesis still on the stack then again the parentheses don't match—there is an extra left parenthesis.

File *ParenMatch.java* contains the skeleton of a program to match parentheses in an expression. It uses the Stack class provided by Java (in java.util). Complete the program by adding a loop to process the line entered to see if it contains matching parentheses. Just ignore characters that are neither left nor right parentheses. Your loop should stop as soon as it detects an error. After the loop print a message indicating what happened—the parentheses match, there are too many left parentheses, or there are too many right parentheses. Also print the part of the string up to where the error was detected.

```
// *****************************************************************
//    ParenMatch.java
//
//    Determines whether or not a string of characters contains
//    matching left and right parentheses.
// *****************************************************************

import java.util.*;
import java.util.Scanner;

public class ParenMatch
{
    public static void main (String[] args)
    {
      Stack s = new Stack();
      String line;                 // the string of characters to be checked
      Scanner scan = new Scanner(System.in);

      System.out.println ("\nParenthesis Matching");
      System.out.print ("Enter a parenthesized expression: ");
      line = scan.nextLine();


      // loop to process the line one character at a time

      // print the results


    }
}
```